MICROSOFT TEAMS QUICK START 2024 GUIDE

JEXONIA GRANEER

Copyright © 2023 Jexonia Graneer

All rights reserved.

INTRODUCTION

Welcome to the "Microsoft Teams Quick Start 2024 Guide," your comprehensive resource for mastering Microsoft Teams in the modern workspace. As we step into 2024, the landscape of collaborative tools is rapidly evolving, and Microsoft Teams sits at the forefront of this change, offering innovative features that cater to the diverse needs of businesses and educational institutions alike.

The Evolution of Communication and Collaboration

In today's fast-paced digital world, effective communication and collaboration are more important than ever. With remote work and digital offices becoming the norm, the need for a robust, versatile platform is undeniable. Microsoft Teams, an integral part of the Microsoft 365 family, has emerged as a leading solution, evolving continuously to meet and exceed these demands.

Why Microsoft Teams?

Microsoft Teams isn't just a communication tool; it's a comprehensive workspace that integrates chat, video meetings, file storage, and application integration. This guide is designed to provide you with a deep dive into the capabilities of Teams, ensuring that whether you're a beginner or an advanced user, you'll find valuable insights and tips to enhance your Teams experience.

Navigating Through the Guide

Our journey begins with an introduction to Microsoft Teams, setting the foundation for newcomers and offering a refresher for seasoned users. As you progress through the chapters, you'll discover the latest features in Teams, particularly those integrated with the newest Windows updates, and learn how to leverage these for more efficient collaboration and communication.

Beyond Basics: Advanced Features and Integration

But this guide isn't just about the basics. You'll explore advanced topics like mastering messaging, engaging audiences effectively, and the strategic use of private channels. We delve into the art of designing with Teams templates, maximizing productivity with Microsoft Viva, and enhancing Teams with powerful apps and bots.

Integration and Management

Integration is key in any collaborative tool, and Microsoft Teams excels in this. You'll learn how to synergize Teams with other applications and services, enhancing your workflow seamlessly. For IT professionals and those interested in a deeper technical understanding, we cover advanced management techniques using PowerShell, ensuring you have the tools to manage Teams effectively in any environment.

Accessibility and Efficiency

To cater to the diverse needs of all users, this guide includes a dedicated chapter on keyboard shortcuts in Teams, promoting accessibility and efficiency. By the end of this guide, you'll not only be proficient in using Teams but also equipped with the knowledge to customize it to your unique needs.

Deep Dive into Microsoft Teams' Features

The beauty of Microsoft Teams lies in its flexibility and the breadth of its features. From seamless integration with other Microsoft 365 tools like SharePoint and OneNote to its robust video conferencing capabilities, Teams stands out as a comprehensive platform for collaboration. In this guide, we explore each feature in detail, offering insights into how they can be utilized effectively in different scenarios. For instance, in our chapter on "Mastering Teams Messaging," we'll dissect the nuances of effective communication within Teams, showcasing how to use chat functionalities, mention tags, and even message formatting to ensure your communications are clear, concise, and impactful.

Engaging Diverse Audiences

One of the critical challenges in any collaborative environment is engaging a diverse range of audiences. Microsoft Teams offers various tools and features to address this, such as live events, webinars, and interactive meetings. Our guide will provide you with strategies and best practices for using these features to captivate your audience, whether it's a team meeting, a large-scale presentation, or an educational session.

Private Channels and Customization

Privacy and customization are at the core of effective teamwork. With Microsoft Teams, you can create private channels for sensitive projects, ensuring that conversations and files are accessible only to specific team members. This guide will walk you through setting up and managing these channels, along with tips on customizing your Teams environment using templates and settings to match your team's workflow and culture.

Leveraging Microsoft Viva for Employee Engagement

In an era where employee well-being and engagement are paramount, Microsoft Viva – an employee experience platform integrated with Teams – offers tools to enhance productivity, learning, and well-being. This guide will help you understand how to leverage Viva to create a more engaging and supportive workplace, whether your team is remote, in-office, or a hybrid of both.

Apps, Bots, and Advanced Integration

Microsoft Teams is not just about internal communication; it's a hub that connects you with a wide array of applications and services. Our chapters on "Maximizing Apps in Teams" and "Enhancing Teams With Bots" will provide you with a comprehensive understanding of how to integrate and utilize third-party apps and bots, automating tasks and streamlining workflows within Teams.

PowerShell for Advanced Teams Management

For IT professionals and advanced users, Teams offers extensive management capabilities through PowerShell. This guide includes a deep dive into using PowerShell for tasks such as automating administrative tasks, managing large numbers of users, and customizing Teams settings at a granular level. Whether you're managing a small team or an entire organization, these skills are invaluable.

Empowering Users with Keyboard Shortcuts

Efficiency is key in the fast-paced digital world, and keyboard shortcuts in Teams are a game-changer. Our guide dedicates a chapter to these shortcuts, helping users navigate Teams more quickly and effectively, thereby boosting productivity.

Staying Ahead in a Dynamic Digital Landscape

As we conclude the introduction, it's essential to recognize that the digital landscape, and with it, Microsoft Teams, is continually evolving. This guide is designed not just to provide current knowledge but also to empower you with the mindset and skills to adapt to future changes. By understanding the core principles and functionalities of Teams, you'll be well-equipped to leverage whatever new features and opportunities come your way in the dynamic world of digital collaboration.

Conclusion

As you embark on this journey through the "Microsoft Teams Quick Start 2024 Guide," remember that the world of technology is constantly evolving, and so is Microsoft Teams. This guide aims to provide you with the knowledge and skills to stay ahead in this dynamic environment, making the most of Teams to enhance your productivity, collaboration, and communication.

With this guide, you are not just learning about a tool; you're embracing a more connected, efficient, and productive way of working. Welcome to the "Microsoft Teams Quick Start 2024 Guide," where your journey to mastering Microsoft Teams begins.

CONTENTS

Chapter 1: Introducing Microsoft Teams 1

Chapter 2: Getting Started With Microsoft Teams 11

Chapter 3: What's New In Teams With Windows 31

Chapter 4: Mastering Teams Messaging 41

Chapter 5: Teams For Engaging Audiences 56

Chapter 6: Focus On Private Channels 79

Chapter 7: Designing With Teams Templates 84

Chapter 8: Leveraging Microsoft Viva 95

Chapter 9: Maximizing Apps In Teams 126

Chapter 10: Enhancing Teams With Bots 137

Chapter 11: Synergizing With Teams Integration 146

Chapter 12: Advanced Teams Management With Powershell 160

Chapter 13: Keyboard shortcuts in Teams 169

Conclusion 173

CHAPTER 1: INTRODUCING MICROSOFT TEAMS

WHAT IS MICROSOFT TEAMS?

In the landscape of digital collaboration, few platforms have made an impact as significant as Microsoft Teams. As of 2024, Teams stands as a titan of teamwork, facilitating communication and collaboration for millions worldwide. But what exactly is Microsoft Teams? Let's demystify this tool that has become essential in many professional environments.

Defining the Platform

Microsoft Teams is an all-encompassing chat-based collaboration platform that integrates the robust Microsoft 365 suite of productivity tools into a single interface. It is designed to enable local and remote teams to work together seamlessly, regardless of their physical locations. With its comprehensive features for chat, video meetings, file storage, and integration with other Microsoft services and third-party applications, Teams is a hub for teamwork and organizational productivity.

Teams as a Collaboration Hub

At its core, Teams is more than just a tool; it is a virtual workspace. It allows for the creation of teams and channels—dedicated spaces for various projects or departments within an organization. Each channel can be customized with tabs for applications, documents, and services that are relevant to that group's work. These features allow for a structured yet flexible approach to collaboration, ensuring that all team members have immediate access to everything they need, from documents to conversations, in a single, searchable location.

The Core Features of Microsoft Teams

Understanding Microsoft Teams begins with its core features, which are designed to support a wide array of business functions:

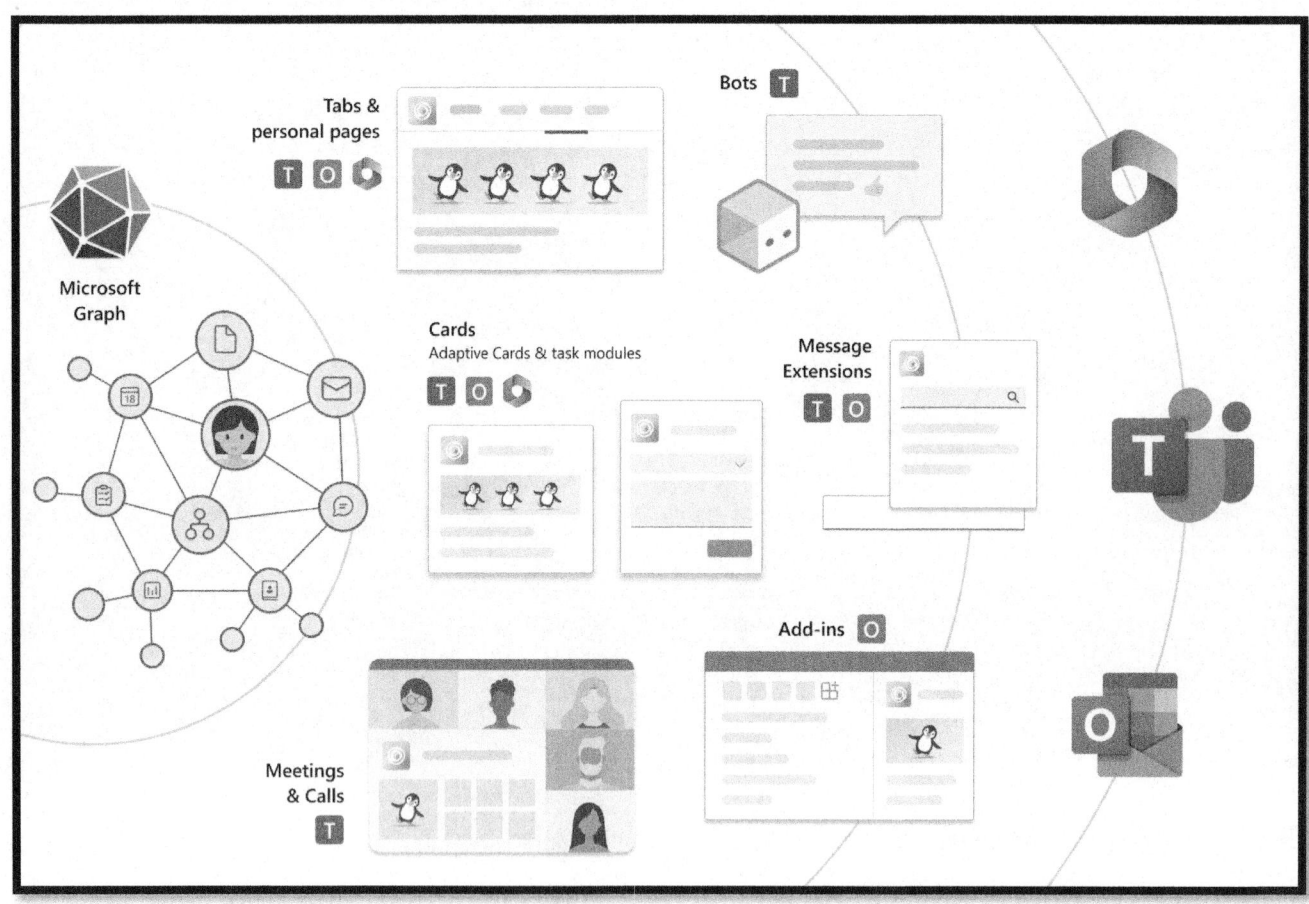

Chat and Communication: Instant messaging, audio, and video calling features enable real-time communication, with the ability to record meetings and save chats for future reference.

Meetings and Conferencing: Teams supports meeting scheduling, screen sharing, live events, and webinars, offering robust capabilities for virtual meetings of all sizes.

File Storage and Sharing: Integration with OneDrive and SharePoint allows for file storage, sharing, and collaborative editing in real-time.

Customization and Integration: With support for Microsoft 365 apps and over 600 third-party applications, Teams can be tailored to include the tools and services your team uses daily.

Security and Compliance: Built on the secure Microsoft 365 cloud, Teams provides advanced security features and compliance capabilities suitable for enterprises.

THE EVOLUTION OF MICROSOFT TEAMS

The journey of Microsoft Teams is a narrative of adaptation, innovation, and growth. It represents Microsoft's response to an ever-changing digital workplace.

From Office Communicator to Teams: A Brief History

Microsoft's foray into office communication began with Office Communicator, which evolved into Lync and later Skype for Business. With the advent of Teams in 2017, Microsoft consolidated the best features of its previous offerings into a single platform, capitalizing on the integrated experience with Office 365 applications. Over the years, Teams has expanded its capabilities, growing from a simple messaging app into a comprehensive collaboration suite.

Recent Updates and New Features in 2024

The year 2024 marks another milestone for Teams with updates that push the boundaries of collaborative work. New AI-powered features assist with meeting summarization, action item tracking, and even emotional tone analysis to enhance communication. Customizable workspaces that adapt to individual workflows and advanced security protocols are some of the innovations that continue to position Teams at the forefront of collaboration technology.

Microsoft Teams and the Remote Work Revolution

The surge of remote work has catapulted Teams into a position of prominence. It has become synonymous with the 'new normal' of remote and hybrid work models, proving to be a crucial tool in bridging the gap between in-office and remote employees. Its features cater to a dispersed workforce, ensuring that collaboration and productivity remain high regardless of physical location.

Teams has not just responded to the remote work trend; it has shaped it. With functionality that mirrors the natural flow of a dynamic work environment, it has set a standard for what remote work can be—flexible, inclusive, and efficient.

Microsoft Teams has, through its evolution, demonstrated a remarkable capacity to adapt and grow in tandem with the needs of modern businesses. It encapsulates the spirit of digital transformation, and as we continue into 2024 and beyond, it stands ready to meet the challenges of a world where teamwork is paramount, yet the definition of the workplace is ever-evolving.

CHOOSING YOUR SUBSCRIPTION

When it comes to leveraging Microsoft Teams within an organization or as an individual, choosing the right subscription plan is critical. Microsoft offers a variety of plans under the Microsoft 365 umbrella, each designed to meet different needs in terms of functionality, business size, and budget.

Understanding Microsoft 365 Plans

Microsoft 365 plans come in several tiers, primarily differentiated by the scale of the business and the suite of applications required. For small to medium-sized businesses, there are plans that offer a balance between functionality and affordability. Larger organizations can opt for more comprehensive plans that include additional security and compliance capabilities. There are also special plans for educational institutions and non-profits.

The plans typically include a range of Microsoft's cloud-based services beyond Teams, such as Exchange for email, SharePoint for document management, and the suite of Office productivity tools like Word, Excel, and PowerPoint.

Comparing Teams Free vs. Paid Versions

Microsoft Teams is unique in that it offers a robust free version that can be quite sufficient for small teams and startups. The free version of Teams includes unlimited chat, built-in online meetings, and 10 GB of team file storage plus 2 GB of personal file storage per person.

The paid versions, included with Microsoft 365 subscriptions, extend these capabilities significantly. They introduce meeting recording, more storage, enhanced security features, administrative tools for managing users and apps, and the full integration with Office 365 applications. For businesses that need to collaborate at scale, the paid version becomes essential.

Enterprise Solutions and Licensing

Enterprises have unique needs, often requiring customized solutions that standard plans do not fulfill. Enterprise plans offer scalability, advanced security, compliance protocols, and premium support. Licensing for enterprises is typically more complex, with options for volume licensing and discounts for long-term commitments.

PRICING STRUCTURE

Understanding the pricing structure of Microsoft Teams and the broader Microsoft 365 ecosystem is crucial for making an informed decision about which subscription to choose.

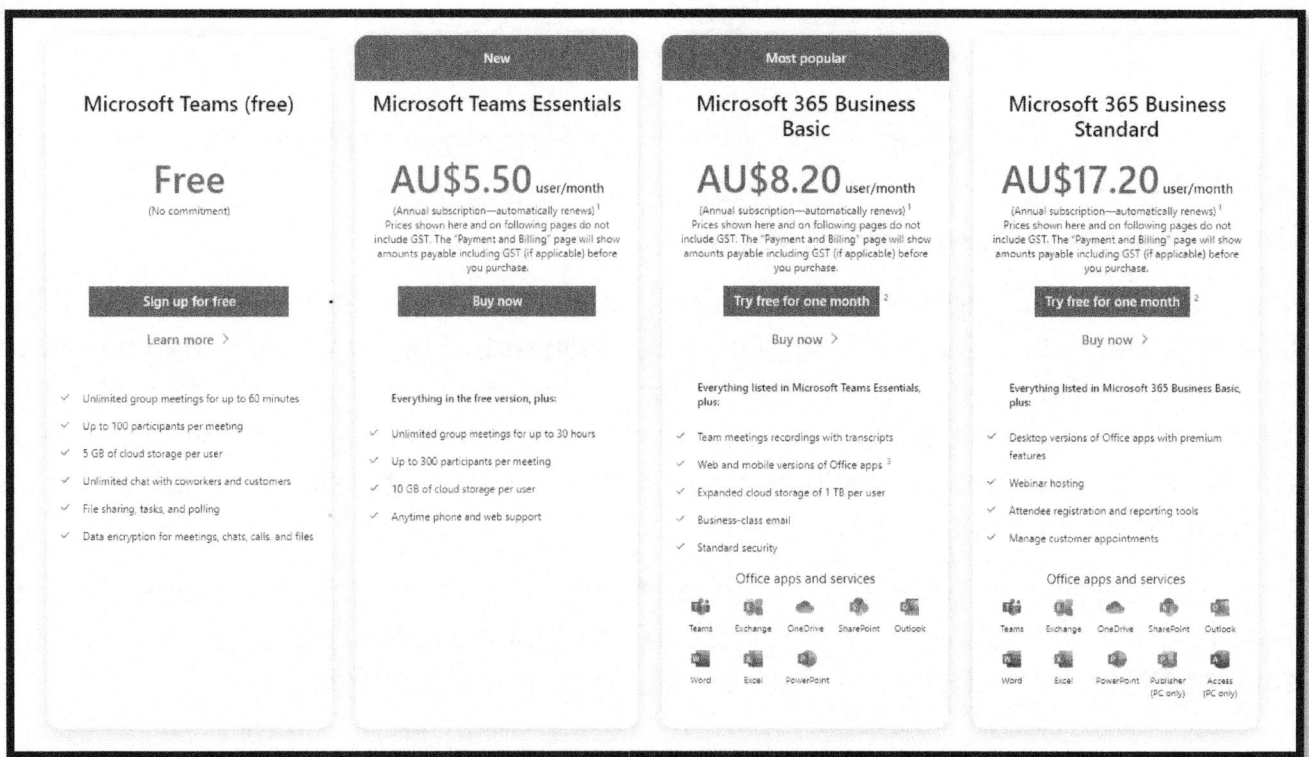

Breakdown of Subscription Costs

Microsoft 365 plans are generally billed on a per-user, per-month basis, with the option to pay annually. Small business plans cater to organizations with up to 300 users, while enterprise plans are for unlimited users. The costs will vary depending on the number of users and the specific services included in the plan.

Evaluating the Cost for Businesses vs. Individuals

For individuals or small teams not requiring the broad array of Microsoft 365 tools, the free version of Teams might suffice. However, businesses will need to evaluate the cost-effectiveness of moving to a paid subscription. This decision will often rest on the need for advanced features, such as additional storage, security, and compliance tools.

Additional Costs and Add-Ons

Beyond the core subscription, there may be additional costs to consider, such as add-ons for enhanced functionalities like advanced analytics, increased storage, or third-party app integrations. Organizations must account for these when budgeting for their Teams deployment.

INSTALLING MICROSOFT TEAMS

Having selected the appropriate subscription plan, the next step is installing Microsoft Teams. Teams is designed to be user-friendly, and installation is typically straightforward across various platforms.

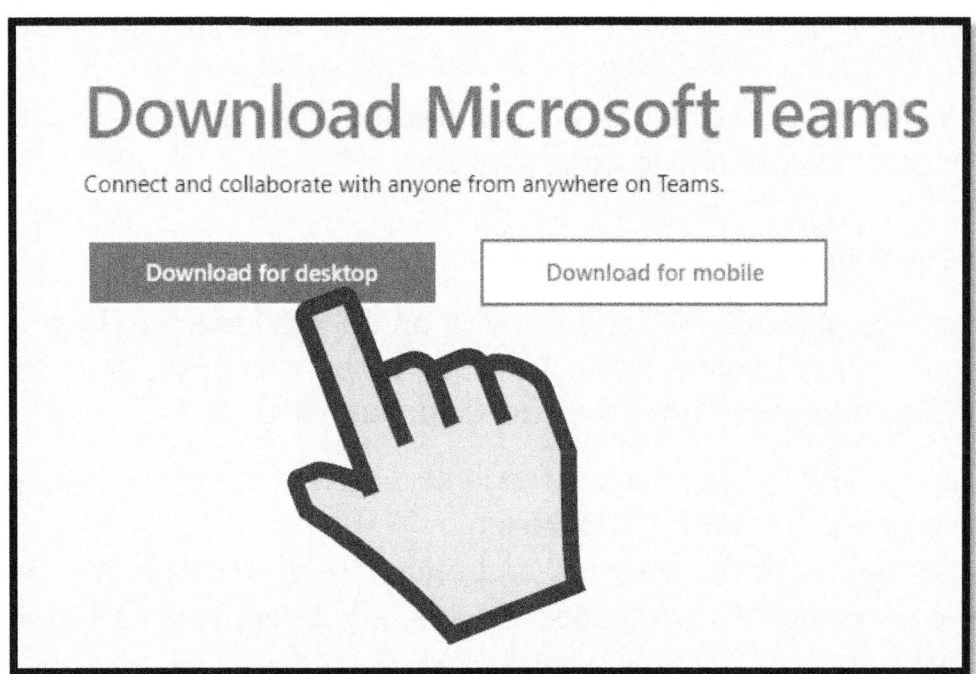

System Requirements for Different Platforms

Teams is available on Windows, Mac, iOS, Android, and as a web application. The system requirements for each platform are published by Microsoft and are periodically updated. It's important to ensure that your devices meet these requirements to experience the full capabilities of Teams without performance issues.

Installation Guide for Windows, Mac, and Mobile

The installation process for Teams involves downloading the application from the Microsoft Teams website or from the relevant app store on mobile devices. On desktop platforms, once downloaded, the installation package will guide you through the setup process. On mobile devices, the process is as simple as installing any other app from your device's app store.

Troubleshooting Common Installation Issues

Installation issues can arise due to outdated operating systems, insufficient user permissions, or network restrictions. Microsoft provides extensive documentation and support for troubleshooting such issues. In most cases, ensuring that your device is updated, you have the necessary permissions, and your internet connection is stable will resolve installation problems.

THE DESIGN CONCEPT BEHIND TEAMS

The design of Microsoft Teams reflects a deep understanding of the need for simplicity, intuitiveness, and efficiency in collaborative software. It's not just about how the product looks, but also how it works and feels to the diverse set of users who rely on it daily for communication and collaboration.

User Interface (UI) Design Principles

The user interface of Microsoft Teams is built on the foundation of Microsoft's Fluent Design System, which emphasizes coherence, responsiveness, and inclusivity. The design principles that guide Teams' UI development include:

- **Simplicity:** The interface is clean and uncluttered, reducing cognitive load and allowing users to focus on their tasks.
- **Consistency:** Familiar patterns and elements are used across the platform, aligning with other Microsoft 365 products, which reduces the learning curve for new users.
- **Visibility:** Essential features are prominently placed and easy to access, ensuring that navigation is intuitive.
- **Feedback:** Interactive elements provide immediate feedback to the user, such as visual confirmations for sent messages or files.

User Experience (UX) Considerations

The UX design of Teams goes beyond the visual aspects and delves into how users interact with the software:

- **Collaboration-centric:** Teams is designed to enhance collaborative efforts, with tools and features that promote easy sharing, communication, and joint work.
- **Customization:** Understanding that no two teams work alike, Teams allows users to customize their workspace with tabs, bots, and connectors to match their workflow.
- **Integration:** Seamless integration with Microsoft 365 apps and services, as well as third-party applications, creates a unified work environment without the need to switch between apps.
- **Efficiency:** Speed and responsiveness are key, with features like slash commands and the search bar enabling users to find information quickly or initiate actions immediately.

Accessibility Features and Inclusivity

Accessibility is not an afterthought in Teams. The platform includes features designed to ensure all users, regardless of their abilities, can communicate and collaborate effectively:

- **Screen Reader Support:** Teams is designed to be fully compatible with screen readers, providing audio descriptions for visual elements.
- **High Contrast Modes:** For users with visual impairments, Teams supports high contrast modes, which increase legibility and reduce eye strain.
- **Closed Captioning and Transcription:** Video conferencing supports live captions and transcription to aid users who are deaf or hard of hearing.
- **Keyboard Navigation:** The interface is navigable entirely by keyboard, accommodating users who are unable to use a mouse.

THE FUTURE OF TEAMS AND COLLABORATIVE SOFTWARE

As the landscape of work continues to evolve, Microsoft Teams is adapting and innovating, shaping the future of workplace collaboration.

Trends Shaping the Future of Workplace Collaboration

Emerging trends such as remote and hybrid work models, AI, and machine learning are influencing collaborative software design. Teams is at the forefront, incorporating predictive text, meeting insights, and virtual collaboration spaces that mirror physical office dynamics.

Upcoming Features in the Teams Roadmap

The Teams roadmap is rich with planned features, including AI-driven contextual collaboration, enhanced virtual reality (VR) meeting spaces, and deeper analytics to help teams work smarter. Continuous improvements in security and compliance ensure that Teams meets the highest standards for data protection and privacy.

Preparing for the Future with Teams

Organizations must prepare for the ongoing changes in collaborative work by leveraging these advancements in Teams. This means investing in training, updating internal processes, and adopting a mindset that is open to digital transformation.

Microsoft Teams isn't just a product of the present; it's a commitment to the future—a dynamic, ever-improving solution designed for the evolving needs of global collaboration. With a strong foundation in UI/UX design principles and an inclusive approach, it stands ready to support the workforce of tomorrow, turning collaborative visions into reality.

Chapter 2: Getting Started With Microsoft Teams

Setting Up Microsoft Teams

If your Microsoft account is linked to your device, the configuration should go smoothly without any problems.

First, go to your Start menu, then to **"Settings"** and navigate to **"Accounts"**. In there, go to the tab that says to "Access work or school account" and if you have any of these accounts linked to your device, you will see them here.

Next, double-click to open Teams. You will get a welcome screen asking you to pick an account to continue. These accounts are the ones already linked to the device and the number of accounts linked to your device will be displayed here. Select an account to proceed. This will link that account to Microsoft Teams and whenever you open Teams, it would automatically log in with that account.

If you follow this step, you may not be asked to enter a password during this process because your account has already been linked to this device. This means your password has also been linked and synchronized with Microsoft 365, so it is more like a single sign-in and you wouldn't be asked to sign in with your password.

However, whenever you change your password from office 365, then Teams would require you to enter your new password.

Team Experience

Now, let's talk about the desktop experience. To understand how it works you should have the Desktop app installed on your computer.

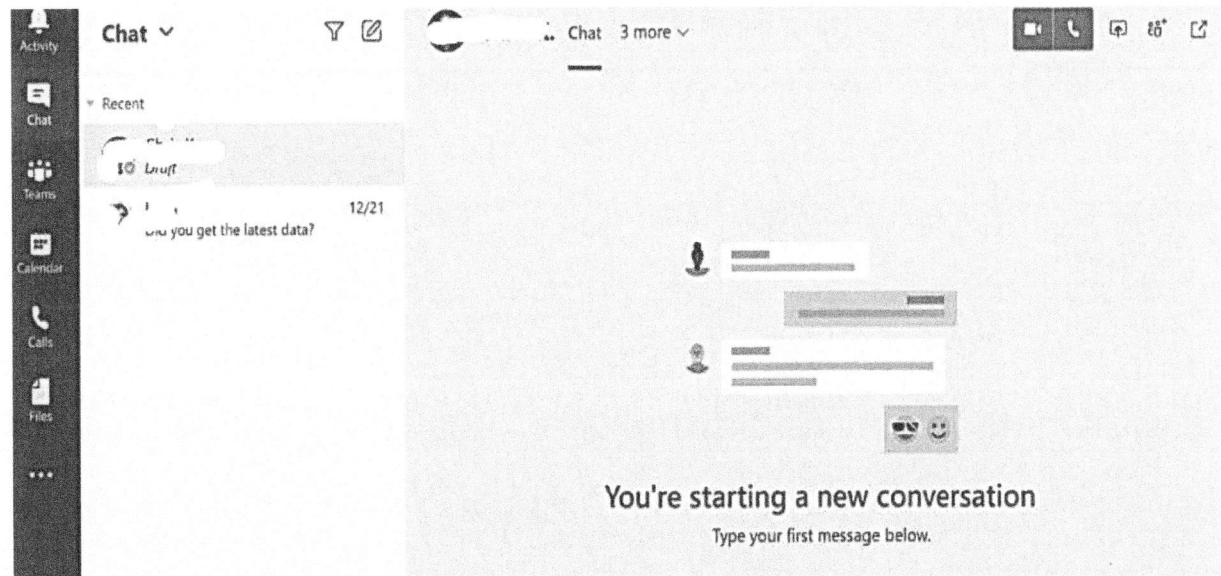

In your Desktop Teams app, if it's the first time you're using this you have to log in and it will take you directly to Teams. On the left side, you have menu options; the one that you're going to use a lot is **Teams**.

Teams

This is where all the actions, collaborations, and sharing happen. This team's view that you're seeing below is for an enterprise account.

If you have an education account you might see the view below instead. You'll just have to click a Team to get to the action.

Back to the business account, you can see the Teams that you're assigned to. So, let's assume you're a finance manager and you belong to two teams. One is a management team that you share with other managers in your organization and the other is a finance team that you share with your direct reports. Usually, each team involves different members and your view of the teams that you see depends on your rights.

Inside a Team, you can have one or more **channels**. These are generally organized by topics. "**General**" is there by default and you can use this as your main channel but you're probably going to have different topics within the team that you want to keep track of. So for example, in the finance team, you want to track project and training conversations separately.

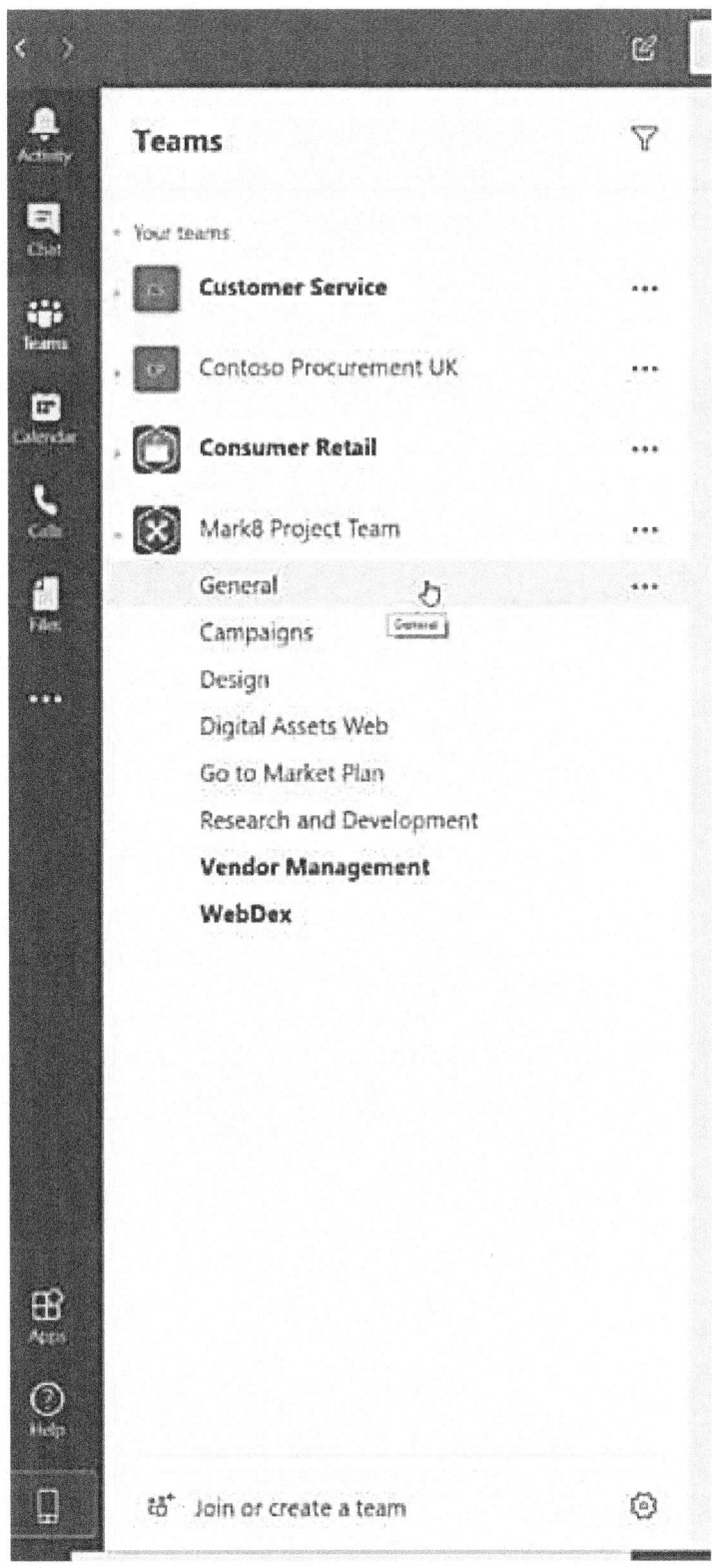

Channels

If you want to add a new channel all you have to do is go to "More options" and add the channel to that. Depending on your rights you might see different options there.

Go to "**Add Channel**", type in the channel name, you can even add an emoji if you want, you can add a description for your channel and update the privacy. Default is that everyone in the team will have access to this channel but you can change that and make it only accessible to specific people within the team. Choose the one that applies to you, and "**Add**" the Channel. Now we can keep conversations around this topic separate from other topics.

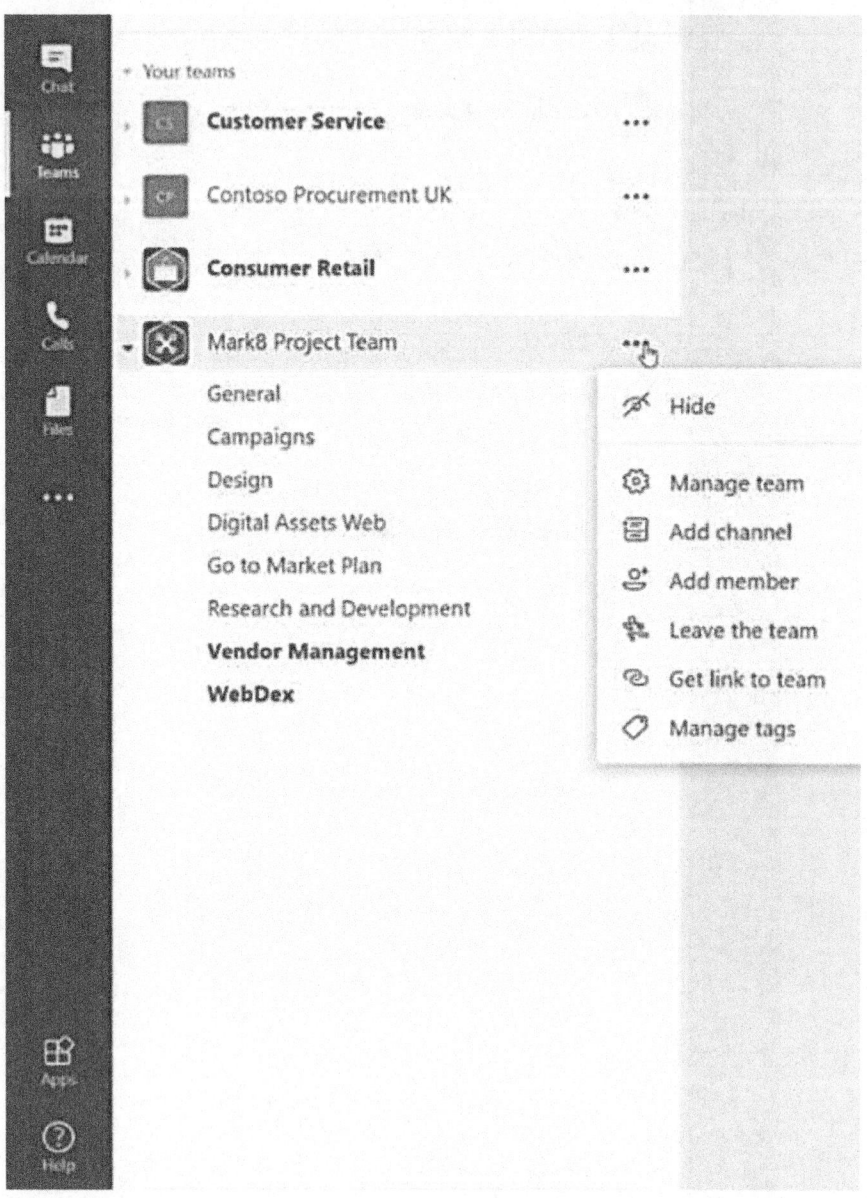

If you're the team owner you can add members to the team. Go back to "**More Options**" and "**Add a member**". You can search for people within your organization by just starting to type their names and then send a request to get them added. You can also add guests by typing in their email addresses once you're done you can send a request. You'll notice if a channel has a guest by taking a look at the top right-hand corner.

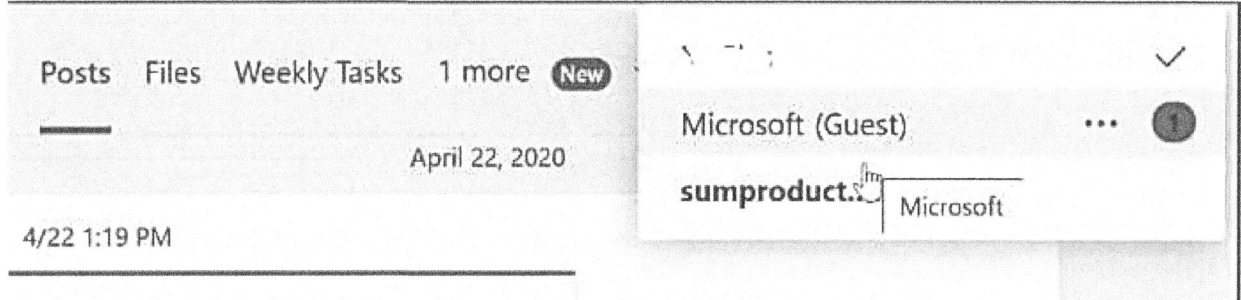

If a channel is in bold it means there is a conversation in there that you haven't looked at yet.

Posts

Once you're in a channel the main view is the **"Posts"** view.

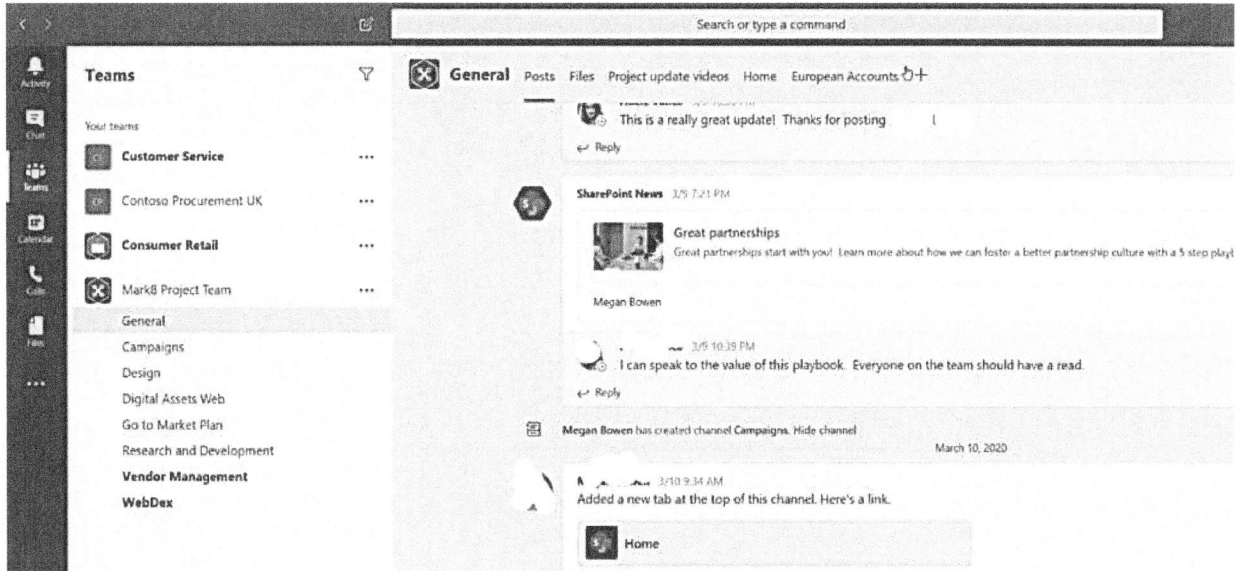

You'll see all the different conversations that are going on and you can reply to conversations. You can also give your feedback in terms of emojis. You also get the option to translate. So if you go to **"More options"**, you can translate a message; it's going to try to figure out the original language and translate it into your team's language.

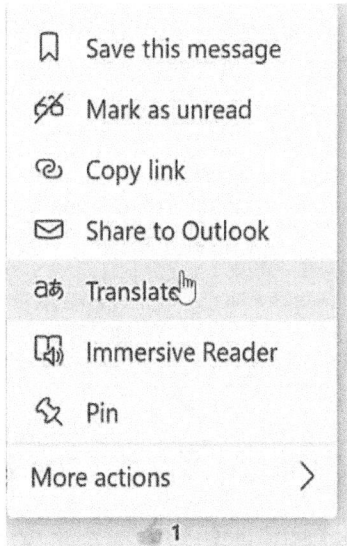

Translated messages have an icon right there, to show this in the original language again goes and select "**See Original Message**".

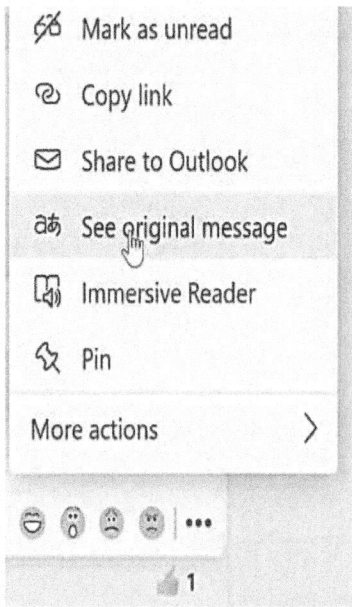

You can start a new conversation by selecting "**New Conversation**". Just type in your text if you'd like to add line breaks use the shortcut key **Shift + Enter**.

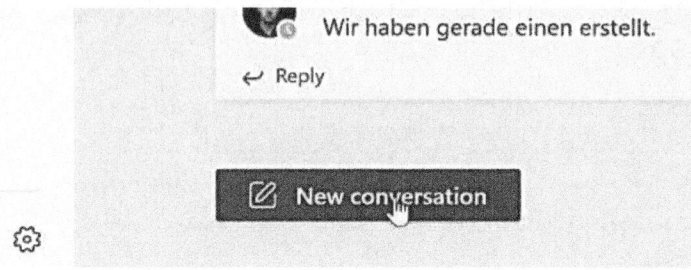

If you'd like to add more text and add formatting, click on the format icon below the text. This is going to give you a lot of formatting options. In addition, you can add a subject that is going to help your message stand out more.

You can also add bullet lists, numbered lists, links, you can even insert tables; pick how many rows and columns you want, and add your table to the message.

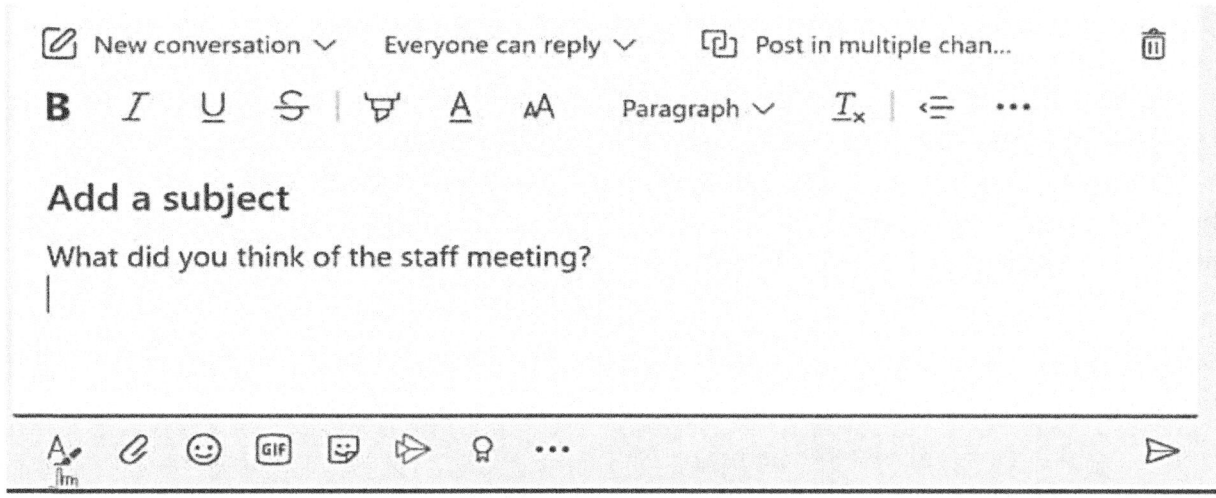

If a message is important, you can **mark it as important**, and you can also post this message on multiple channels. Just select your channel and click on **"Update"**.

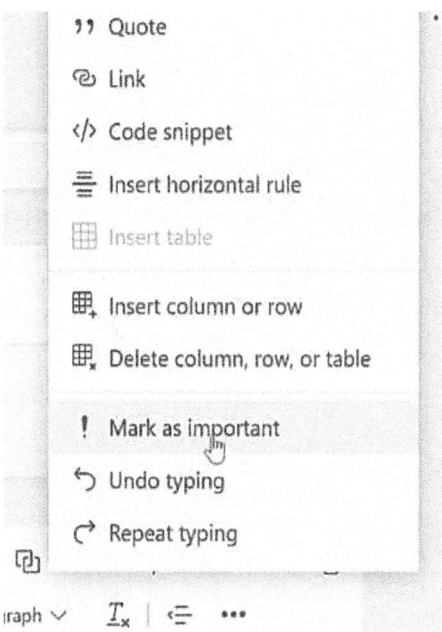

Default messages are shown as Conversations; you can change that to Announcements as well. This makes it even bigger and more noticeable. You can give your announcement a headline, select the color scheme that you want and even add a background picture.

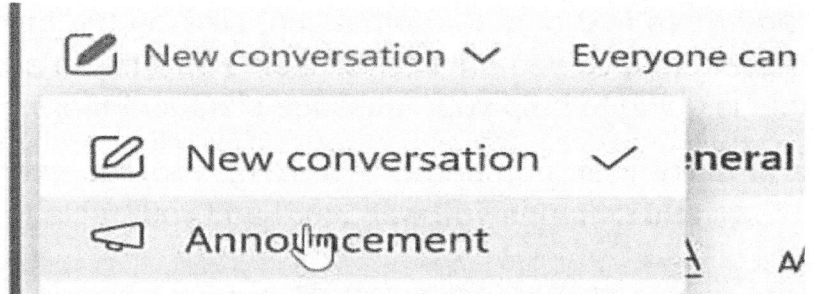

In addition to this, you can also mention specific people to make sure that they are notified about this message. Just start typing their name or select them from the list. If you want to send everyone in the team a notification, mention the channel name. Here you can use enter without problems, and once you're done with your message click on "**Send**".

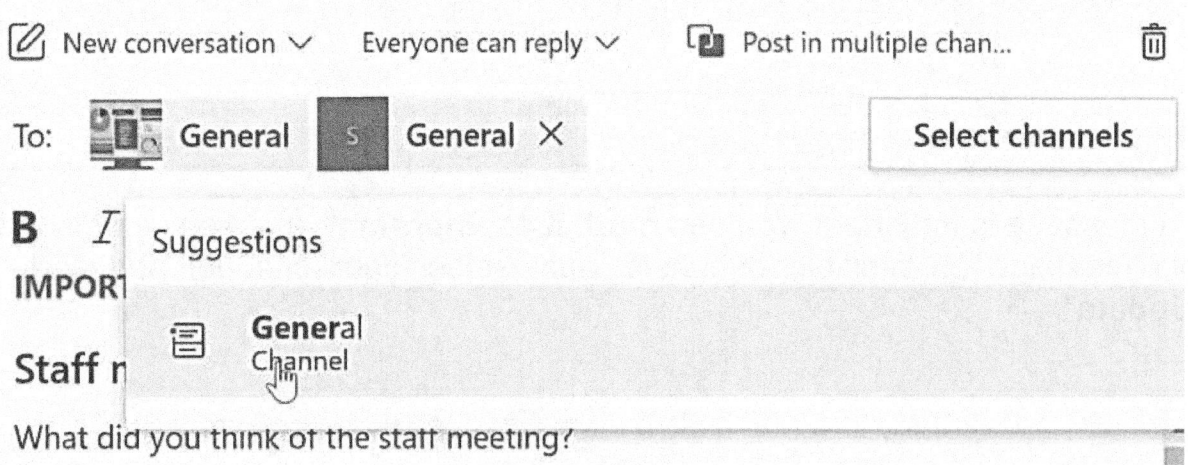

Sometimes, notifications can get out of hand. So, to manage your channel notifications go to "**More Options**", and then "**Channel Notifications**". You can turn these off if you want, or customize the notifications depending on how and when you want to see these notifications.

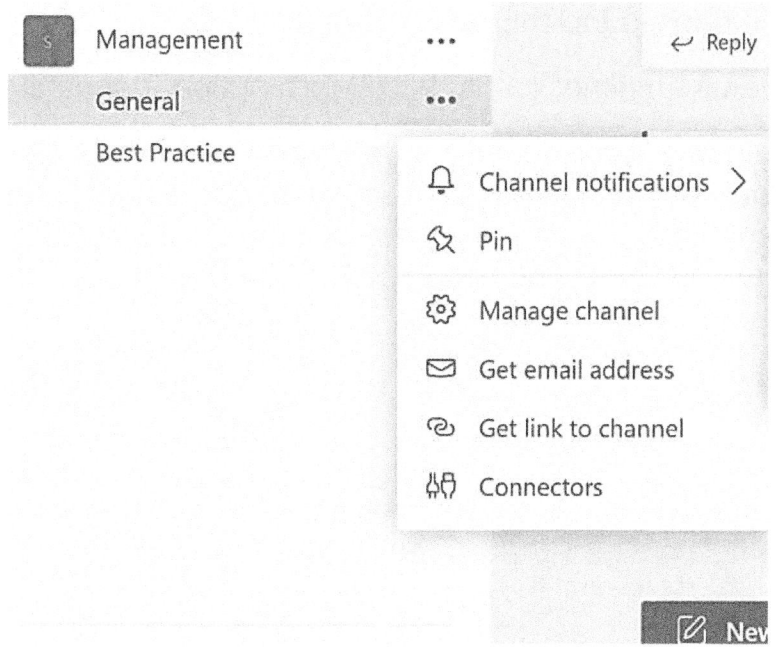

You can also pin important messages in a channel. If you want to pin a message, go to more options and pin it. Pinned messages are going to get a green border and green icon, but they will also disappear from view as more messages get added.

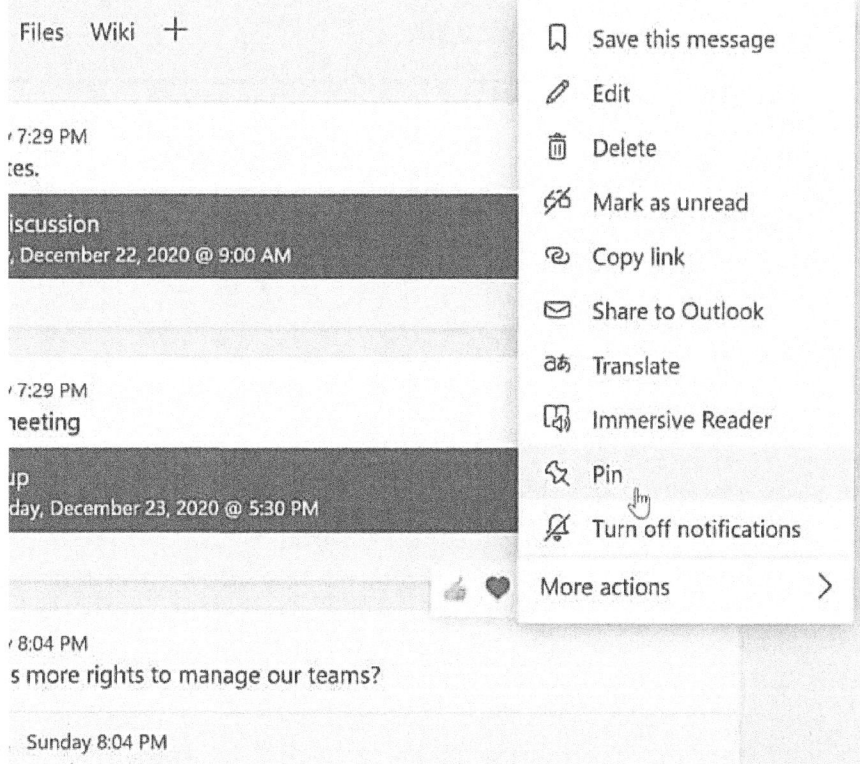

To view all your pinned items, go to the Information icon at the top and you can see your pinned messages on the bottom. When you select the message, it's going to take you back to the original message.

You can unpin items anytime; go back to "More options" and select "**Unpin**".

In addition to sending a formatted text as you saw before, you can also send attachments. You can upload these from your computer, OneDrive, or Teams and Channels.

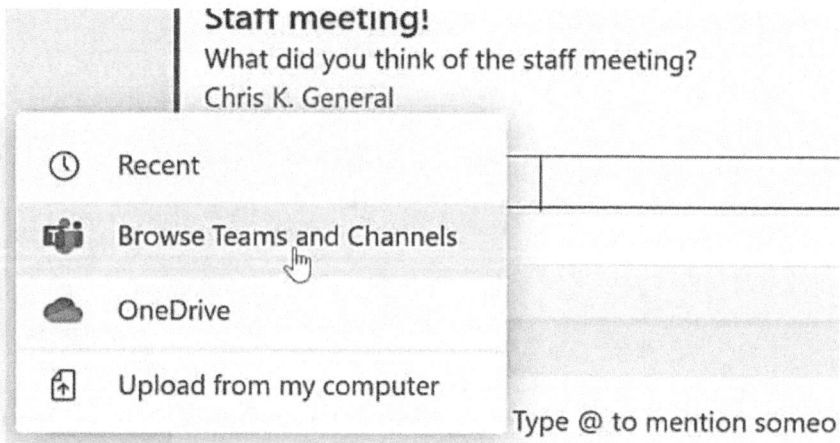

You can also send animated emojis. You also have the option to search for and add Gifs. Another cool feature is the ability to add stickers and memes. A lot of these are customizable; just select the one that you want, update the text, click on "**Done**" and you can send this through.

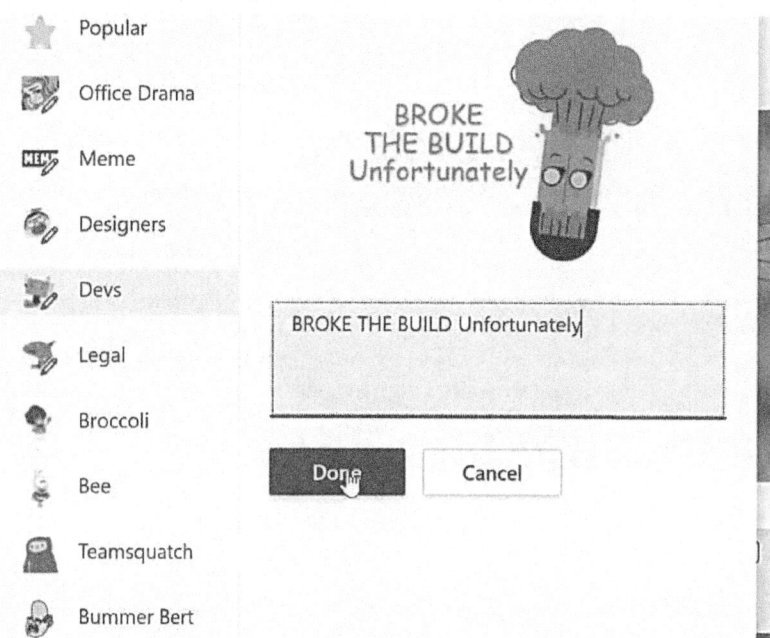

Another thing you can do from here is to schedule a meeting. You can "**Meet now**" and have an online meeting right away.

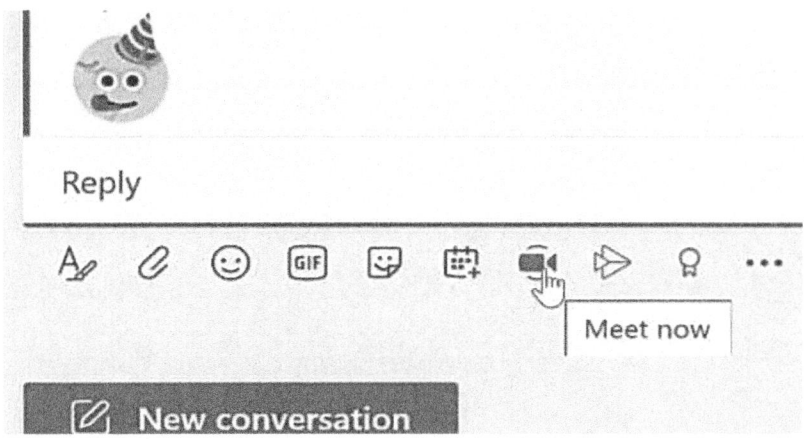

You can also add a link to a Microsoft stream video. So if you've previously recorded a meeting, you can add the link to that meeting in your other channels.

Another cool feature is to **send praise** to people. It's a nice way to say thank you, recognize people for their courage or just tell them that they're awesome. You can type their name here, add a personalized note, preview it, and then send it.

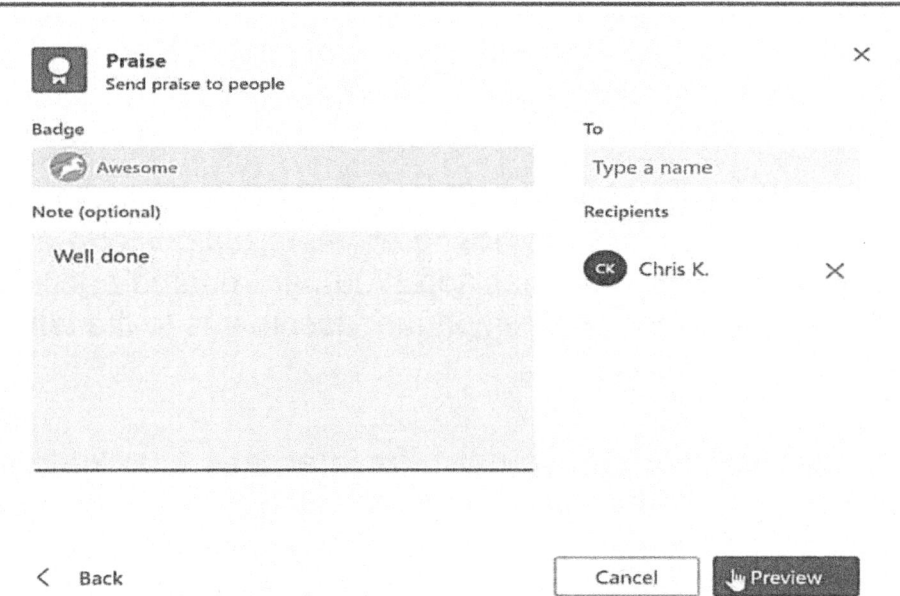

These are the main features in Post view. Now let's take a look at **"Files"**.

Files

The Files tab is available by default for all your channels. Whenever you or other members share documents in a chat, you can see them automatically in the Files view.

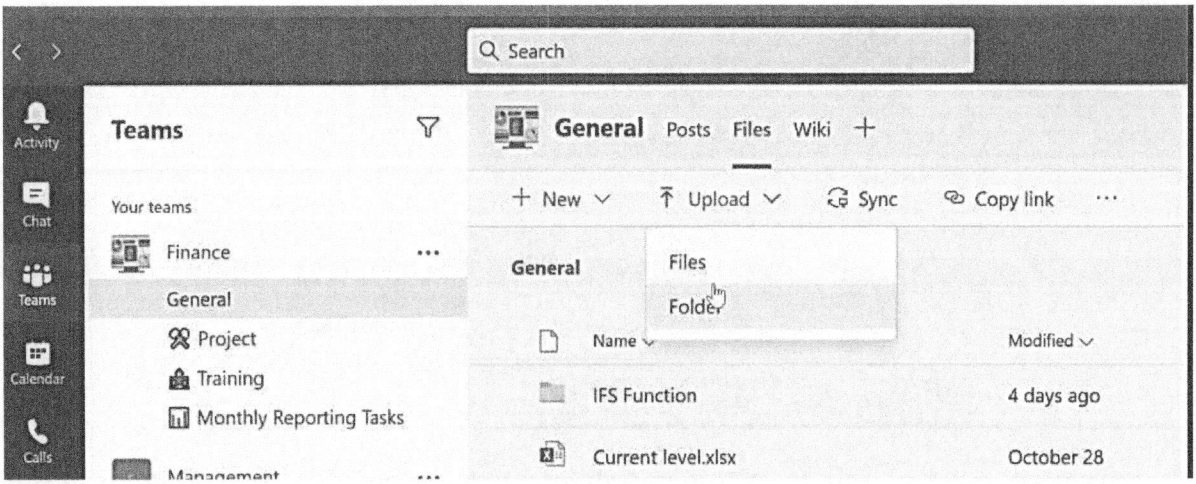

You can also directly upload files and folders from here, you can add new documents directly from here, and any files you create here are automatically uploaded to the SharePoint drive for this group. You can collaborate live on a document here and your changes will automatically be saved in SharePoint. This is great because you have protections as well as collaboration benefits.

So, let's say right now another team member is in a document, you can have a conversation with them right inside this file. Any changes you make to this file are automatically saved in SharePoint. Now let's say you are done with the file; you just need to click **close**.

If you don't want to make changes directly to a file but instead you want to create a copy, you can do that by clicking on more options and copying it. You can also download a copy to my desktop. You can rename documents directly from here, delete documents, or pin important documents to the top.

Wiki

If you have a business account you also have access to Wiki. If you have an education account, you see other tabs like Class Notebook, Assignments, and Grades. The purpose of Wiki is like a notebook; you can use it as a central place to share things you don't want to get lost in conversations, for example, best practices, important decisions, and the like.

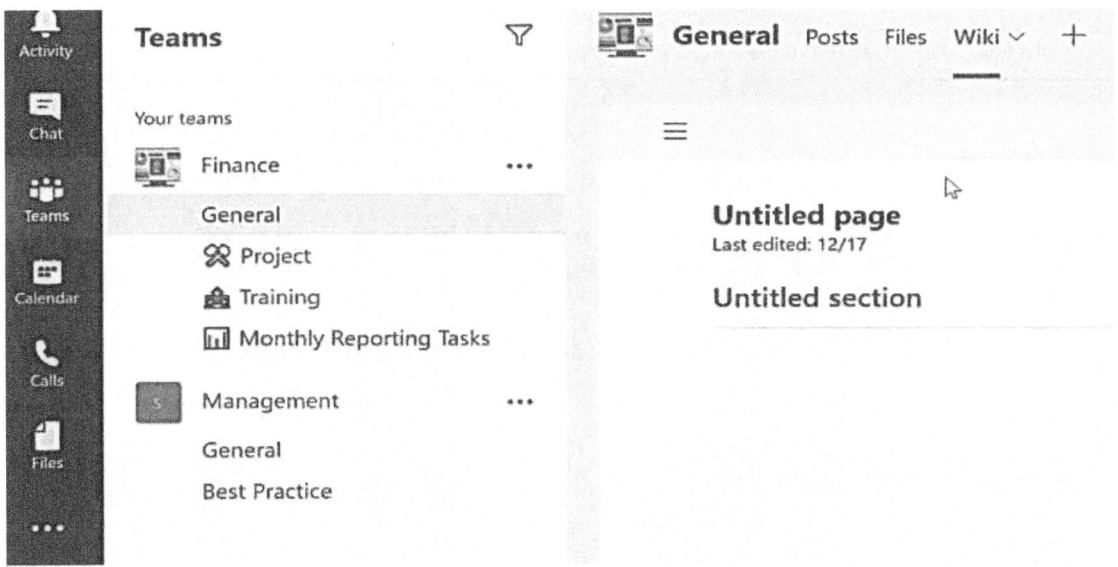

Every channel has its Wiki. It acts as a central hub for important information.

Workspace

The best part of teams is that you can customize your shared workspace by adding other apps. These can be Microsoft or other third-party apps, so notice you have access to a lot of apps here. The reason you'd want to do that is so you don't have to leave Teams to get to your other apps; you have one location where you can access everything. If you want to use any of these apps, you can add that app directly here so all your team can access it. First, you need to log in with the app, then you need to select the board that you want to share with your team. This is going to add the app board directly in here, now your team members will have to log into the app for authentication, and then they can work with this board directly from within Teams. If it's hidden, click on **"more options"** and you can see the board.

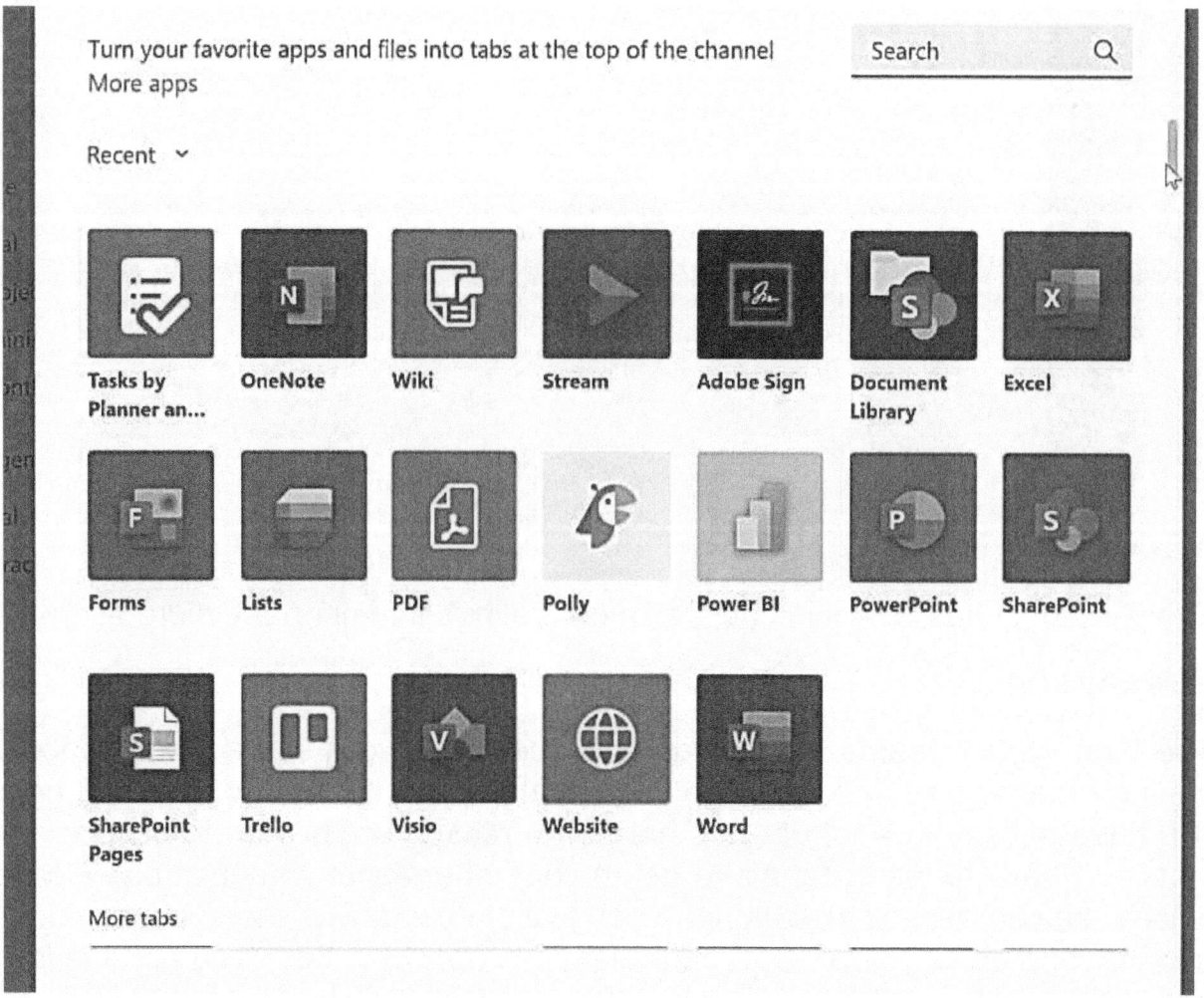

If you're using Microsoft Planner, you can add that as well. Select **"Tasks by Planner"**, use an existing plan or create a new plan, and click on Save.

There are some great apps here that you can use. You can also directly add files as a separate tab to this, so for example let's say there is a specific Excel file that you want to make available as a separate tab, select that file, this could be a file that you've already uploaded to your files drive and Save.

This file is now available as a separate tab in your project channel. You can also rename these tabs by clicking on them and renaming them.

There are other actions you can perform within a channel such as creating and joining an online meeting and using the joining Chat feature. This will be discussed in subsequent chapters.

Now, let's move on to the other tabs in the Teams.

Calendar View

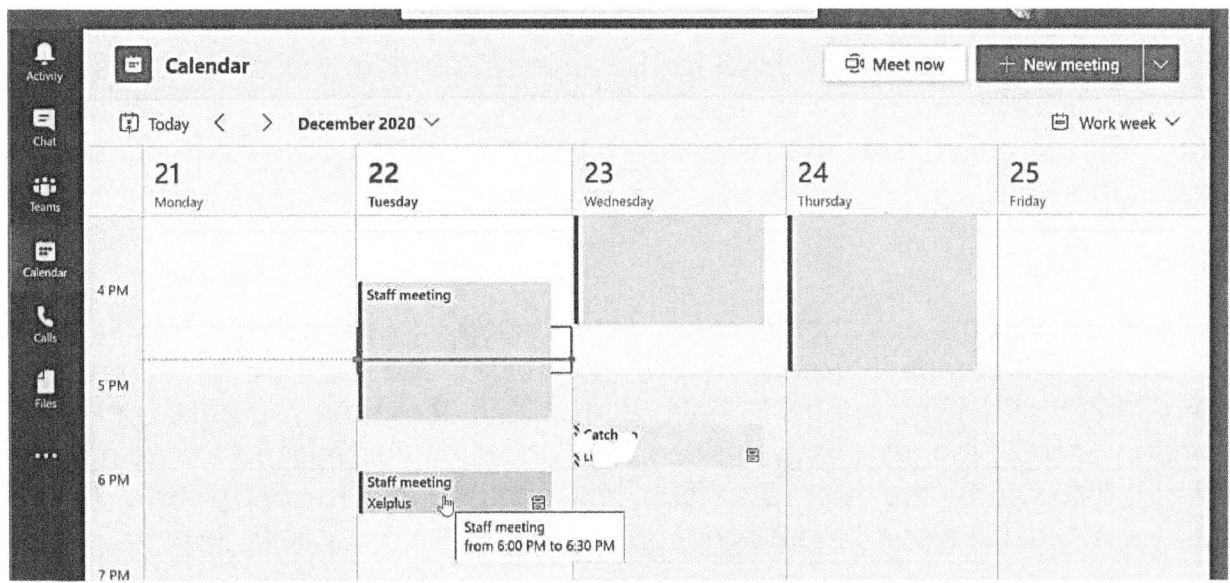

If you go to the Calendar view you will see all your scheduled meetings. This is synced to your exchange account, and with all your meetings in one place, you can manage them from here or from outlook directly.

Chat View

Here you can have private one-on-one chats or group chats with specific people. This helps reduce the number of emails that are sent around. To search for someone you haven't chatted with yet click on "**New Chat**", then search for their names and add them; you can also add multiple people and create group chats. Anything related to a Team topic t should stay in a team unless you need it to be private because the last thing you want is to manage multiple chats and multiple Teams.

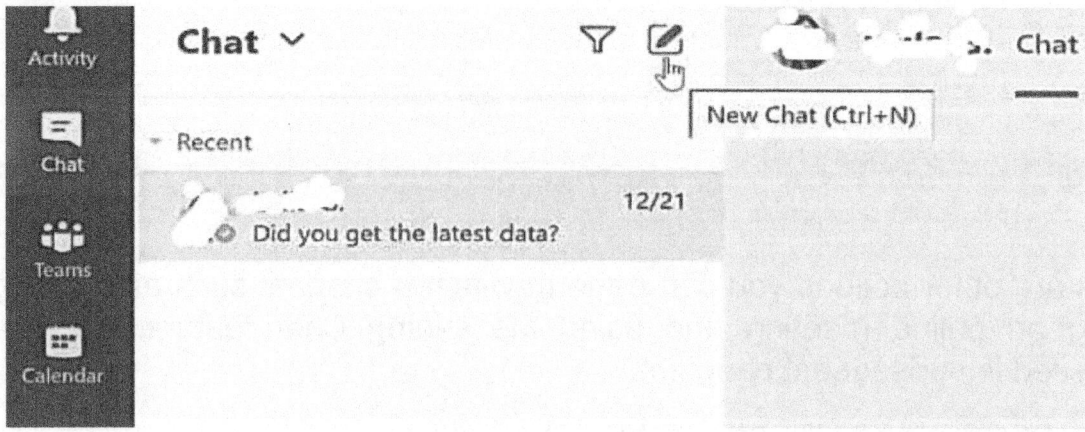

Here you have the same messaging options that you saw before. If you're typing too much back and forth, you might as well have a video call or an audio call. Any files that you share with a person are going to be inside files. These are saved to your personal OneDrive for Business. You can see all of these files if you log into **office.com**, go to OneDrive, under "**Shared**" and then "**Shared by you**". You can also see the files that have been shared with you directly in OneDrive as well.

Activity Tab

To keep up with the activity that you missed when you were away, this is where the activity tab comes into play. Here in "**Activity**", you can see the summary of everything that's going on. If you have a red circle, it means you have a new app mention or reply that you haven't seen. Any activities you missed are going to be in bold, followed by the latest activities. You can use the "**more options**" here to filter for a specific type of message; you can also filter by specific text.

The search box at the top has multiple purposes; it can search for a specific text or a specific phrase, you can also send direct messages to someone from here. Start with "@", type in their names, and type the message. This means you don't have to switch to a chat view and find the person to send them the message, you can send that message directly from search.

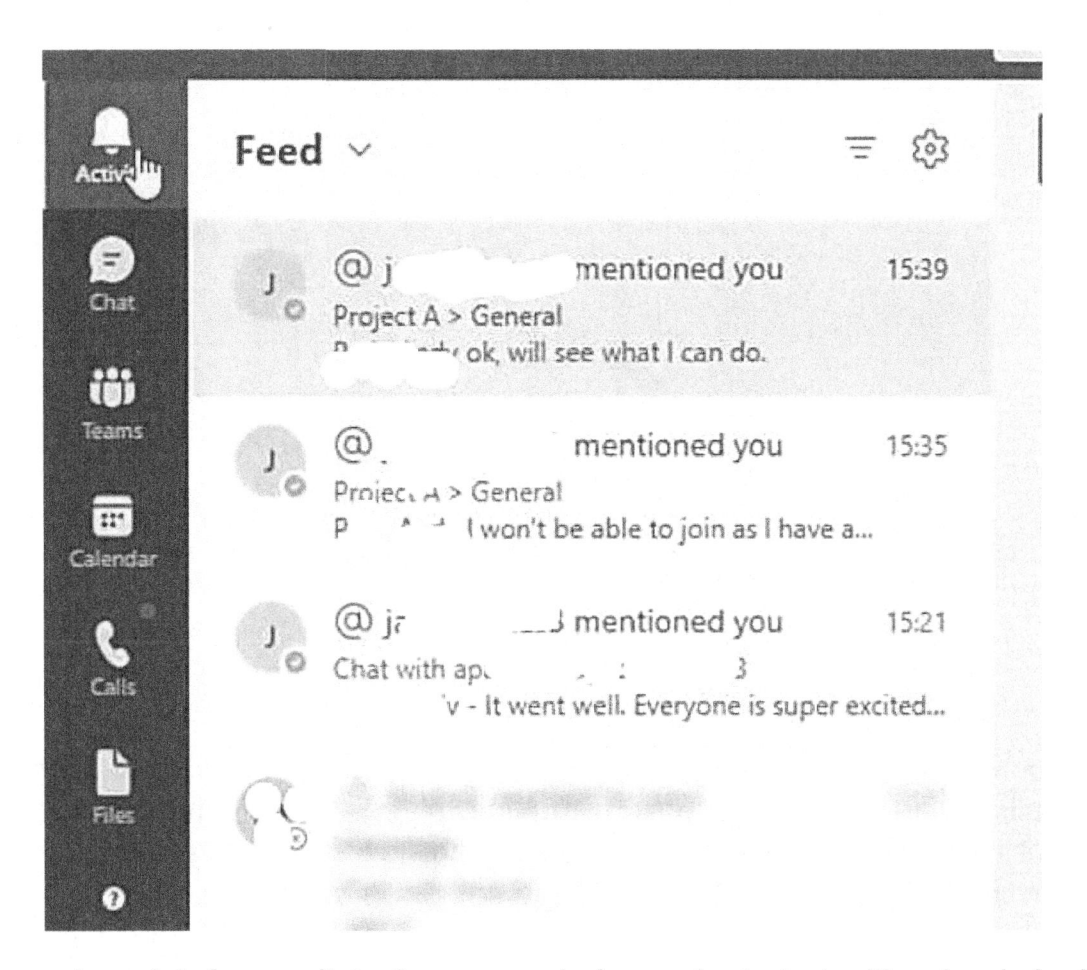

You can also pick from a list of commands here. Just start with a backslash and pick or type a command. To filter for unread messages, just type in "**unread**". To change your status from "**Available**" to "**Do not disturb**", type in a backslash and "**dnd**"; that changes your status to "**do not disturb**".

Calls Tab

Here, you can see your contacts, your history of calls, and you can quickly call any of your team members.

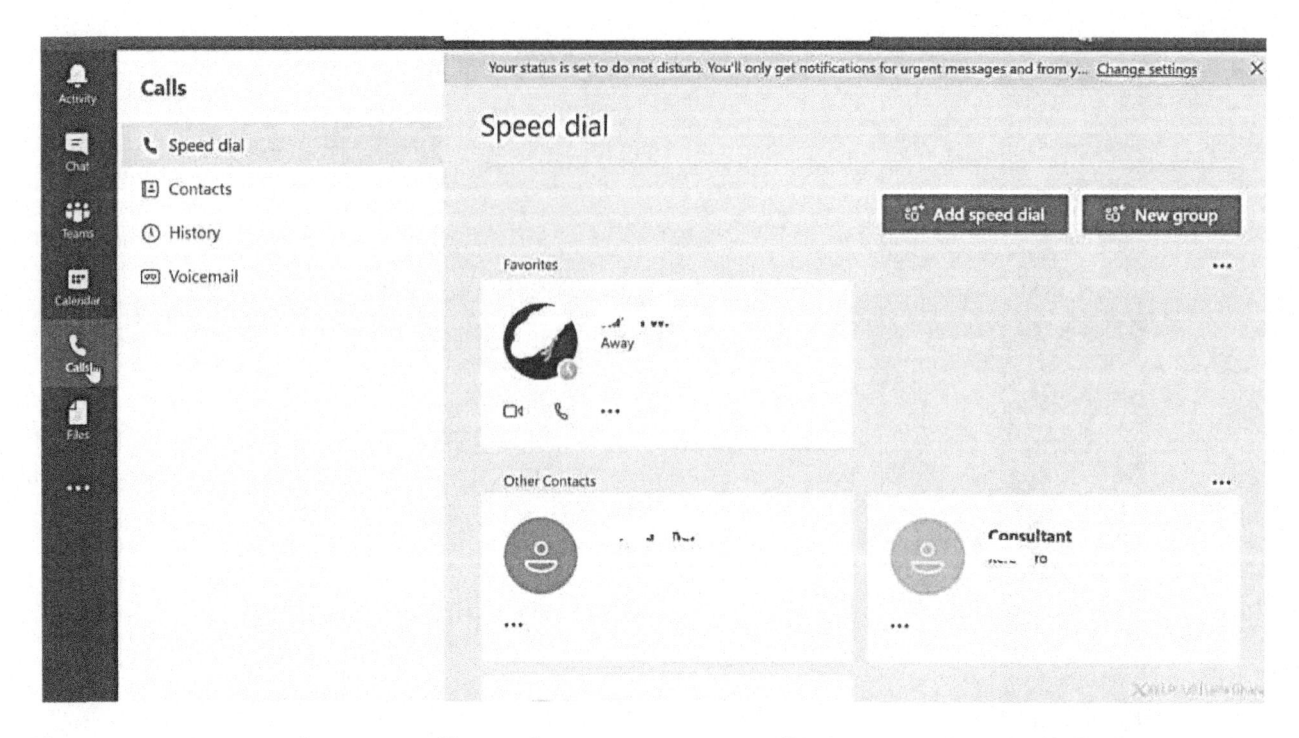

If your company has a calling plan, you can call any number by dialing it from here. Calling can also be done from multiple places, so if you're in a team and you want to call a specific person in that team just hover over their name and call them directly from here, either a video call or an audio call.

Files Tab

Under **"Files"**, you get to see all the files you've recently worked on regardless of whether this was in teams or outside teams. You also get to see your private OneDrive for Business.

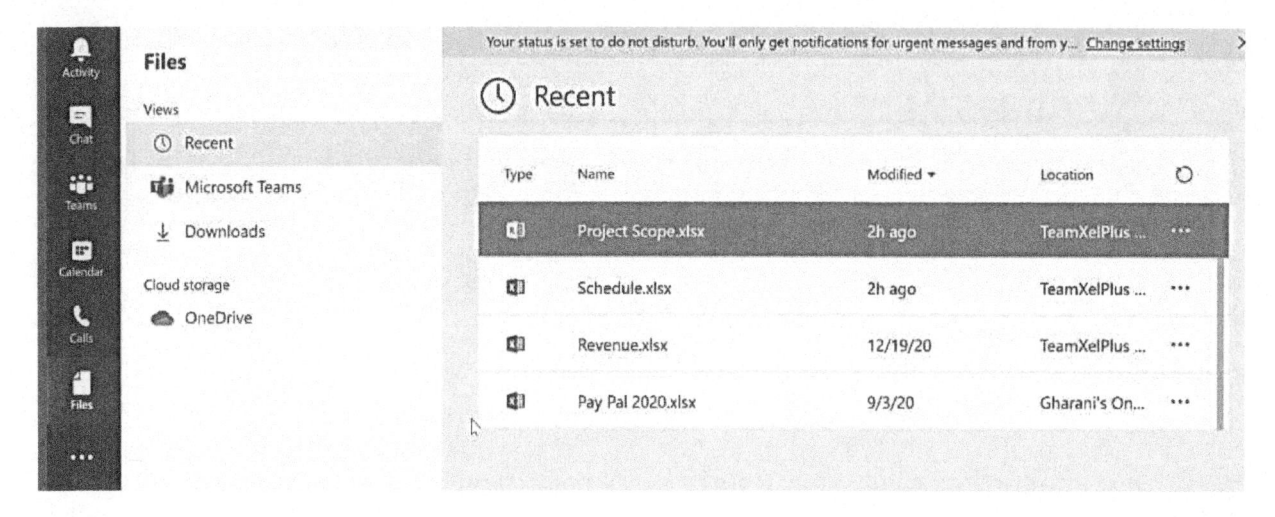

If you belong to different organizations with the same email address you can switch your organizations by clicking on the organization name at the top right-hand corner and switching.

If you're using a different email address for the Teams of another organization, you have to sign out of Teams and then sign back in with the alternate email address. You don't have to install another Team's software, no matter if it's education or business; just sign out and back in with the other email address.

Summary

In this introductory chapter, you learned

- What Microsoft Teams is and does
- How to get Teams
- How to install Teams
- The interface and the elements such as Teams tab, Chat tab, Calendar view, Calls tab, Activity tab, and Files tab and their specific functions.
- What a channel is and how to get familiar with using Channels in Teams

Chapter 3: What's New In Teams With Windows

In this chapter, I'll be showing you the new features in Microsoft Teams. This includes the new search experience, the Q & A app, the new Viva apps, and a whole lot more. Please note that all these will be discussed separately in subsequent chapters. With that in mind, let's get started.

Improved Search Experience

The first new feature is a significant overhaul of search in Teams, and this makes it much easier to find things. In teams, up at the top, there's a search bar, and if you type in a certain term and hit enter, you'll notice that it's much more laid out. Before now, it used to be all crammed in on the left-hand side.

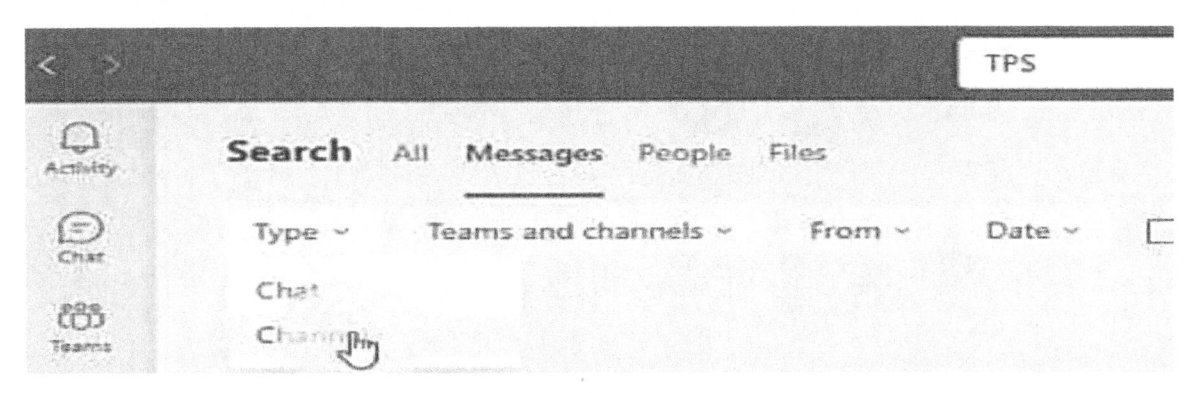

You can also do things like search across messages or filter by people or by files. Under **"Messages"** there's a bunch of new filters right there, you can filter by type, so if you just want to look at the channel versus chat, you can do that. You can also search across teams and channels, and you can filter by **"From"** and **"Date"**. So, if you click here and type in a certain name, this will filter all of the messages that have the initial term you search for across both chats and channels. If you want to clear everything, just click **"Clear all"**.

In the specific messages themselves, If you click on the little arrow, it shows other conversations that might be related to these messages. You can click to go directly to that message and this takes you right into a chat where you're talking about the term you searched for.

Q&A App in Teams Meetings

The second new feature is the just-launched Q&A app that you can add to a Team's meeting. This allows you to easily manage questions and answers during a webinar or a rather large meeting where there are a lot of questions happening. After you've set up your meeting right here as the organizer, you're going to click it and choose to edit. This is before the meeting starts, so you will go up to the plus menu in your channel and there's a new app called Q&A.

If you don't see it just search for it at the search bar and click on it when found and then add. You will see the setup screen for the app. Here you can choose to allow attendees to ask new questions and respond to conversations. You can turn these on or off during the meeting or before a meeting. The other option below, allow organizers to moderate attendee conversations, and if you check this one on, you cannot turn it off once the meeting starts. Now click **"Save"**.

What this does on the meeting organizer's side is that it adds the Q&A tab. Now you have a clue of what you can do; some questions are in review, questions that would be published and there are questions that you could dismiss. So, if you are the moderator, you have the choice to **review questions**, **publish them**, and **dismiss them**. You can also click on the drop-down and you can ask a question or start a discussion.

Word Cloud for Forms Poll in Teams Meetings

If you have a meeting you've set up, go to the plus tab and choose "**Forms**"; If you don't see it just search for it. In the Forms Window, click "**Save**" and this sets up your forms tab.

What you're going to do is to join the meeting and create a new poll in the meeting and then you're going to gather responses to show that word cloud.

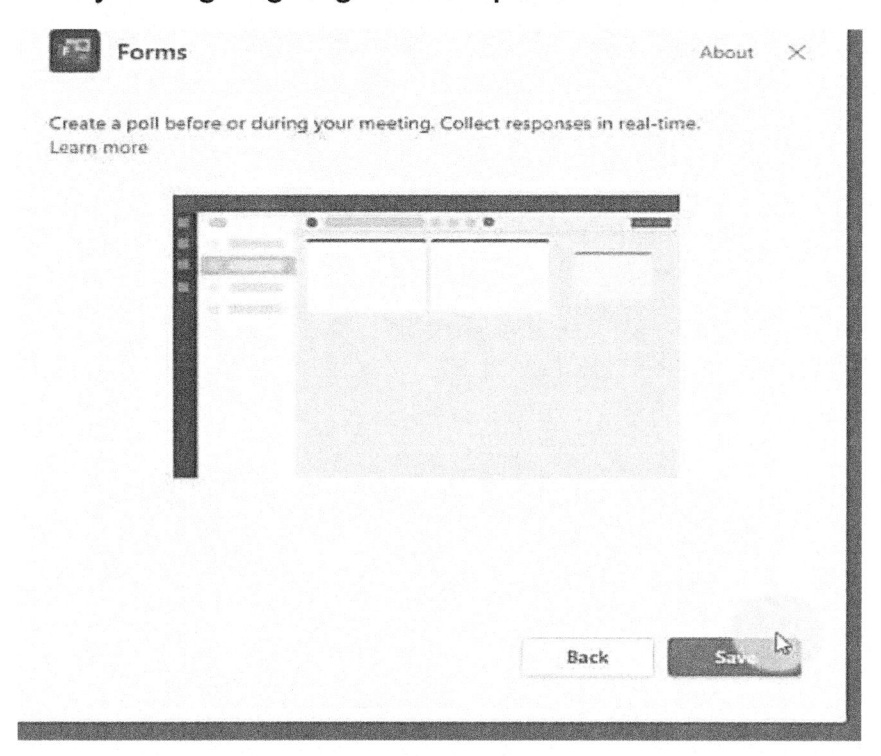

If you're the organizer in the Team's meeting, at the top you'll see the forms app that you added. So, click on it, now go down and click "Create new poll". You'll see the new option "**Word Cloud Poll**", so click on that and give it a question, then click "**Save**".

If there are many different responses your Word Cloud will be very distributed and it's great to gather all that information quickly. When you leave the meeting, you will also have that copy of your Word Cloud Poll right there in the meeting under polls, where everyone else can see it as well.

Transcription Support in Channel Meetings

Channel Meetings are very popular in the education world but also there are some in main commercial organizations. So, if you've got a new meeting and you've given it a title, you can add a channel to make this a channel meeting and click "**Send**". This creates the meeting in your calendar but let's switch over to the Team so you'll see how to launch the channel meeting there and then do transcripts.

In the Teams tab, you will see that scheduled meeting for transcripts in the channel, If you click it to start it up and now click "**Join**". This will take you to the Teams meeting and If you go to the three-dot menu, there is a choice to Start transcription. If you choose "**Start recording**", it will also start the transcription.

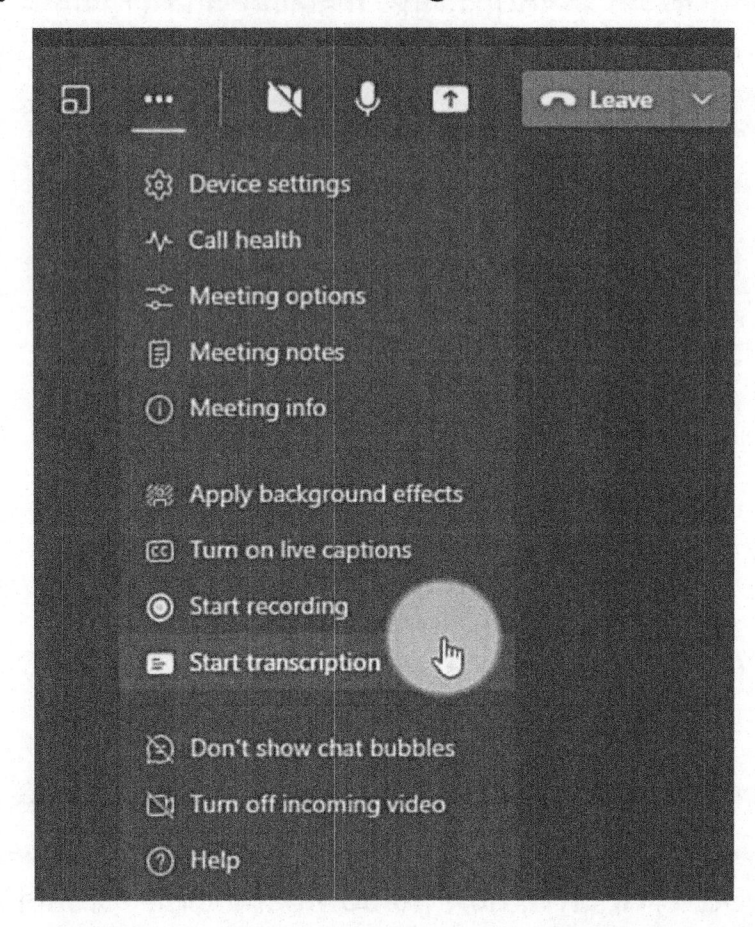

When you do this, there is a bar across the top with the transcript pane opened and as you're talking, all of the transcripts are captured. If other people are talking as well, their name will appear next to it just like normal Teams transcription works.

If you leave the meeting and go back to that channel, you can see that not only does it have the attendance report but the meeting transcript is right there and if you click on it, it opens up this transcript tab, with the entire transcription is right there and anyone can view it later. You can also download it as a VTT file or a Word document.

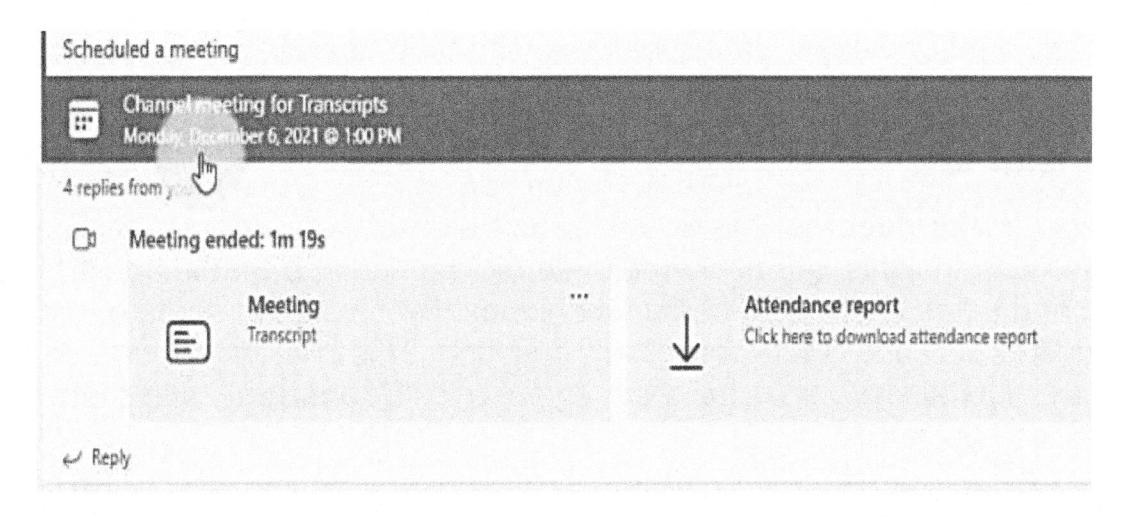

Please note that your IT administrator may have to enable the transcription across your tenant in general so make sure to know how to enable transcripts in your tenant.

Viva Learning

Viva Learning helps employees make learning a natural part of the day and brings it into the flow of work and tools that they already use like Teams. To find Viva Learning, go to the three-dot menu on the left side of your Teams app and choose Viva Learning.

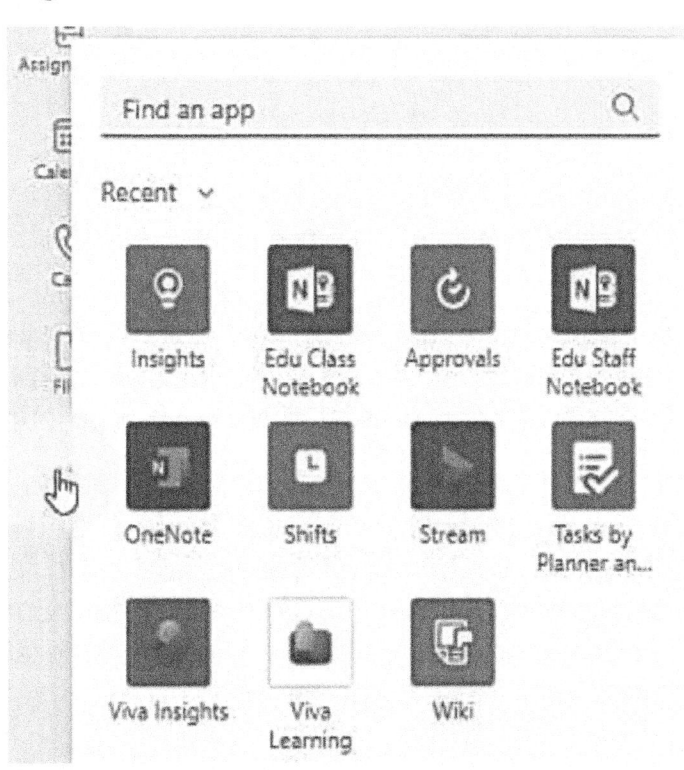

If your company has other courses they can plug those into viva learning. So you can have all your learning right here within Teams in Viva Learning.

There are a much deeper set of features with Viva Learning and we will go into detail in subsequent chapters.

Viva Insights

If you go to the three-dot menu on the left side of your Teams, click on Viva Insights. Viva Insights is a new employee experience app that is again built into Teams and takes a lot of the same techniques if you've seen some of the things around **"Reflect"** and **"Well-being"** in Education. This is more about a corporate or organizational view or a staff view if you're in **"Education"**, and there's a set of activities you can do.

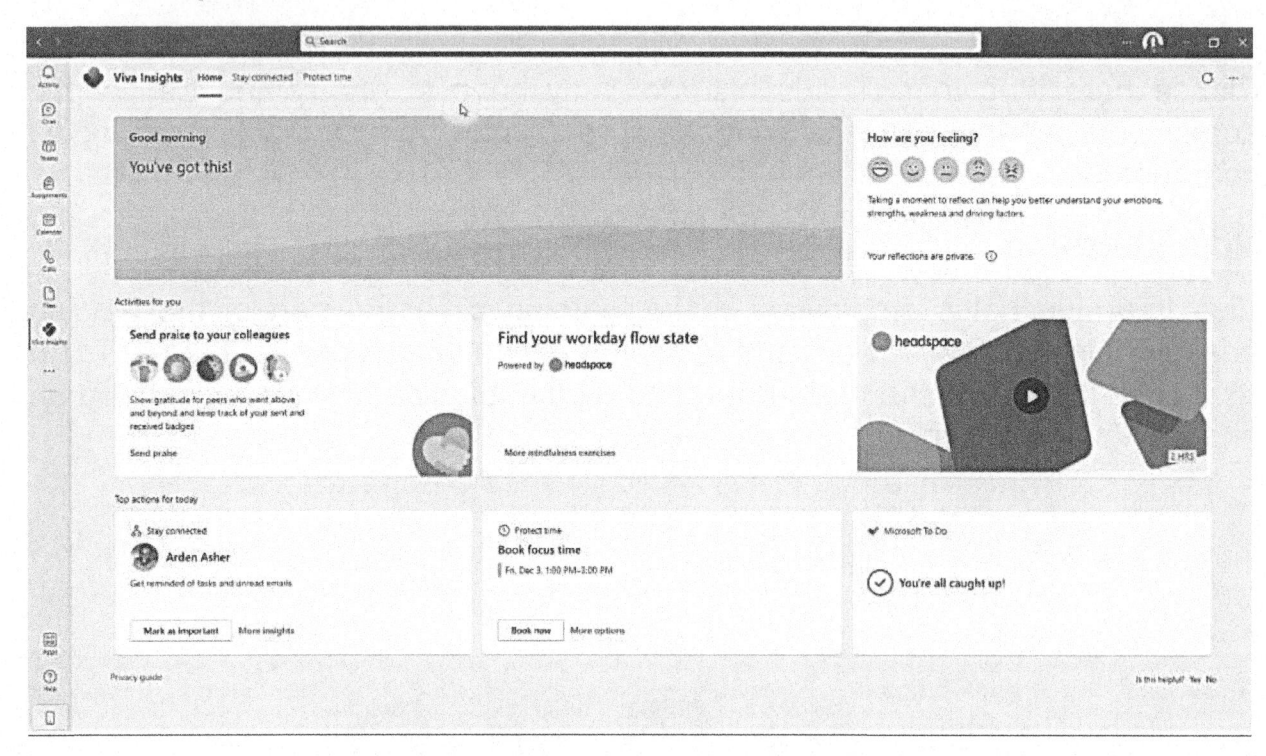

You can take a reflection and even see history, so you can track how you've been feeling over time. During pandemic work, feelings can be up or down and so there are a lot of things you can do just to track your emotional state.

Another option is sending **"Praise"** to your colleagues. Sometimes when you get busy you can forget to do that. Click **"Send Praise"** and you can send out awesome praise to your co-worker. After you've searched for your co-worker's name, you can choose to send it one-on-one in a chat to them or you can send it to the team. If you choose the team, it'll put it in the general channel, you can add a personalized note, hit preview, and hit Send.

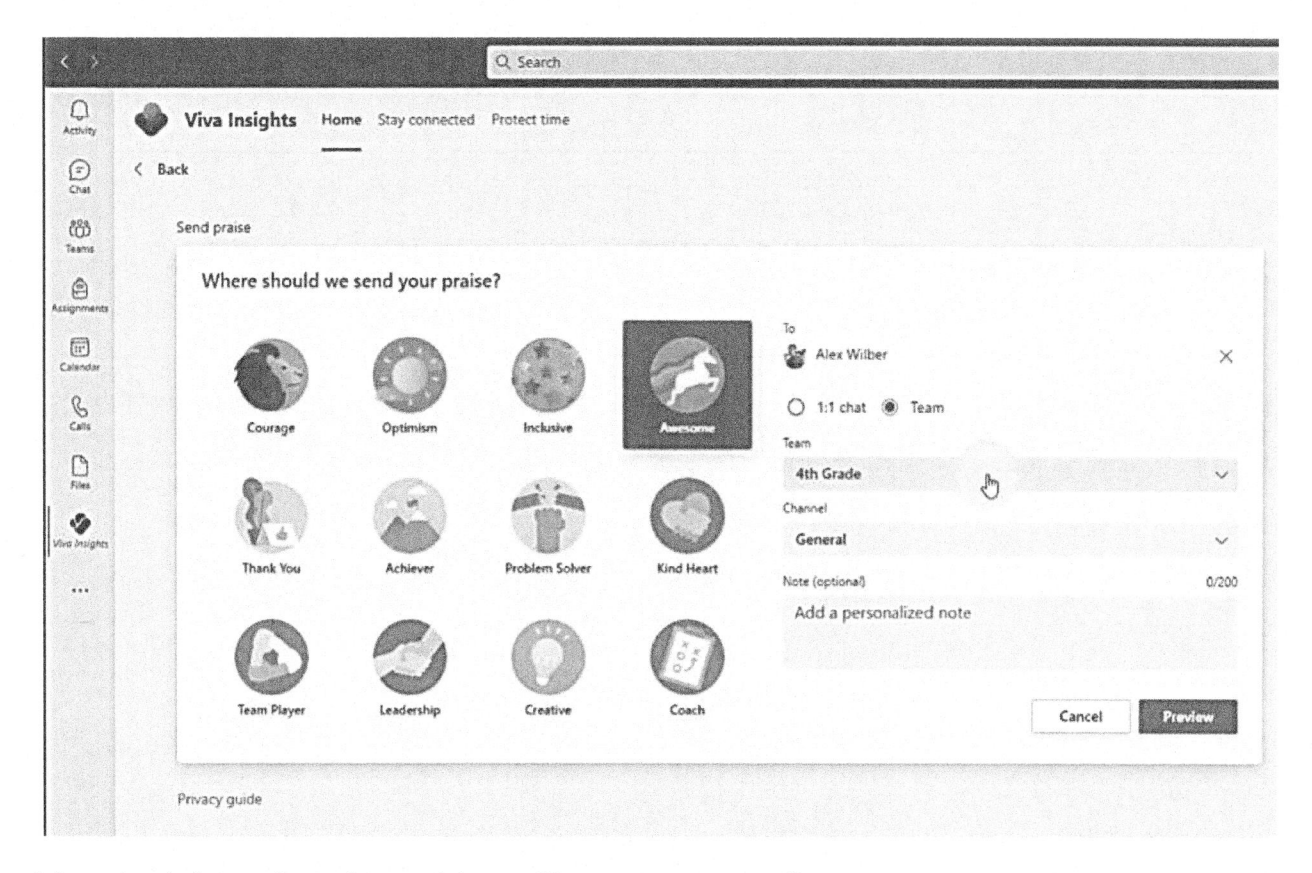

Viva Insights also does things like recommending you to stay in contact with certain colleagues. This means that if you haven't stayed connected with a colleague, you're going to get reminded to work and collaborate with them. So, you mark that colleague as important, to make sure you stay connected with him.

Another important one is Booking Focus Time. This falls under the **"Protect Time"** tab. To ensure that you have extra focus, you can use this to give yourself focus time. If you want to see more options, click the appropriate button and this takes you into the Protect Time tab.

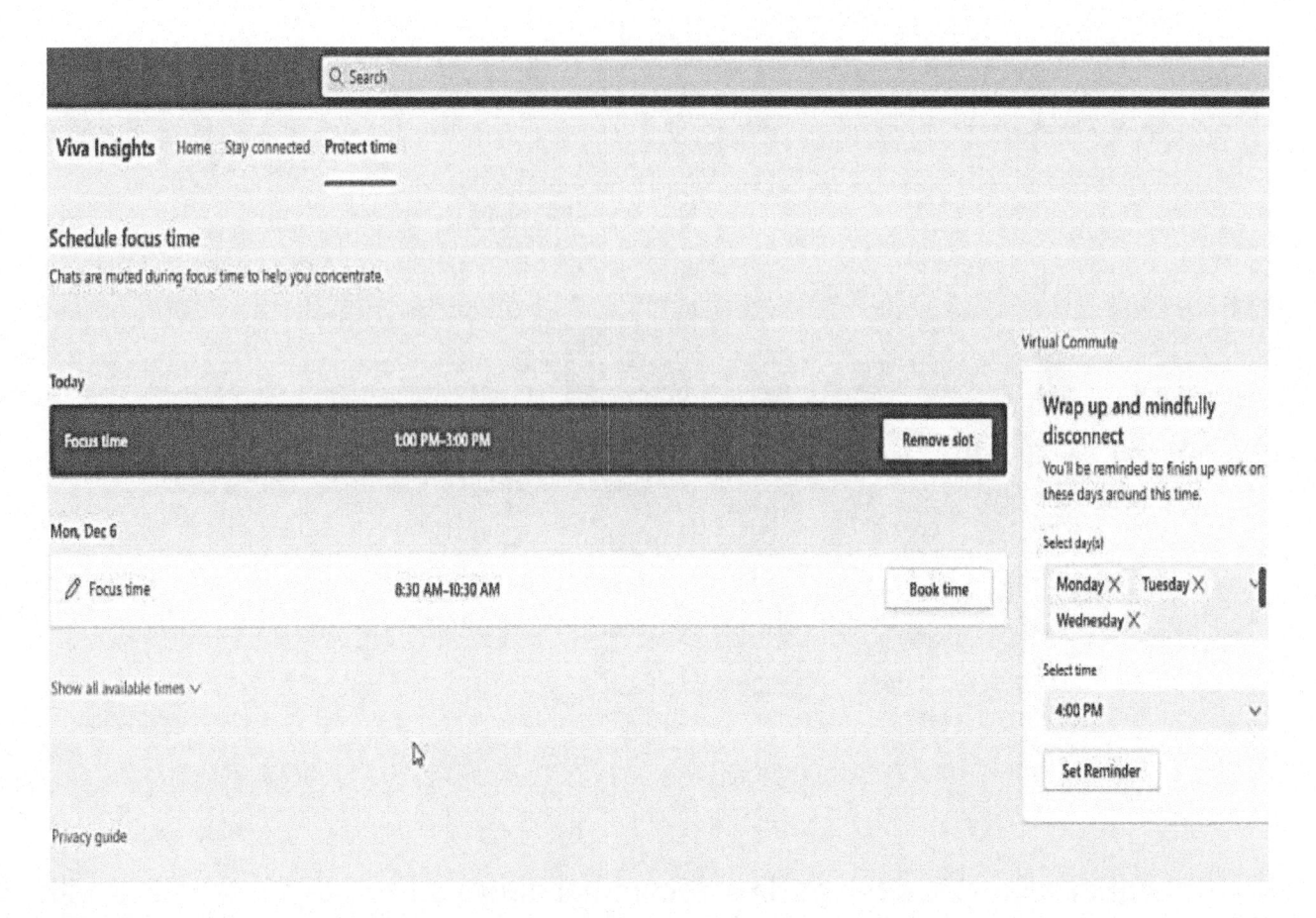

This is a great way to keep yourself focused and not let your calendar explode with meetings.

Mirroring Video for your Team's Calls

So, you're getting ready to join your team's call and if you go to settings here, you're going to see a new option that says **"Mirror my video"**. By default, it is mirrored.

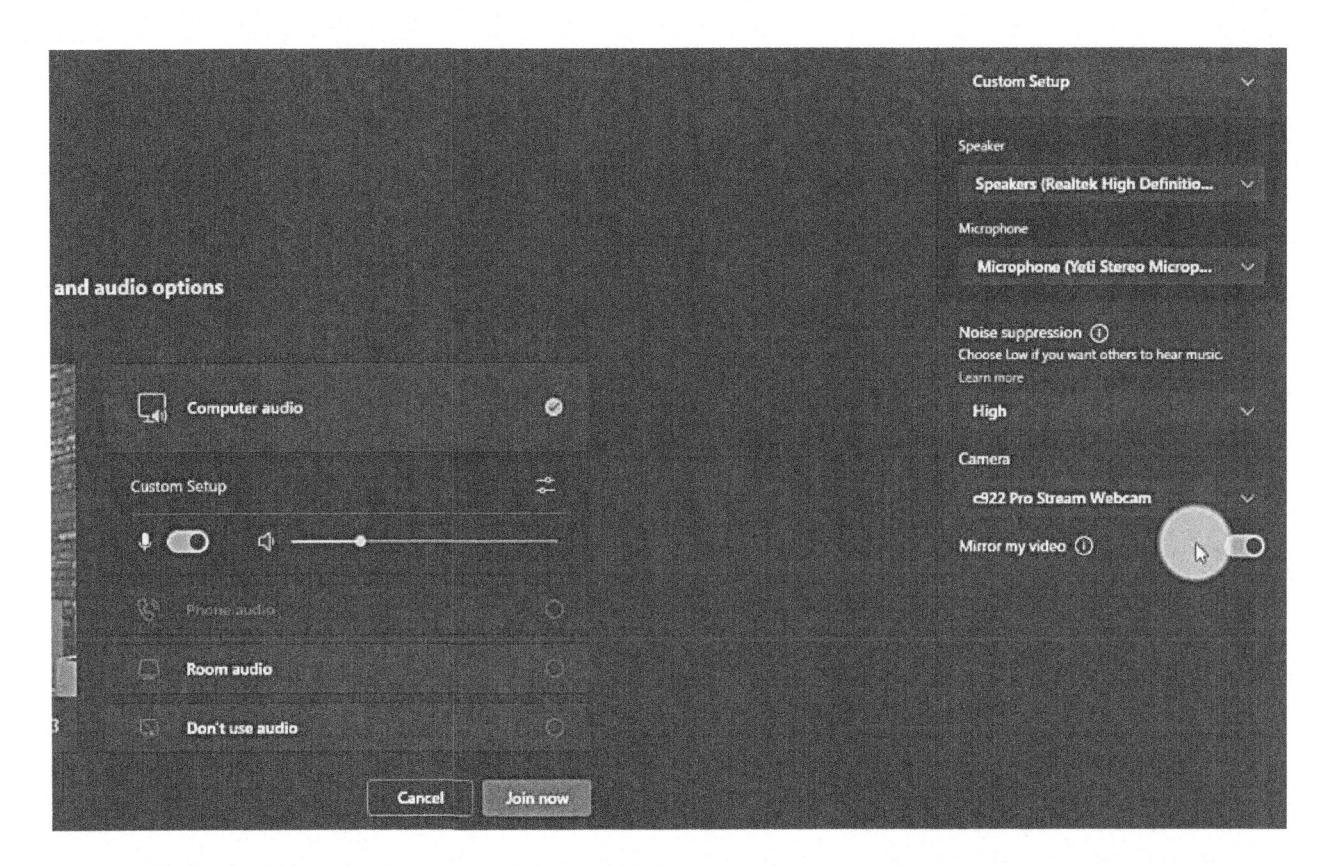

If you turn this off, this feature is switched off. So, you can mirror yourself or not.

Clippy in Teams

If you have a message that you want to reply to, click **reply**, now go and choose stickers.

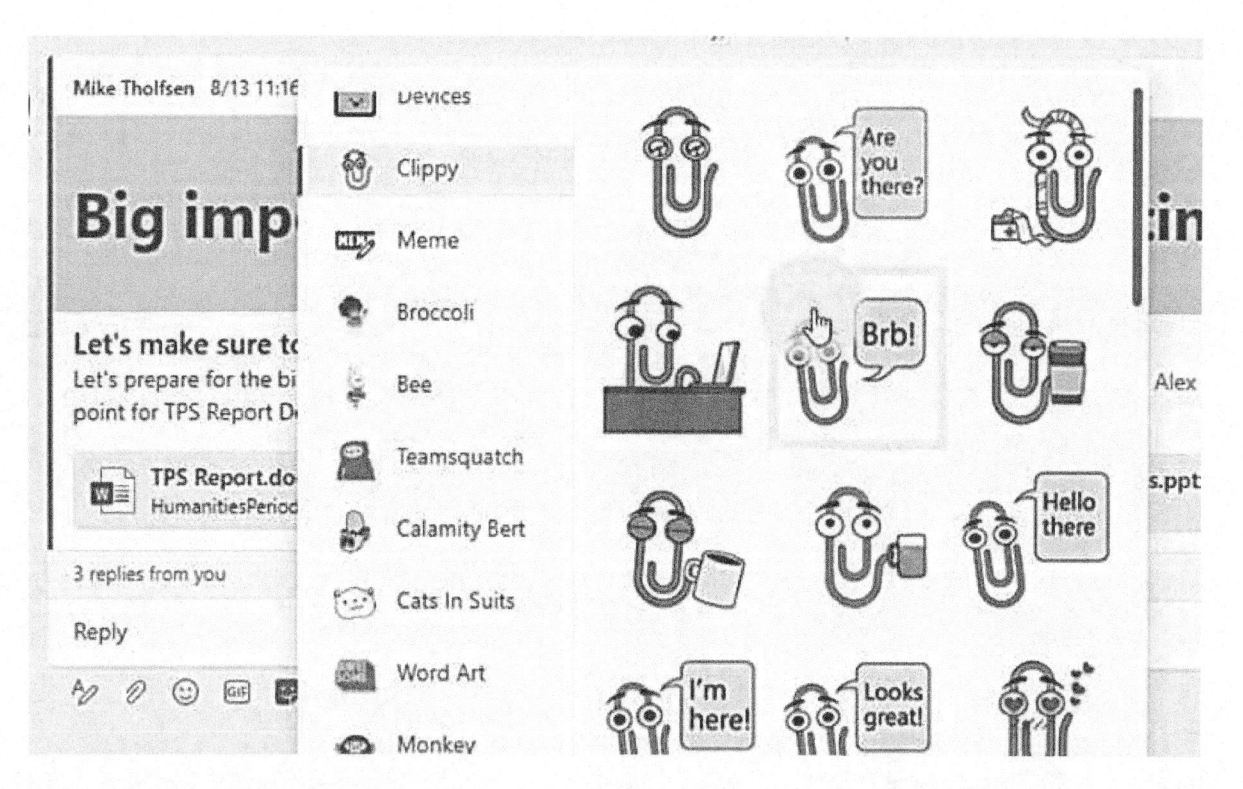

As the sticker dialog launches, if you scroll down, you'll find Clippy, click on here and you'll see all of the great things that Clippy always offers. He is so helpful; you can scroll down to find your favorite.

Summary

In this chapter, you learned about the new features of Microsoft Teams

especially for the Windows 11 operating system, as this is the latest version of Windows. The features covered were:

- Improved search experience
- Q&A App in Teams' Meetings
- Word Cloud for Forms Poll in Teams' Meetings
- Transcription Support in Channel Meetings
- Viva Learning
- Viva Insights
- Mirroring Video for your Teams' calls
- Clippy in Teams

Chapter 4: Mastering Teams Messaging

In this chapter, you will get full details on how to use Microsoft Teams chat and conversations. Here, we'll focus on the following: Starting a chat and conversation in Teams, responding to a chat, searching for chats and conversations, notifications, chatting with guests and groups, and other topics which you will learn as you go through this chapter.

Chat Vs Teams Conversation

The first thing you should know is that you can have an individual chat with one other person or a group chat with multiple people and you can also have a conversation within a Team's Channel. Think of a chat as a private message between you and someone else or a group of people, whereas Team's Channel conversation is more public that can be viewed by everyone who belongs to the teams.

Chat Features

To start a new chat, go to the chat tab and click on the chat icon. You can enter the name of the person you want to chat with, you can also enter their email group or tag. Don't worry about all these different options, for now, we'll come back to it later. As you type, Team suggests different people from the organization's contact list and it'll also suggest guests who have been invited. If this is a group chat and you want to include additional people, you can continue to enter their names.

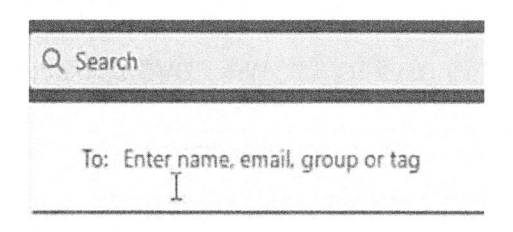

If this is a new chat and you've never had a chat with this specific person or group of people, the main window will be blank; but if you had previously chatted with this person or group, chat history will show here.

Composing a Message

Now you're ready to compose your message. You can simply enter your message in the message box and either hit enter or press the airplane icon.

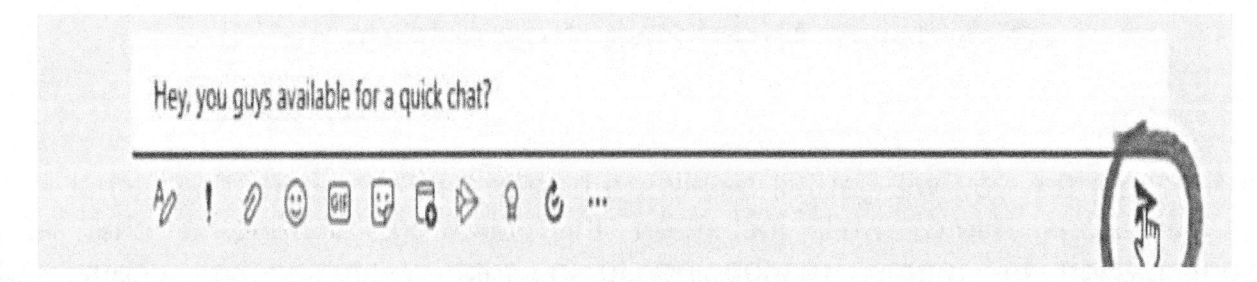

One note of caution here, do not make the mistake of hitting enter thinking it'll create a new line, because it ends up sending the message prematurely. For a new line, you need to press **Shift + Enter**. But this is easy to forget, so what I suggest is for you to get in the habit of sending the message from the expanded compose box, and here you can press enter for a new line and it won't send the message until you hit the airplane. A shortcut to expand the compose box is CTRL + SHIFT + X.

Formatting your chats and Conversations

In this expanded window, you have the basic formatting options such as bold, italic, and underline, and these have the same keyboard shortcuts as anywhere else like Word and Outlook.

The next set of formatting tools allows you to highlight, change the font color, and font size. For highlights and fonts, we have a basic 10-color palette, and for size, we are limited to just small, medium, and large. You can also choose different outline levels for writing a long announcement. You can indent and outfield, and add bulleted or numbered lists. If you want to quote someone, you can highlight the text and select the quote button. If you have a long hyperlink to a document or website and want to replace it with shorter, more descriptive text, you can enter it by choosing the link button. The three-dotted menu will reveal more options to include code snippets, horizontal rules, and a table. Finally, you have the undo and repeat options but it's just easier to use **CTRL + Z** and **CTRL + Y**, rather than digging through these menus.

Delivery Options

Next, you can set delivery options. There are three to choose from. The default of course is standard, but you can choose Important or Urgent.

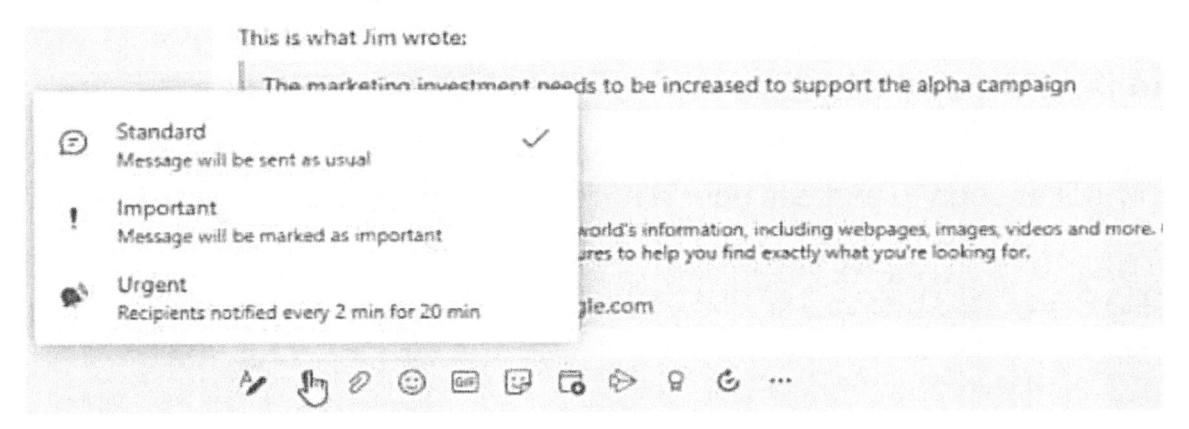

Urgent will notify the recipient every two minutes for 2 minutes for 20 minutes. If your goal is to annoy somebody you can choose this option, otherwise, you should stay away from it.

Attachments

For Attachments, you can choose to pull files either from OneDrive or upload from your computer and if you're in a team's conversation you have an additional option to pull from a team's SharePoint site as well, and you're not limited to the team's channel that you are having the conversation in. You can navigate to other teams and channels and copy the file over, in this case, you would be creating a duplicate file not linking to the source.

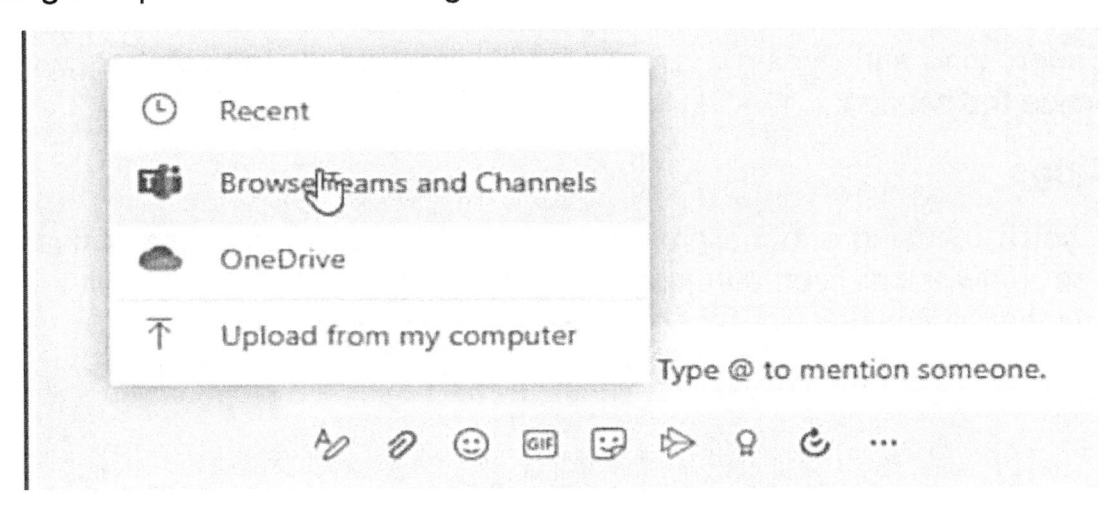

Here's something worth mentioning. If you're in a one-on-one chat or a group chat, the uploaded file will be saved in the OneDrive of the person who uploaded the file. This means if this person leaves the organization or otherwise makes changes to their OneDrive, the file will no longer be accessible by the other people in the chat. In contrast, files uploaded in a channel conversation will be saved to the team's channel SharePoint site and live in the document library. Even if the person who uploaded the file leaves the organization or leaves a team site, the remaining members will still have access to the file.

Emojis, Gifs, and Stickers

When typing, you can scroll through and search for emojis and if emojis are simply not enough to express your emotions, then Gifs might do the trick.

You can browse or search for the appropriate Gif to make the message a little more interesting and dynamic, and you can also add stickers that allow you to customize the caption.

Meetings

While you're chatting about a project, if you decide that a meeting is needed to align on a few things, you can just click the meeting icon here and it'll launch a new meeting dialog box.

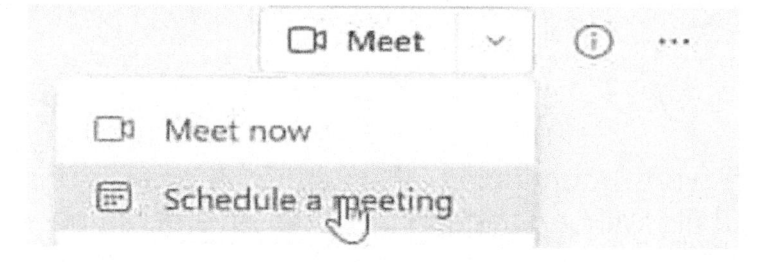

All people in the chat are already added to the invite, so you just need to fill in the rest and send it.

Deleting a chat

You can always delete a chat draft by hitting this trash can icon here.

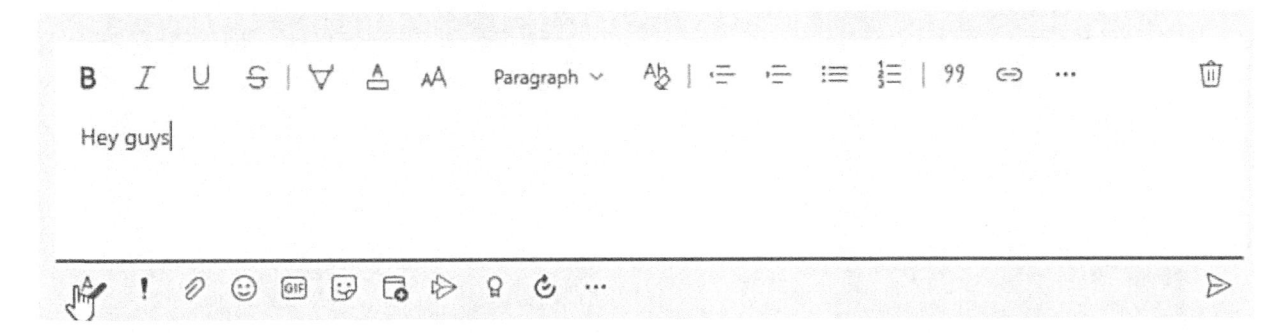

Streaming

Stream is a video platform. All meetings you record in Teams will be saved to this platform. If you want to share a specific recording, you can go to streams to copy one of the URLs to the video and paste it here.

You can open up Microsoft Edge, navigate to your Office 365, click on the app launcher, and choose **Stream**.

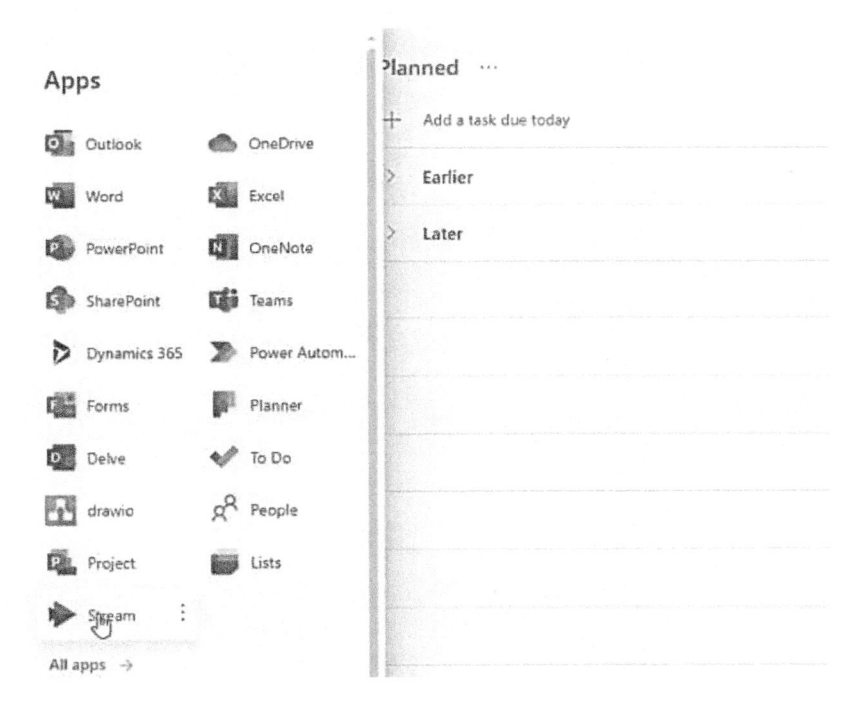

Here you can go to **"My content"** for your video recordings, click on **"Video"** and here you'll see a list of all of the videos that you've recorded.

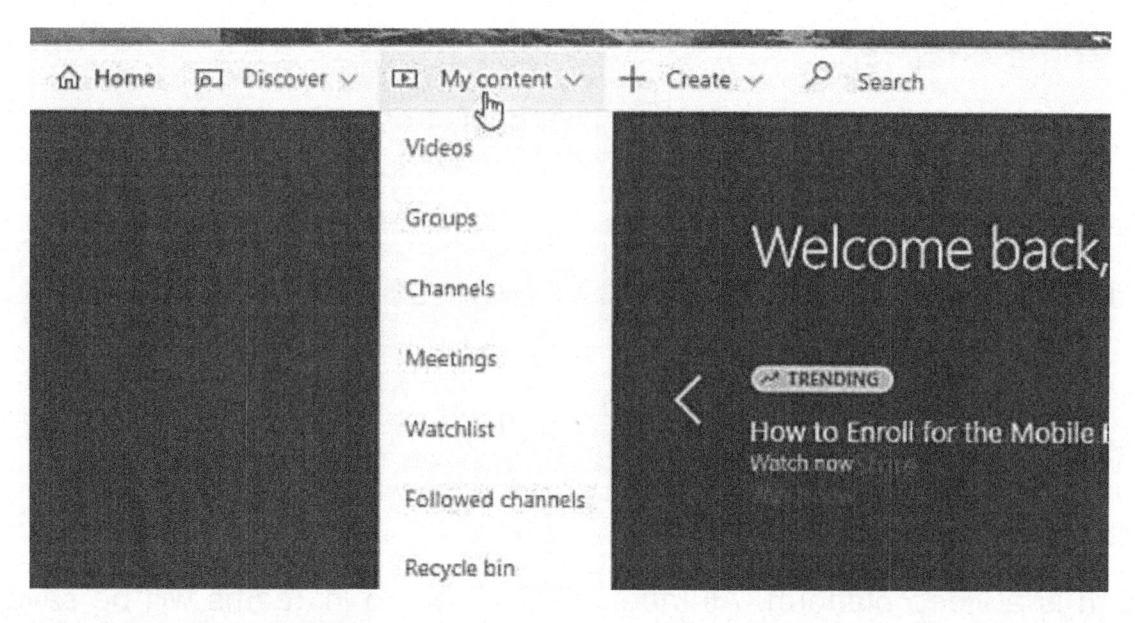

Click on the three-dotted, then share and copy the link. Now, go back to Microsoft Teams, click on Stream and you can paste the link here.

Sending Praises

You can send a batch to someone. Rather than simply typing **"Good job"**, a badge will add a fun element to it.

Click on the badge icon, choose your badge, type the name of the person that you want to send the badge to and they have to be part of the chat, and type in the optional note. Review your badge and hit Send.

Approvals

The very last icon here on the bottom of your chat box is for approvals. If you ever need approval from someone within this chat you can click on the approval's icon, type in the name of the request, and enter the names of your approvers. You can have one approver or multiple approvers; they all need to belong to this chat.

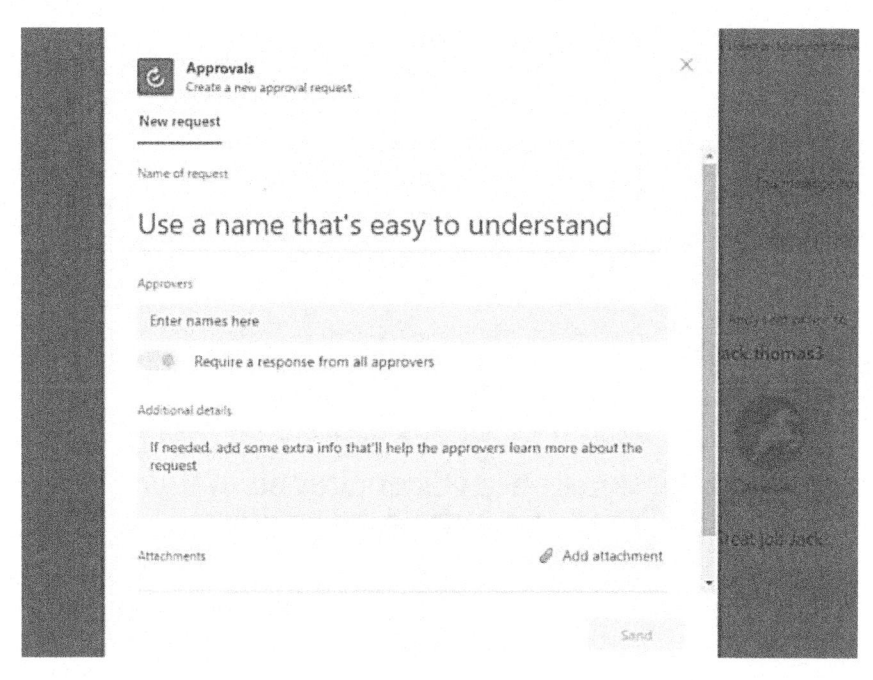

If you have multiple approvers this toggle button will be enabled, where it allows you to require a response from all approvers. You can type in additional details and you can add an attachment. You can choose a file from OneDrive or upload a file from your computer, and you can enable custom responses from the approver.

You can always come back to this chat if you want to check the status of this approval request or you can go to your side pane, go to your applications and launch the Approvals app from here, and it will list all approval requests. You also have the option to cancel the request if it's no longer needed.

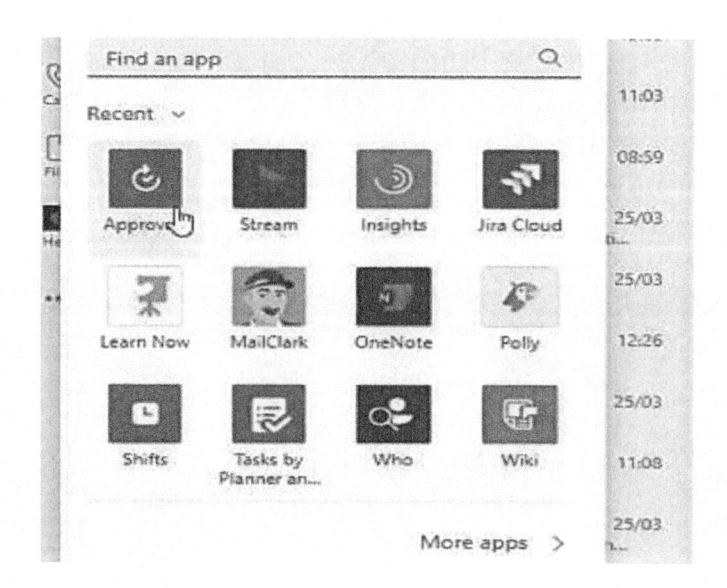

Pinning Chats

Back in the chat window, going through the options on the bottom, if you click on the three-dotted menu, it will reveal additional apps that you can pin. So, if you want to pin an app, right-click on it, hit **"Pin"** and it will appear on the bottom.

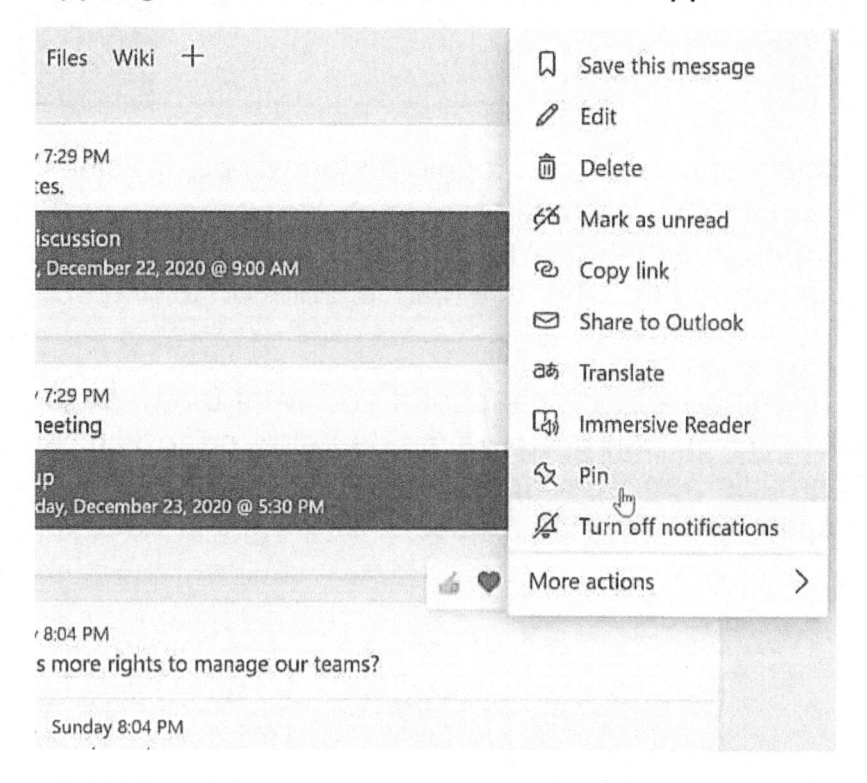

In the first part of this chapter, we explored all the things that you can do in a private chat message, and in this part, we're going to start by switching over to the Channels Conversation and you'll get to know some of the unique features.

Starting a Conversation

If you go to the General Channel of your team site, right at the button you'll see a button to start a New Conversation.

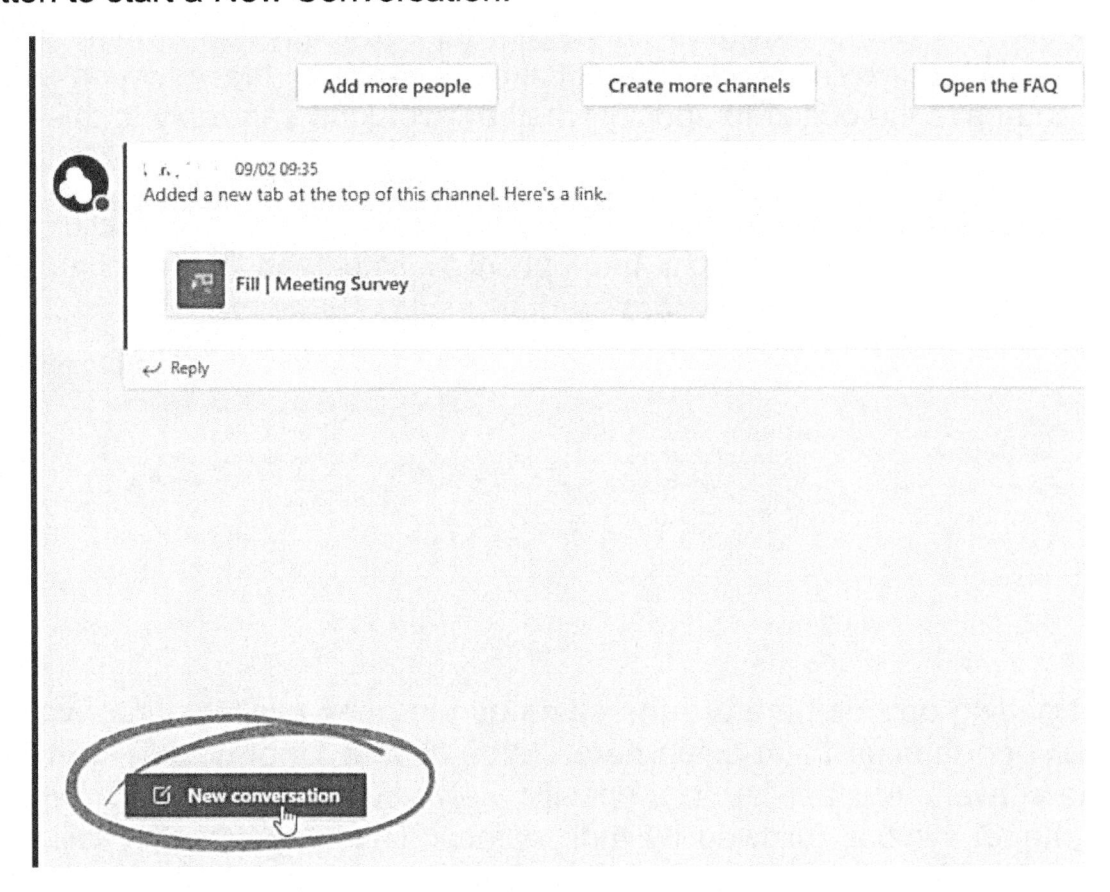

The first thing you should know is that everyone on this team site will be able to view and participate in this conversation. If you want to see the list of people who belong to this team, the simplest way is to click on the Info button on the top right.

Conversation Features

As with the chat, you have the option to expand the compose box. Here, you have the option to change this from a normal conversation to an announcement.

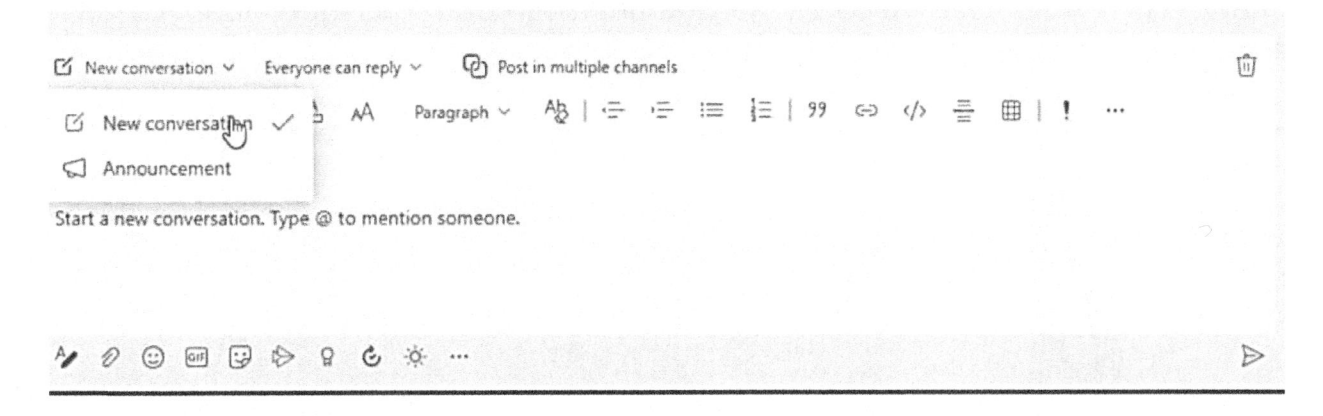

In the default choice of a new conversation, you have the option to include a subject. In the announcement, you can add a headline and customize the banner color, or add a background image. You can even add a subhead if we choose. Whether you're in the announcement mode or the new conversation mode, you have the option to specify whether everyone can reply to this post or just you and the moderator can reply.

You also have the option to post this in multiple channels; if you click on the corresponding button, you have the option to select additional channels by navigating to it and clicking "**Update**".

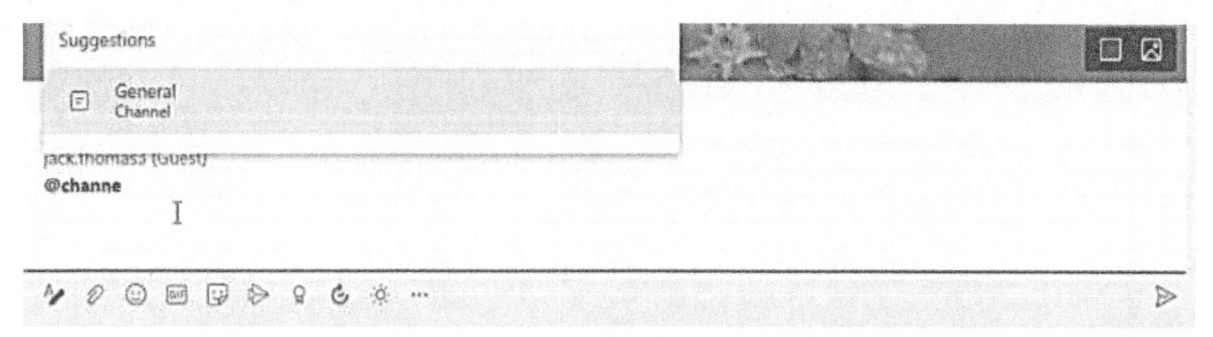

The formatting options here are the same as the ones available in private chat so I won't go through them again here. If you have a lot of people in this team and the conversation applies to a specific view you can "**at mention**" them by hitting the @ symbol, followed by their names. This way, not only will the "at mentioned" person or people get notified, but the other team members can see that the conversation does not apply directly to them. If you want everyone in this channel to get notified, you can "at mention" the channel either by just typing in "**@ channel**", or by specifying the channel name. If you have multiple channels in these teams and want to include all team members, you can "at mention" the team.

Responding to a Chat or Conversations

When you have a new chat message, it'll be indicated by a red circle next to the chat icon. The number indicates the number of unread messages that you have and the unread messages will be indicated in bold.

You can simply respond by typing in our response in the compose box.

Responding to a team's conversation is a little different. First, if you notice that in the Teams icon that there is a little red "@" symbol, this indicates that someone had mentioned you in a Channel conversation.

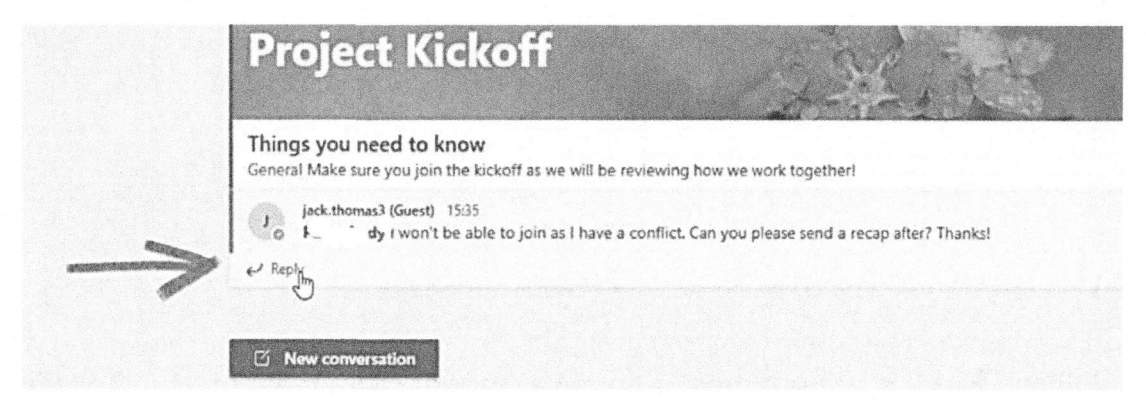

Team's Channel allows for multiple conversations to take place, so the conversations are threaded. If you're replying to an existing conversation you need to use the reply field at the bottom of the thread rather than starting a new conversation at the bottom. You don't always need to respond to a chat or conversation with texts; sometimes a simple acknowledgment will suffice. In this case, you can choose from one of several emojis and when the conversations get long, you can always collapse the thread and expand it back when you want to.

Notifications

Here, I'll just quickly highlight two things. In Chat, you can select any chat and go to the three-dotted menu for more options and choose **"Mute"**. For Teams Channel, you can select the appropriate channel, hit the three-dotted menu for more options and you can customize your notification settings here.

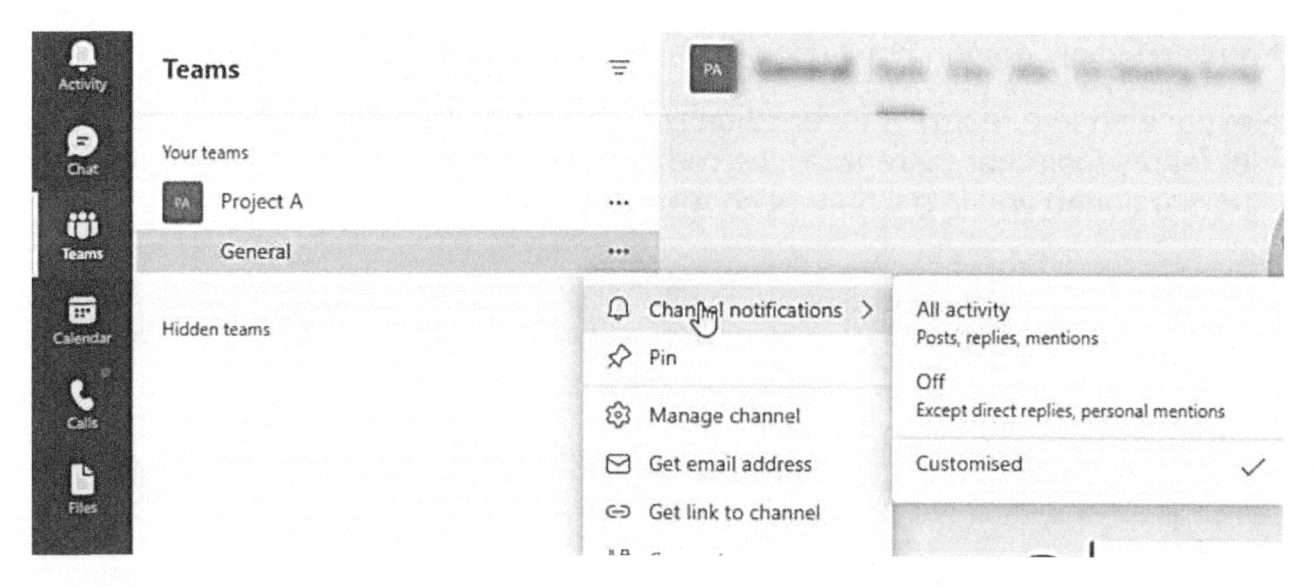

The activity feed is where you can see recent activities in the Teams and Channels you belong to. It will also show Chat messages and reactions you may have missed.

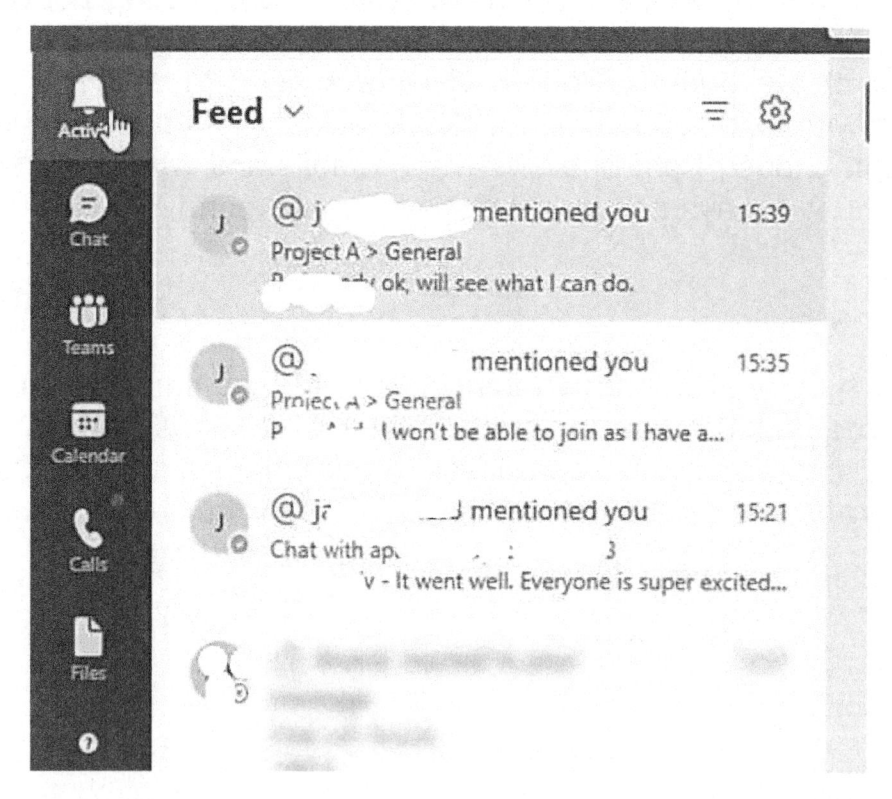

There are a few ways you can search for a chat or conversation. Chats are organized by date order and your most recent chats will appear on top. If there are a lot of chats on the list, you can apply a filter; you can filter by the person's name, group, or meeting name where the chat took place, and if you hit the three-dotted menu, you can further filter by unread chats, took place in a meeting, or have been muted. Chats can take place inside meetings and they behave the same as a regular chat.

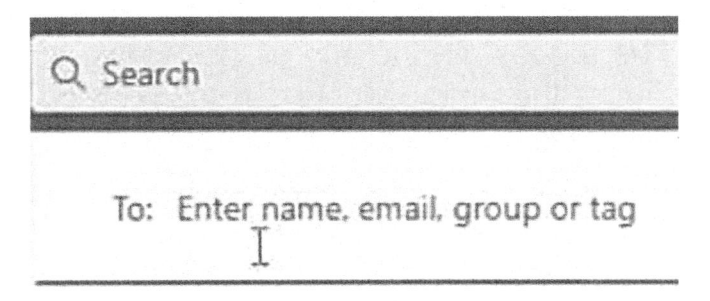

In Teams, you can filter either by the Team name or the Channel name and from there you can see your posts and conversations. If we belong to a lot of Teams you can choose to hide those that are inactive for a better organization. Similarly, you can hide chats as well. Chats that you use most frequently can be pinned to the top, and of course, Channels can be pinned to the top as well. Specific messages within a chat or conversation can be saved to favorites, just hit the three-dot menu beside it and click **"Save"**. These saved messages can be found by clicking on your icon and selecting "Saved messages".

The search Bar

This offers an easy way for you to send and search for chats all from one place. To send a simple chat, click forward-slash(/) chat, followed by the name of the person and message.

To see all unread messages, enter the forward-slash symbol, followed by **"unread"**.

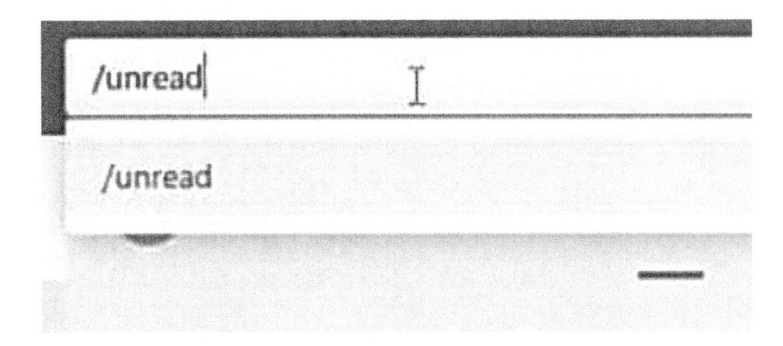

To see all conversations where you were mentioned, enter the forward-slash symbol, followed by **"mentions"**.

If you enter a simple forward-slash, you'll see the full list of things that you can do in this search bar.

Advanced Features

When you create a new chat, you can search for people's names, emails, groups, or tags. For the name and email, it'll only list people who belong to the organization. If you want to chat with someone from outside the organization, they must be invited as a guest first to any of the teams. You can go to Teams, **"Add member"** and enter the email address. If teams recognize that the email domain is external it'll suggest adding as a guest the guest then will receive an invitation and will need to agree to the organization's terms and services before they can join.

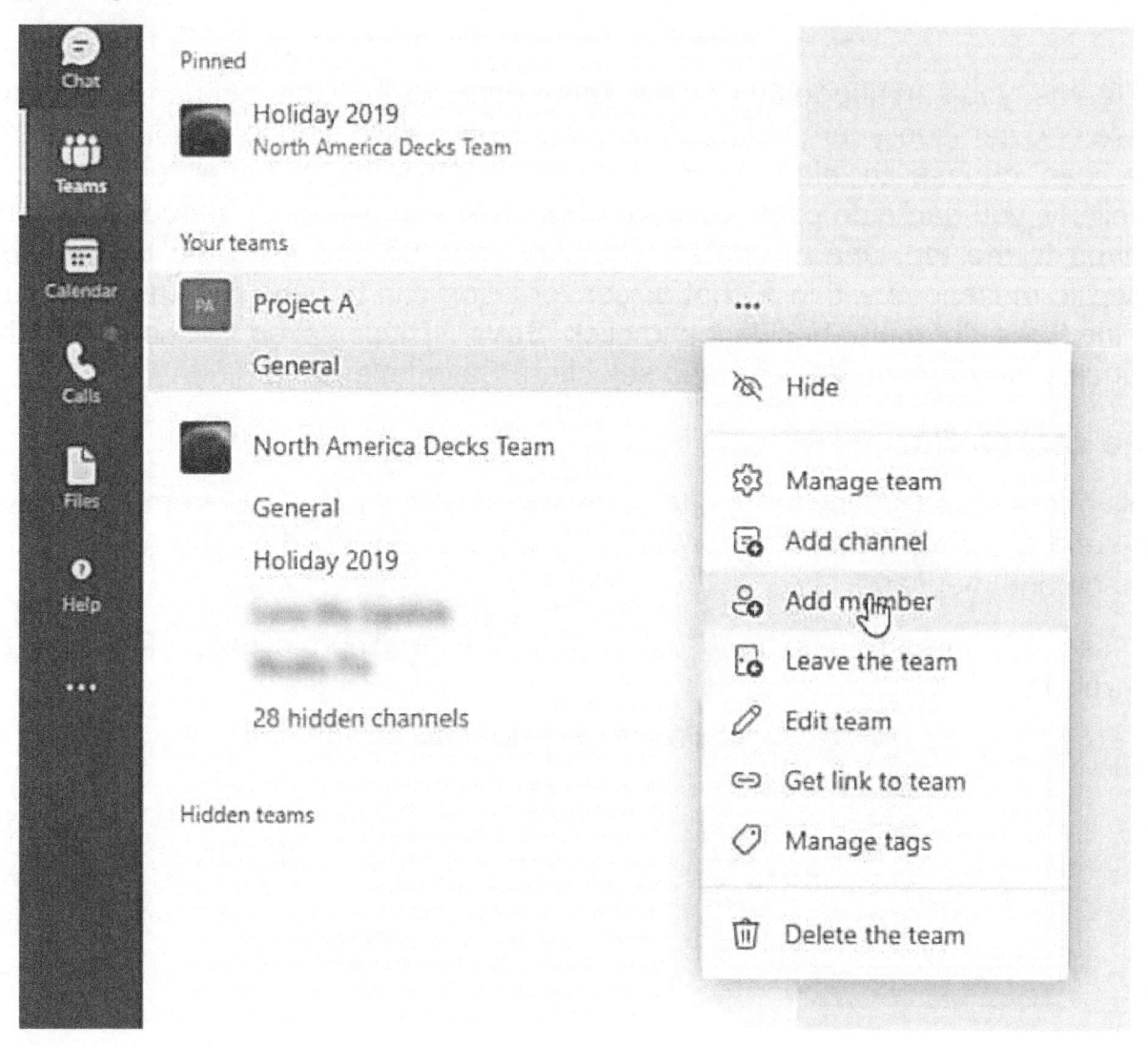

Group is any Microsoft 365 group and can be created from a variety of tools including Outlook, SharePoint, Planner, and Teams. So, just know that you can start a chat using a group name.

Tags let users easily connect with a subset of people on a team. You can create custom tags and assign them to people. It's a way to categorize people based on attributes such as their role or function. To create a tag, go to Teams, select a team and go to the three-dotted menu. Go down to "**Manage tags**", create a tag, give it a name and start adding people to it. You can use this tag to create new chat messages or "**@ mention**" them.

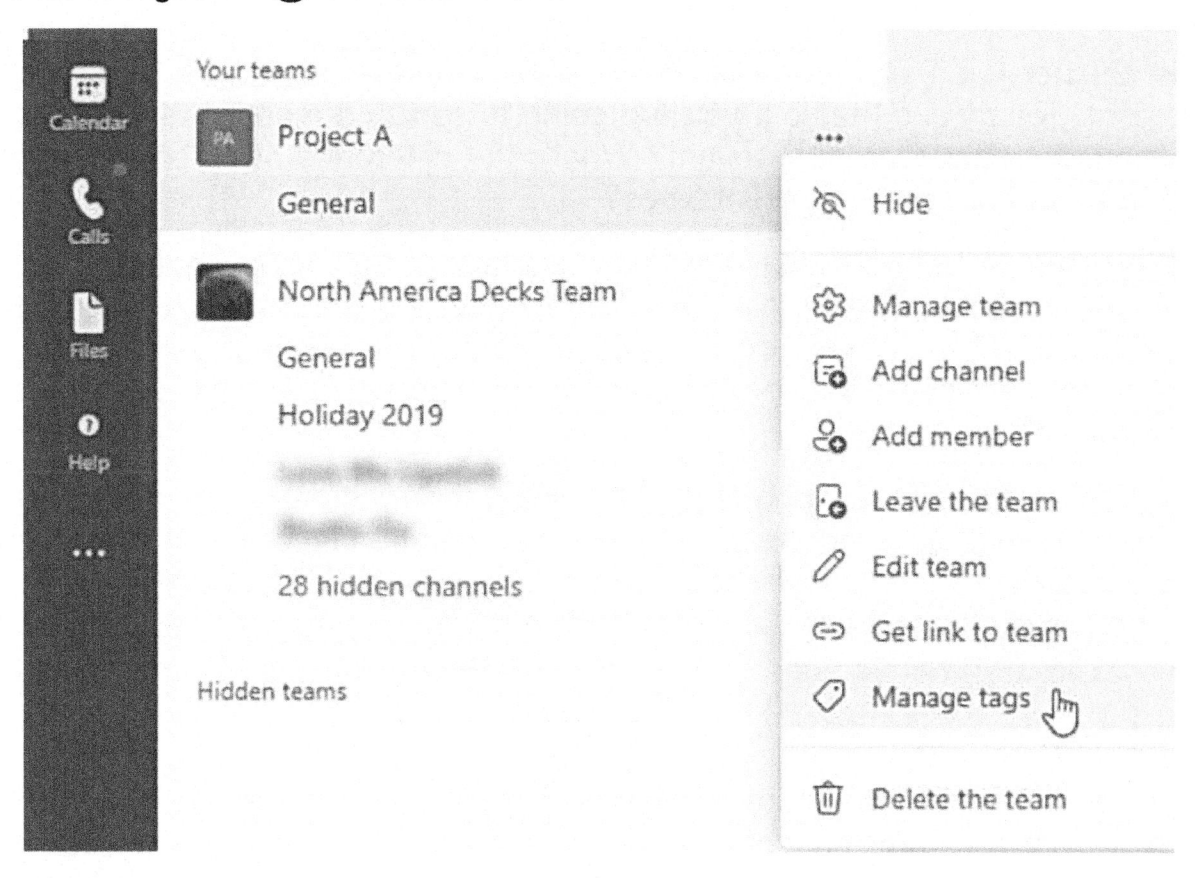

Summary

In this chapter, we went further to explain all about the Chats and Conversation platforms in Teams.

We looked at the features of these platforms, how to start up chats and conversations and how to make your chats and conversations fun and creative.

Chapter 5: Teams For Engaging Audiences

This chapter is all about one of the most popular questions when it comes to Microsoft Teams and that is if you are going to set up a meeting, should it be a meeting, a webinar, or a live event? What's the difference between these three and why are there three different types?

We're going to be analyzing each one, explaining the disadvantages and the advantages of each, we're going to be creating a Meeting, a Webinar, and a Live event, seeing these events or meetings from the side of the organizer and the side of the attendees. You're also going to see when you should use one over the other.

The main thing to understand is why there are three different types of meetings and it all comes down to the participation of the attendees during the meeting and the control the organizer has over the participation of the attendees. So, let's get started so that you can figure out which one of these you're going to use the next time we want to run a live event or a meeting.

Meetings

First, you'll see how to create a scheduled meeting using the Team's Channel. You can do this from any channel because all of these channels except for a private channel. In Private Channels you cannot schedule meetings; however, from any of the other channels you can and the most common one is going to be the General Channel, but in any case, it makes no difference. Now, you'll go to the General Channel, click the **"Meet"** icon at the top right corner, and **"Schedule the meeting"**. Next, enter the details of the meeting, such as giving the title, adding your attendees, but because you used the General Channel, you can see it's already added the channel for you and if you try to change the channel then it's going to replace this one with whichever other one you're going to choose. So if you choose a Channel, you cannot add another channel; you can only use one Channel. You're going to see how you can add more channels from different teams by using Outlook to schedule the meetings but for now, let's continue with this. After you have entered the details of your meeting, click **"Send"** and that's going to schedule.

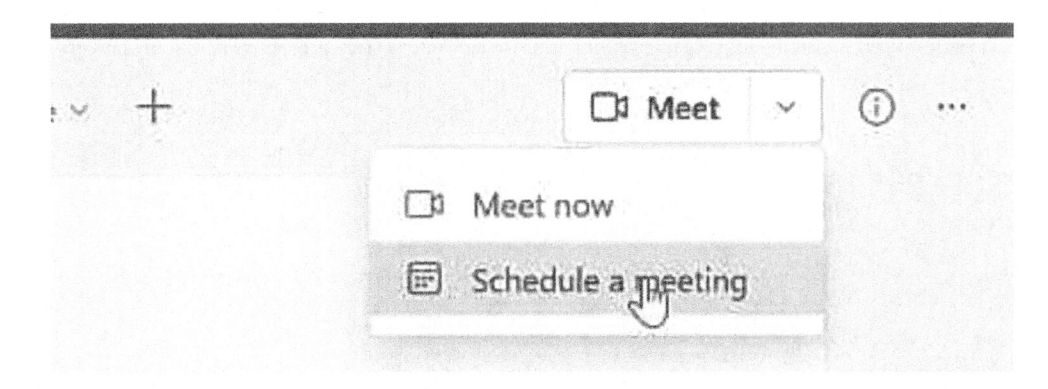

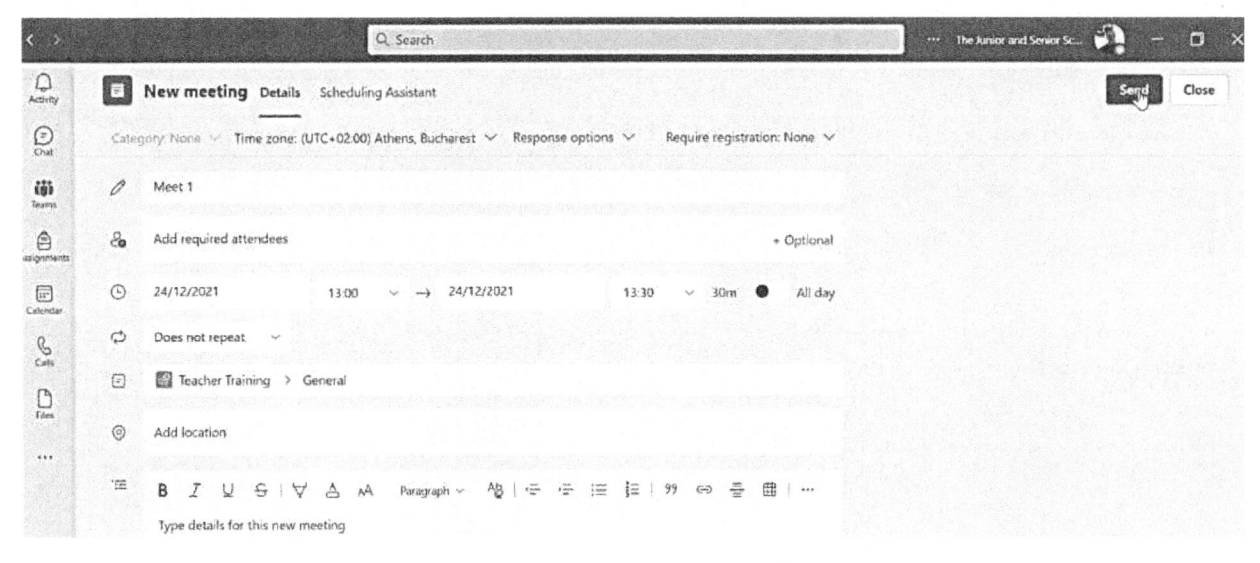

If you go to your Calendar, you can see it scheduled here. And if you go to the calendar of members of that Channel, you should see that meeting scheduled in their calendars as well.

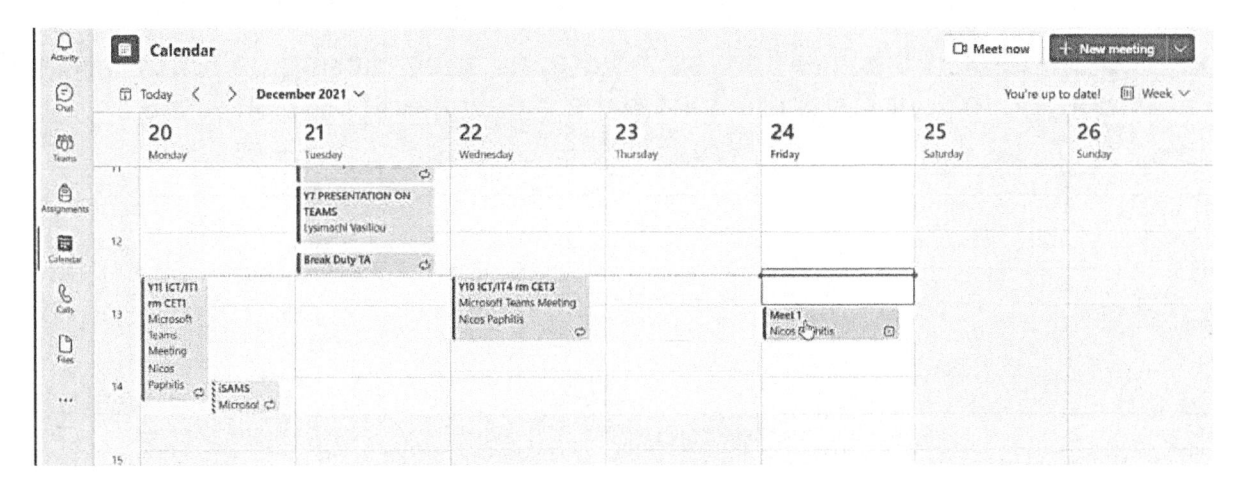

Before you start the meeting, you are going to go back as the organizer, open this meeting and you've got your meeting options. If you go to your meeting options, by default you can see that everybody is allowed to be presenters. If you don't want that, click on that and put **"Only me"**, meaning only you are the presenter.

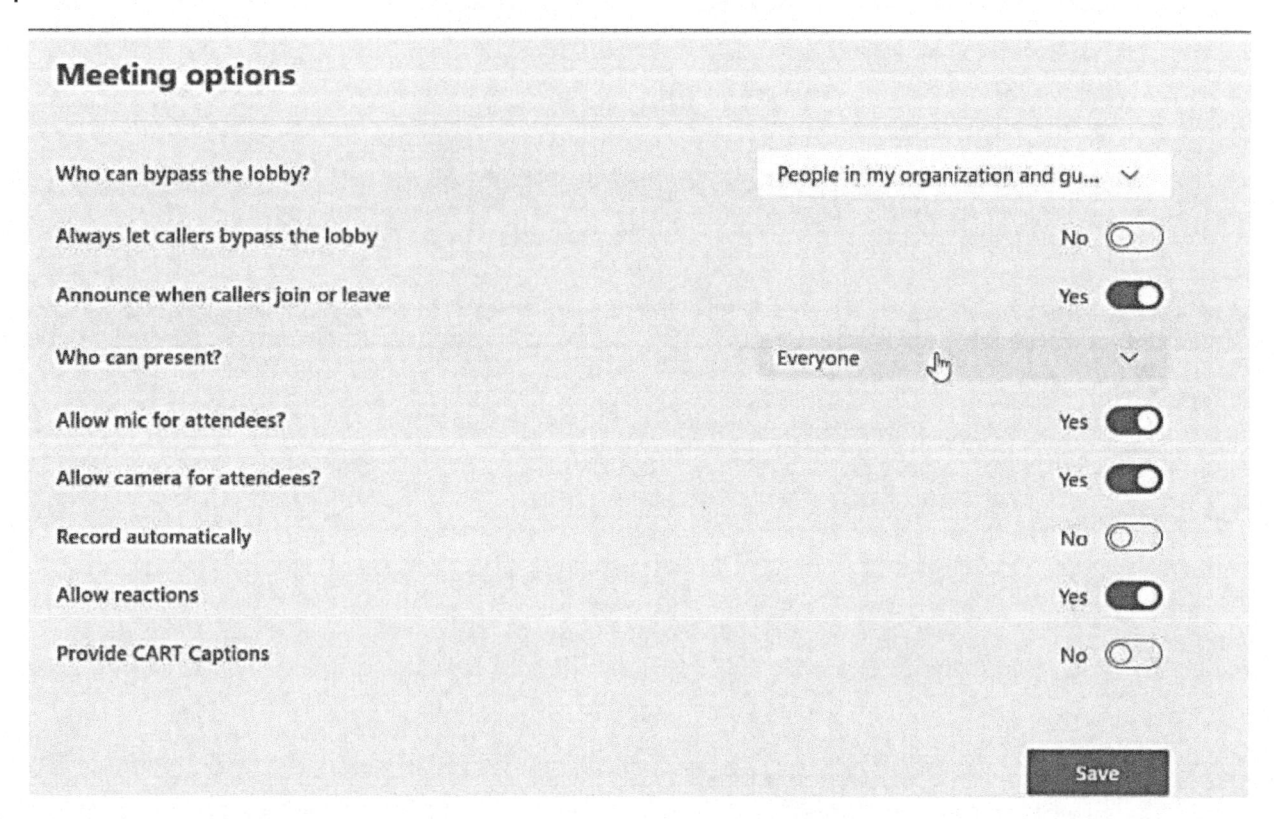

Meeting options	
Who can bypass the lobby?	People in my organization and gu... ˅
Always let callers bypass the lobby	No
Announce when callers join or leave	Yes
Who can present?	Everyone ˅
Allow mic for attendees?	Yes
Allow camera for attendees?	Yes
Record automatically	No
Allow reactions	Yes
Provide CART Captions	No

Save

Now, that also enables the two features below, which is to allow the camera or allow the mic for attendees. If you turn these to **"NO"**, that means that attendees will not be able to turn on their microphones and cameras until you say so. When you are done going through the other options, click **"Save"**.

Now, you are to start this meeting, as the organizer by clicking on **"Join"**. And as an attendee, go to your Calendar, locate the meeting and click on **"Join"**.

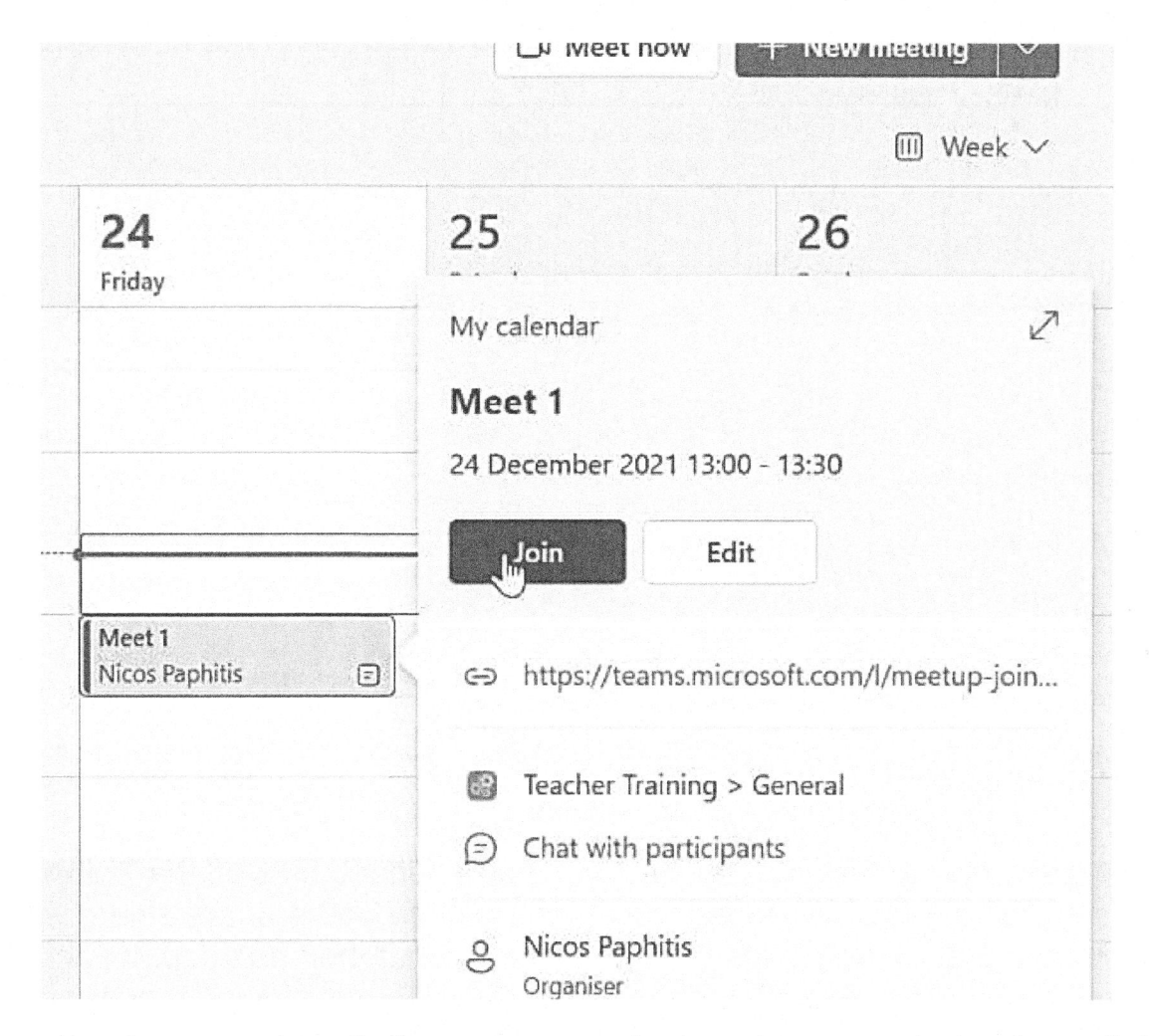

Your attendees can turn their cameras and microphones on but only until they start the meeting. As soon as the meeting starts, the cameras and microphones are now disabled for them; the only way that they can turn on is if the organizer does that.

So as the organizer, you'll go to the **"Participants"** and from here you can see the attendees it's got here. If you click the "more options" menu, you can "allow mic" or "allow camera". So, if you turn on the "**allow mic**", on the attendee's side the microphone can now be turned on and off and you can do that for the camera as well.

Meeting options

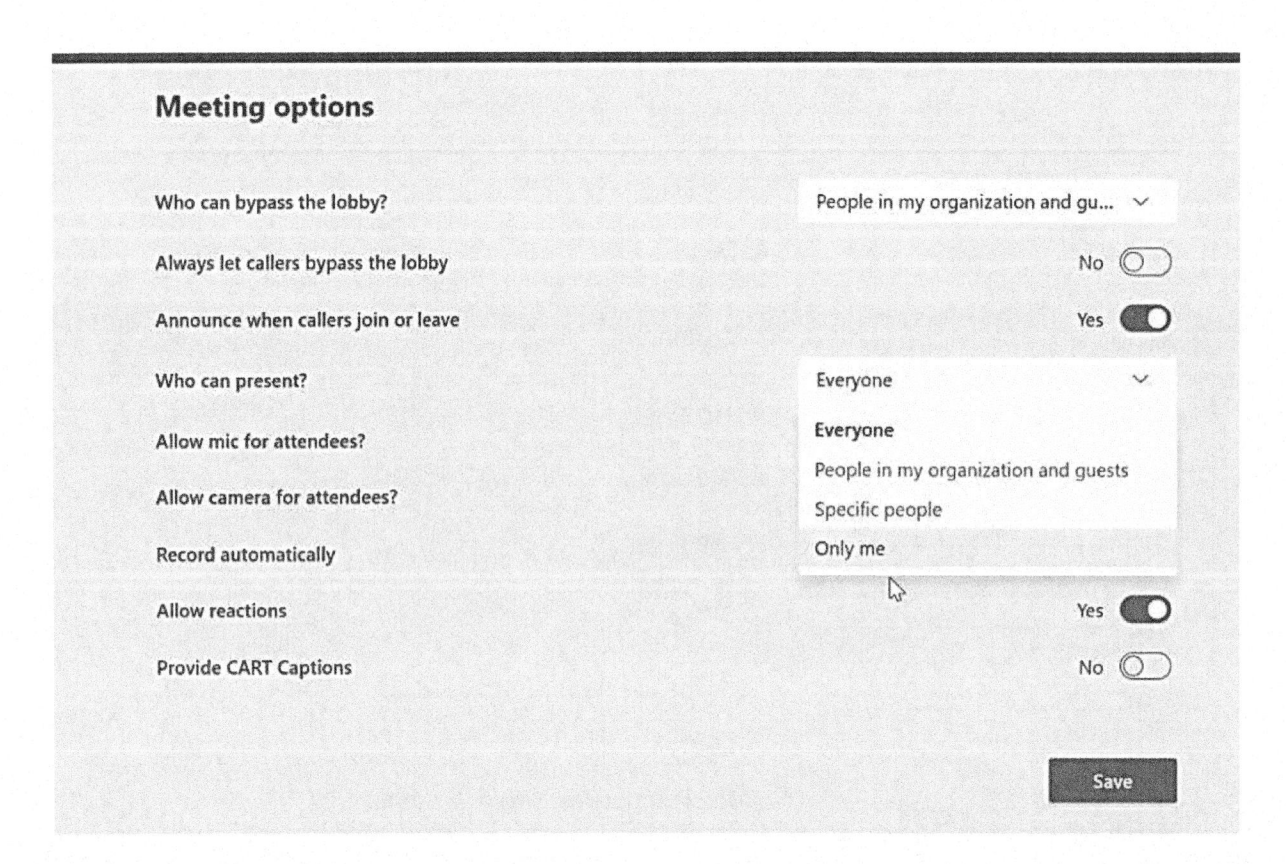

Who can bypass the lobby?	People in my organization and gu... ⌄
Always let callers bypass the lobby	No ⊙
Announce when callers join or leave	Yes ⬤
Who can present?	Everyone ⌄
Allow mic for attendees?	Everyone
Allow camera for attendees?	People in my organization and guests
	Specific people
Record automatically	Only me
Allow reactions	Yes ⬤
Provide CART Captions	No ⊙

Save

Now here's another little fantastic feature. If an attendee puts on the **"hands up"**, from the organizer's side you can see that the hand up here has a number one. That means this attendee was the first person to put their hand up. If somebody else puts a hand up as well, then that person will have a number two, and that way you know as an organizer, you've got the order of who to allow to ask a question first.

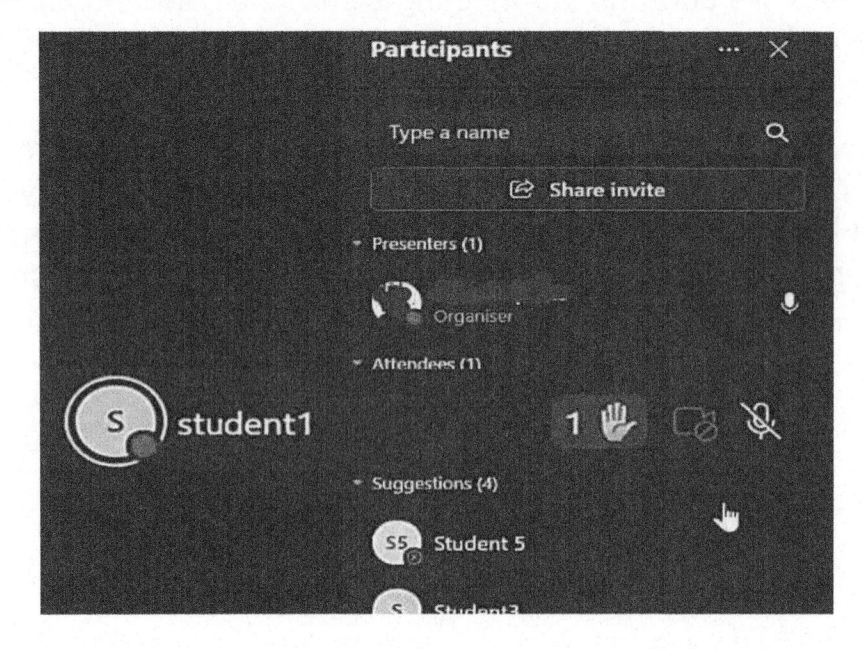

Turning these things on and off, one by one for each attendee can be tedious but it does give you good control so you can just turn the camera or the microphone on only for the attendee asking the question, and then you can disable the microphone so they don't say anything else. But if you want to open up for group discussion then the easiest way is if you simply go to the top, in the three dots at the top, click here and **"Allow mic for attendees"** and that will enable the microphone for all the attendees, and if you allow camera for attendees that will allow the camera on for the attendees.

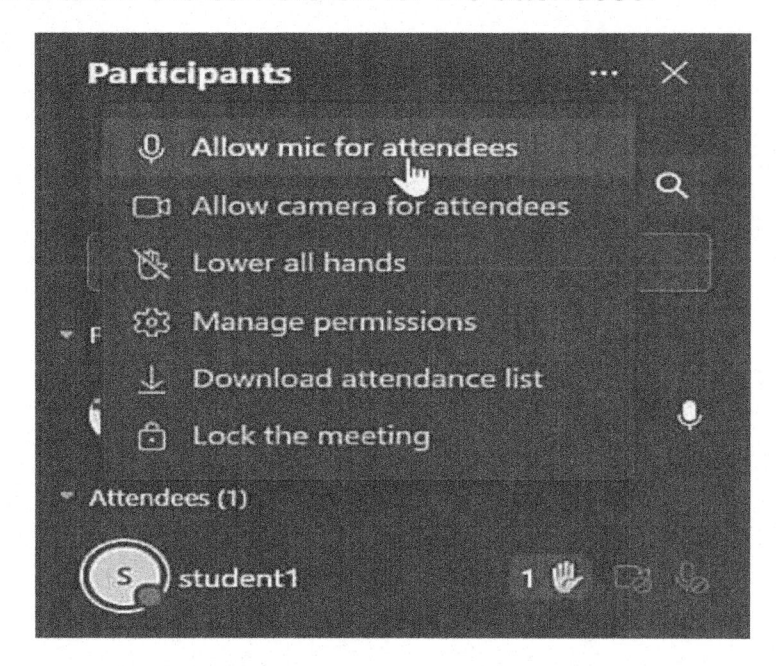

So, there you go. That's a meeting using a Team's Channel.

Before we proceed, what I want to show you now is another little feature, we don't use this feature for meetings but it's there and it does cause confusion. If you go back to schedule a meeting and you get to the point of adding the meeting details, you've got this option at the top that says **"Require registration"**. Now if you do require registration and you're going to put **"For everyone"** or **"For everyone in your organization"**, what that means is people receive an email they will have to fill in that form that they get to register for the event and then they will get an email.

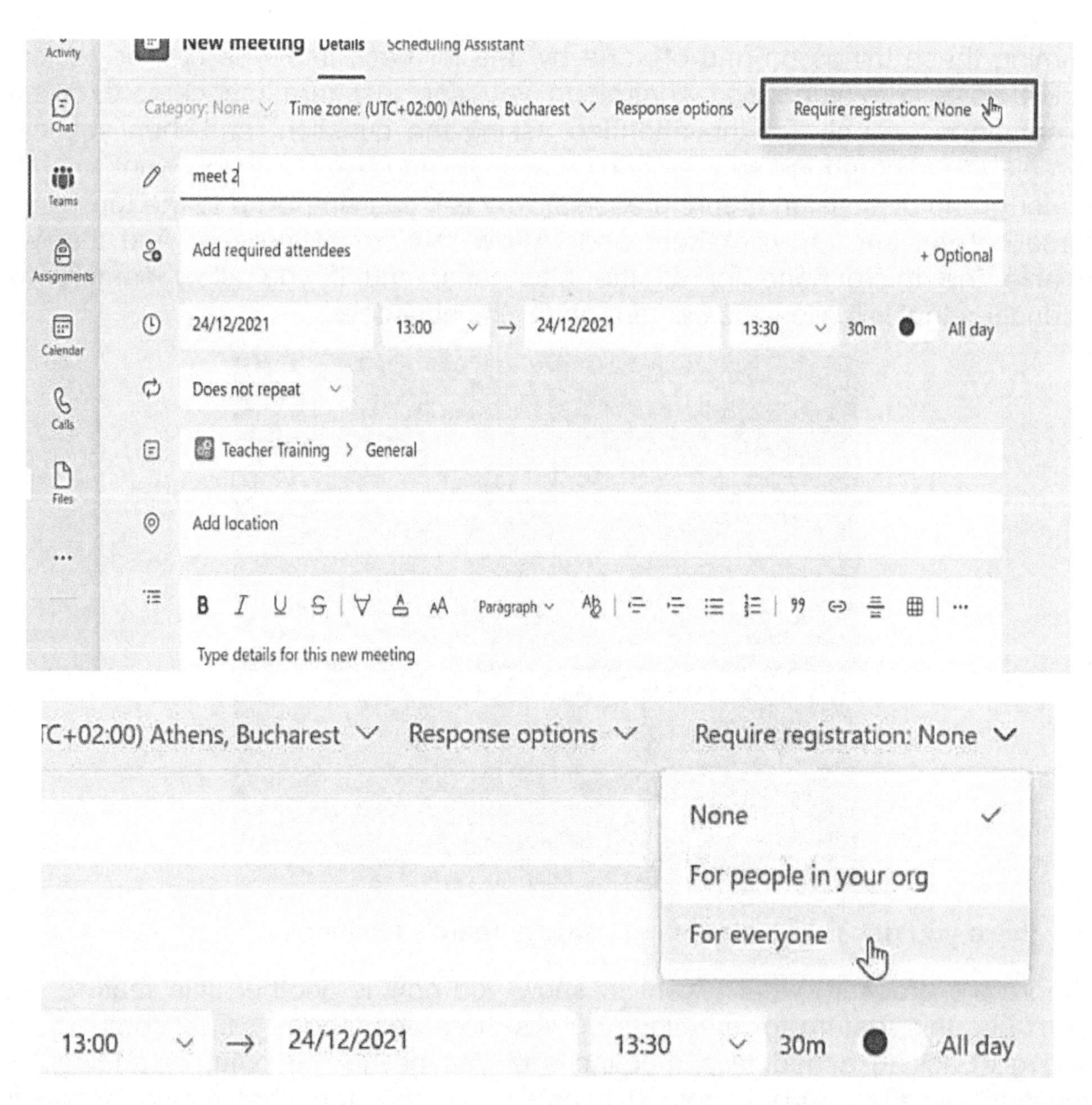

This is a webinar and that's what we're going to look at a bit later on but if you try to change this now, it's not going to work because you've got a Channel that has been added for this meeting. So if you try and do that now you'll get an error message because you can't add people automatically and that's what this is doing from the Channel.

If you go to your Calendar and create a scheduled meeting, because you don't have a channel here, you'll be able to choose this. But what's going to happen here is that initially, it says **"New meeting"** at the top, as soon as you require registration, it starts loading and you will see it's now become a **"New webinar"**.

We're going to complete this when we go to webinars, but because that option is there it does cause a bit of confusion. So, if you do want registration, you're going to use a Webinar and not a Meeting.

The next thing you should know when it comes to meetings is how to schedule a meeting for many Class Teams. Notice I said class teams; it can only work for class teams.

You need to do this through Outlook, as you can't do it from Teams. In Microsoft Outlook, go to your calendar and what you're going to do is to start a new calendar entry. You'll do this for a scheduled Teams Meeting so you can either click at the top, where it says **"New Teams Meeting"** or you can double click on a calendar entry and say this is going to be a Teams Meeting, and as soon as you do that it's going to add the Teams Meeting link down here in the body of the email.

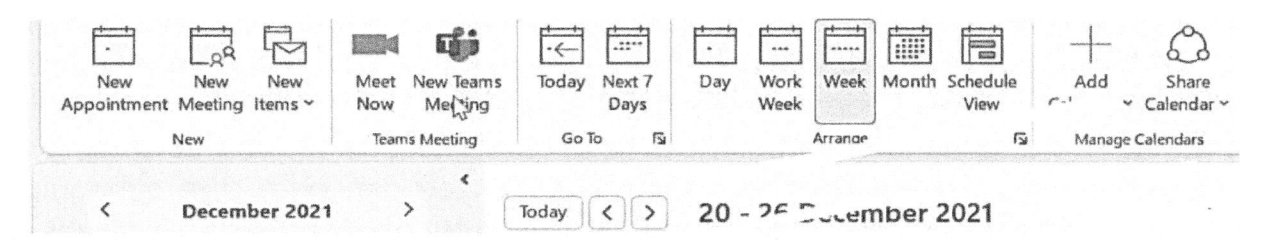

The next step is to give it a title, and for the **"Required"** field you're going to type the email addresses of the Class Teams of which you want the participants or the members of those teams to be able to get a scheduled entry in their calendar. Remember I was very clear about that; it's Class Teams only. For any other kind of Team such as Staff Teams, this will not work.

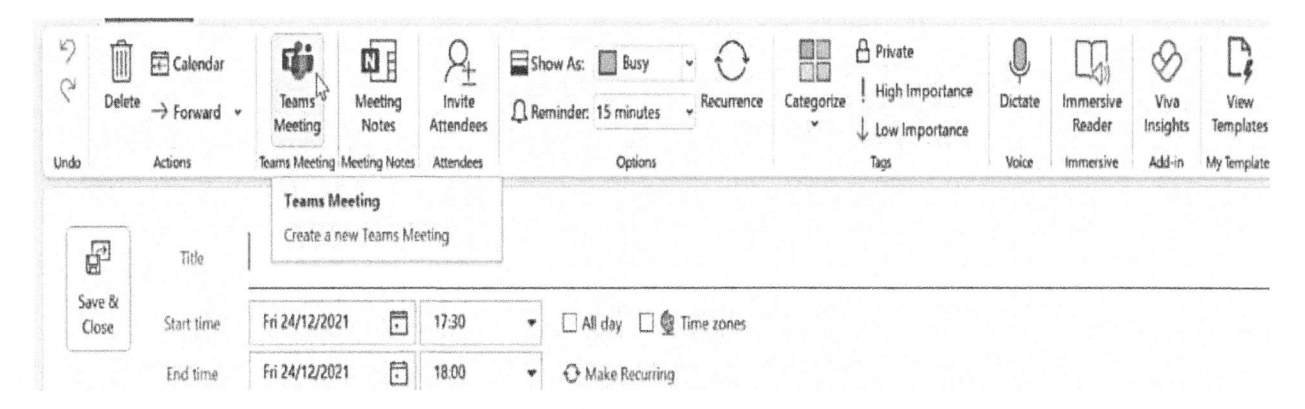

The next part is simple; you simply send this email and everybody who's a member of that team will receive this calendar entry.

If you go over to the student end you can see that this meeting has been set up, and it's just like any other scheduled meeting. So why go to the hassle of adding this? Well, the reason is that as a student and a member of this team, if you double click on this, you can join this meeting just like any other meeting.

However, as the organizer, if you now go to your teams, you can see the meeting that has been scheduled. If you open this up, you can see up here that although you've got the meeting options just like before where you can set them up like the normally scheduled meeting, if you look on that top line here you can see more items have been added. For example, a whiteboard is automatically included, the attendance module is automatically included for you there so you can see after the meeting at any point in time, you can go to the scheduled meeting open it up click on the attendance module, and see who's present in this meeting and for how long and some other information as well. What else is fantastic about scheduling meetings this way is you've got this plus sign up so you can add new apps to this scheduled meeting.

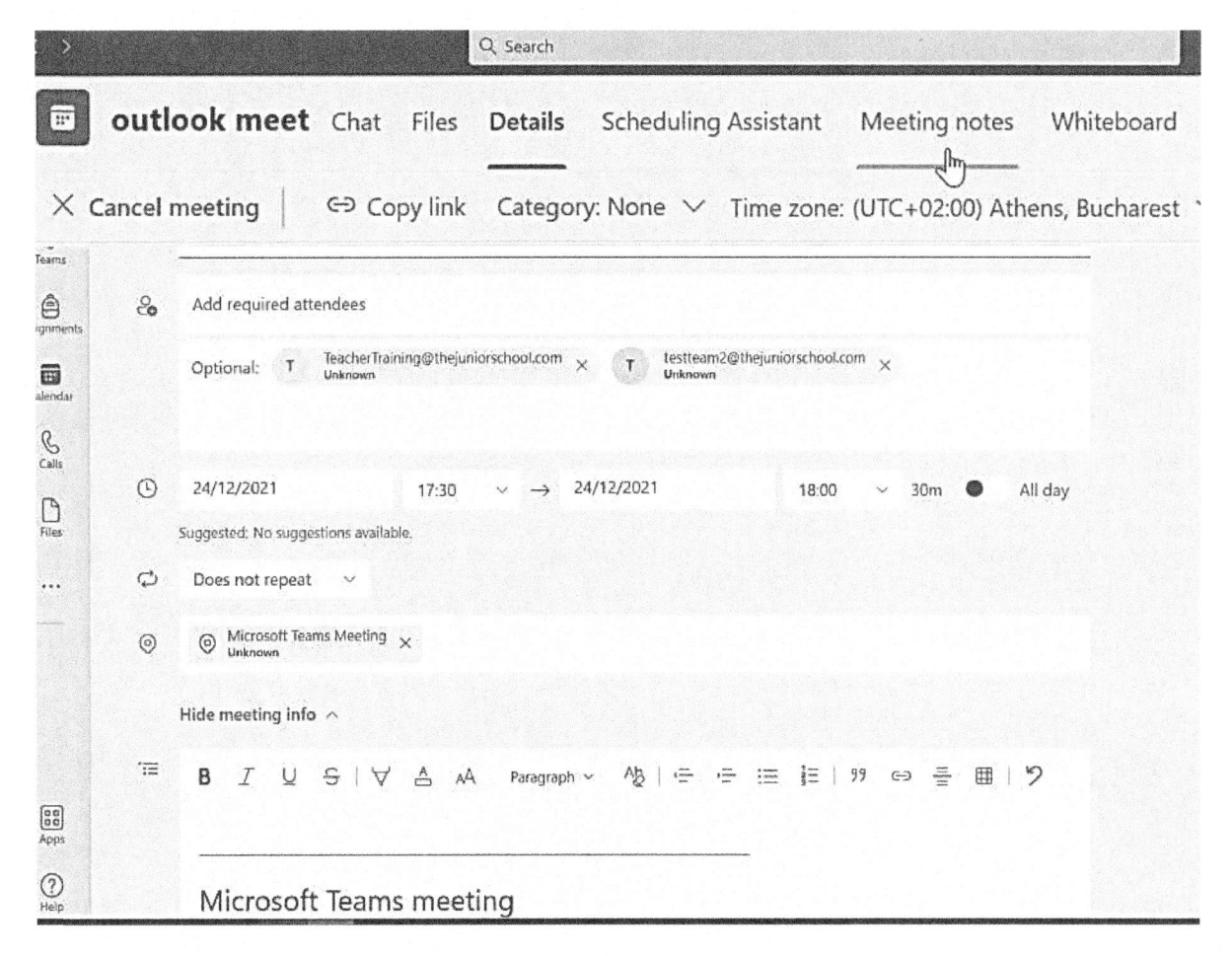

This is something that you can't do when you schedule the meeting through Microsoft Teams either through the channel or through the Calendar; it can only be done if you do it through Outlook and use the Team's email address. Remember, only Class Teams.

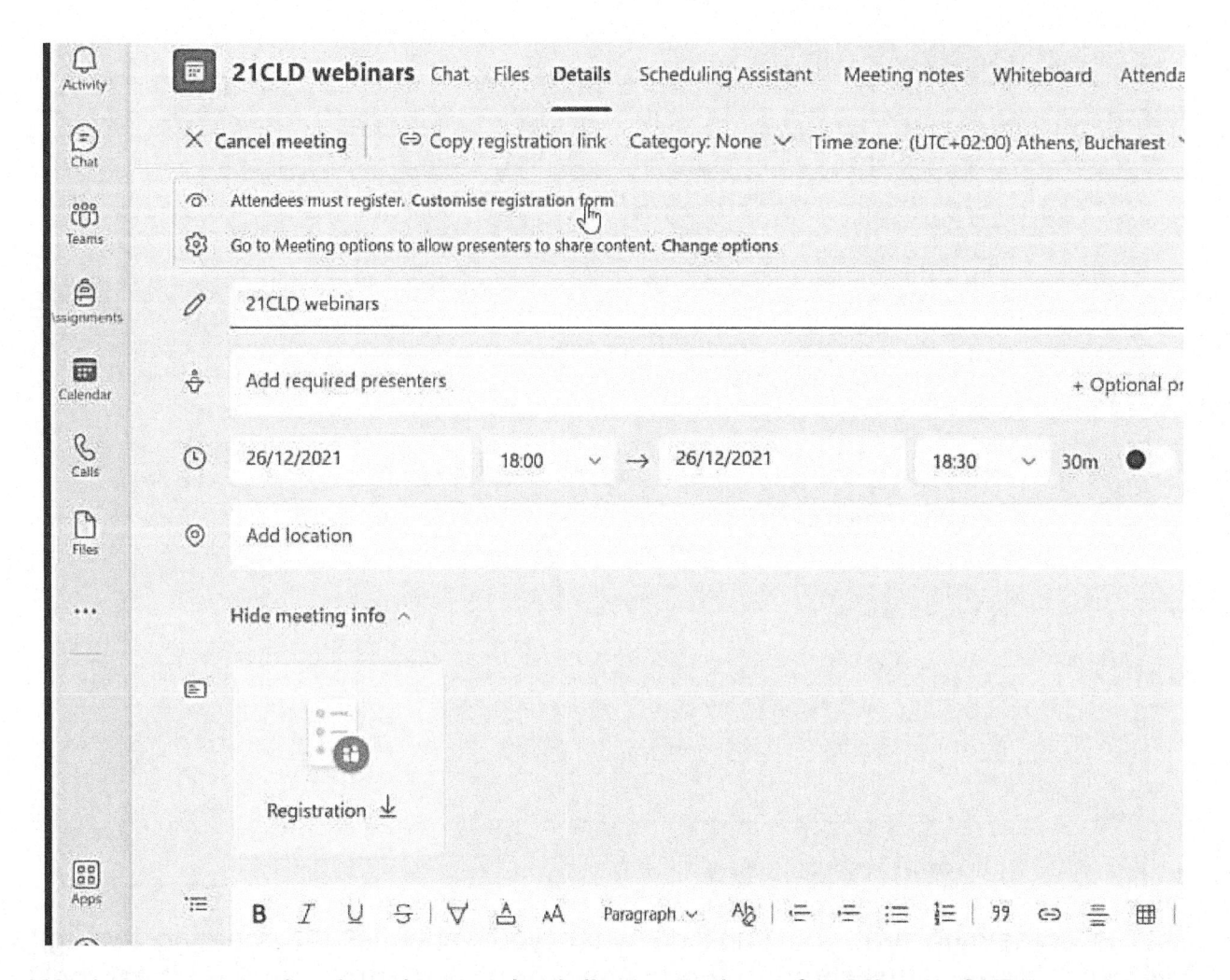

We have covered a lot about scheduling meetings for Microsoft Teams. We're going to look at the differences in the number of participants or attendees that can join a meeting, a webinar, or a Live event towards the end of the chapter, so now let's go to Webinars.

Webinars

To create a webinar, there are two ways to do that, and you've already seen this. So, from your Calendar, you can go up there where it says **"New Meeting"** and you simply click on it, and you can see this is the classic meeting that we've just finished in the first part of the chapter, but if you add **"Require registration"** and you choose any one of these two here **"for people in the organization"** or **"for everyone"**, automatically it becomes a new webinar. So that's one way.

The other way is to go to **"New meeting"**, click on the drop-down list, and choose Webinar. It's the same thing. This will take you to the webinar setup and you're going to create it from here.

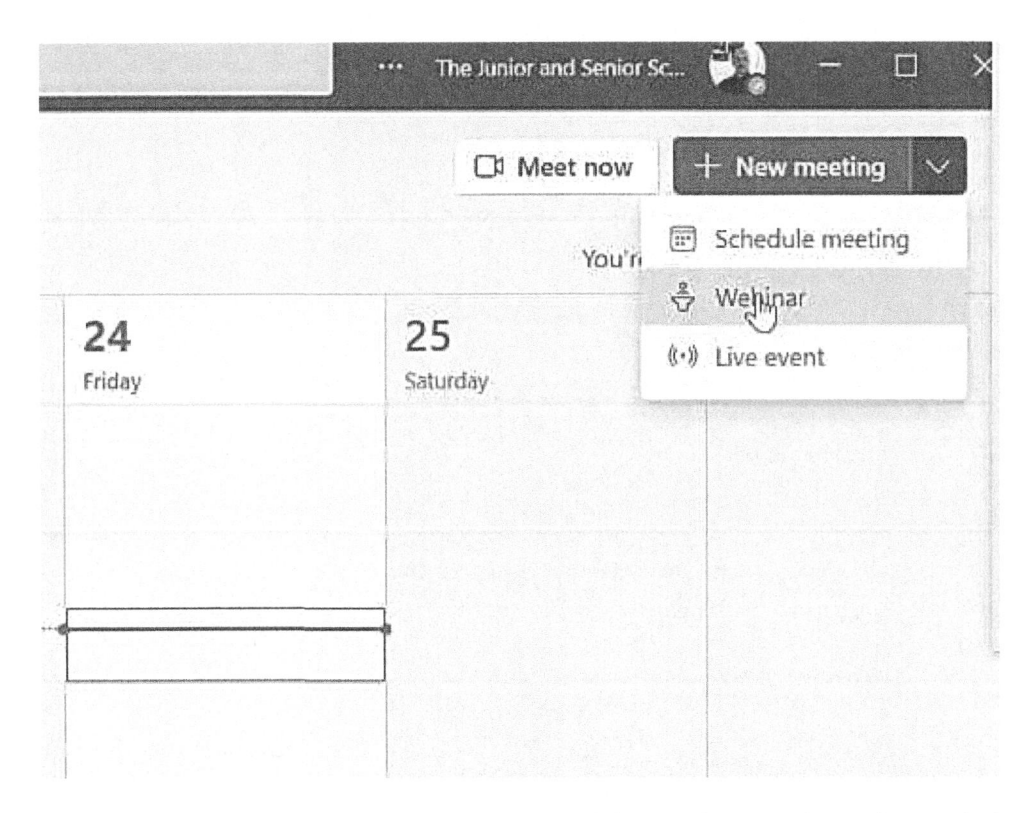

You can see that because you chose the webinar, the registration tab is already selected here for everyone and you can choose for people in your organization only. This will make it so that only people in your organization can attend this webinar and if you do it for everyone then it will allow for people in your organization and anyone who has the registration link.

The first thing is you're going to put a title. Next, you're going to add presenters, and if you've got other people presenting, you can add their email addresses here so they will receive the link so that they can join the webinar, not as an attendee but as a presenter. The next thing is you're going to put the date. Lastly, you can put some details. If you click on **"Send"** directly it's going to create the webinar with the default registration form. If you want to modify that form, go to where it says "**View registration form**" and from here you're going to prepare your registration form.

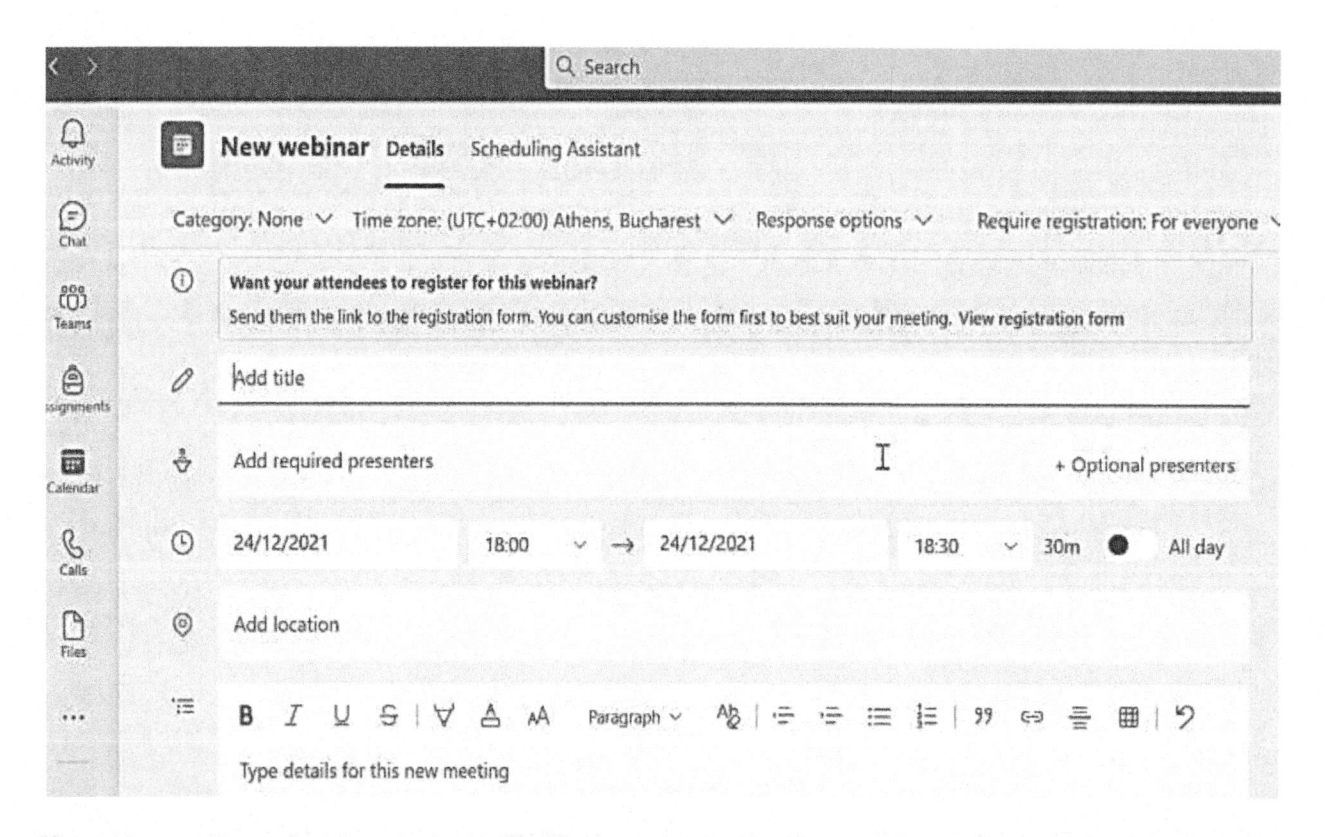

If you've got an image set up that's good, as it personalizes the webinar. So you can upload an image, and notice here that the perfect size for your image is **918px by 120px**. The next thing is the event details; give this a title. It's always good to give a title. You may have a series of webinars. The next part is you're going to put the date, and in the description, it's good to put a little description about what this webinar is all about.

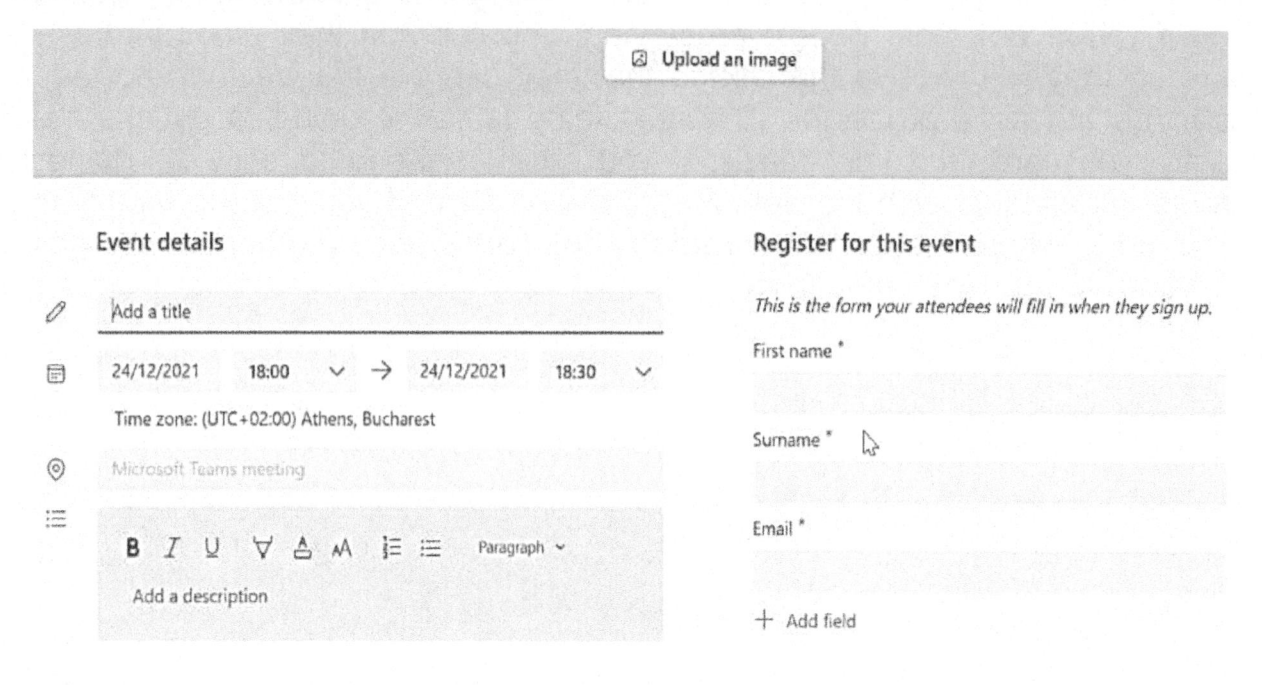

The fields on the right side which includes first name, surname, and email are added by default and you can add any other fields that you want to collect because all of these are going to be collected by the registration form, and as an organizer, you'll have access to this in the form of an excel spreadsheet. To do that, click on **"Add field"** and you can add some of the pre-set fields here, and if you go to the customized option, you can choose another **"Input"** and it is the style where it gives a title and the person who's filling in will add something in here, but you can add the **"Choice"** option instead.

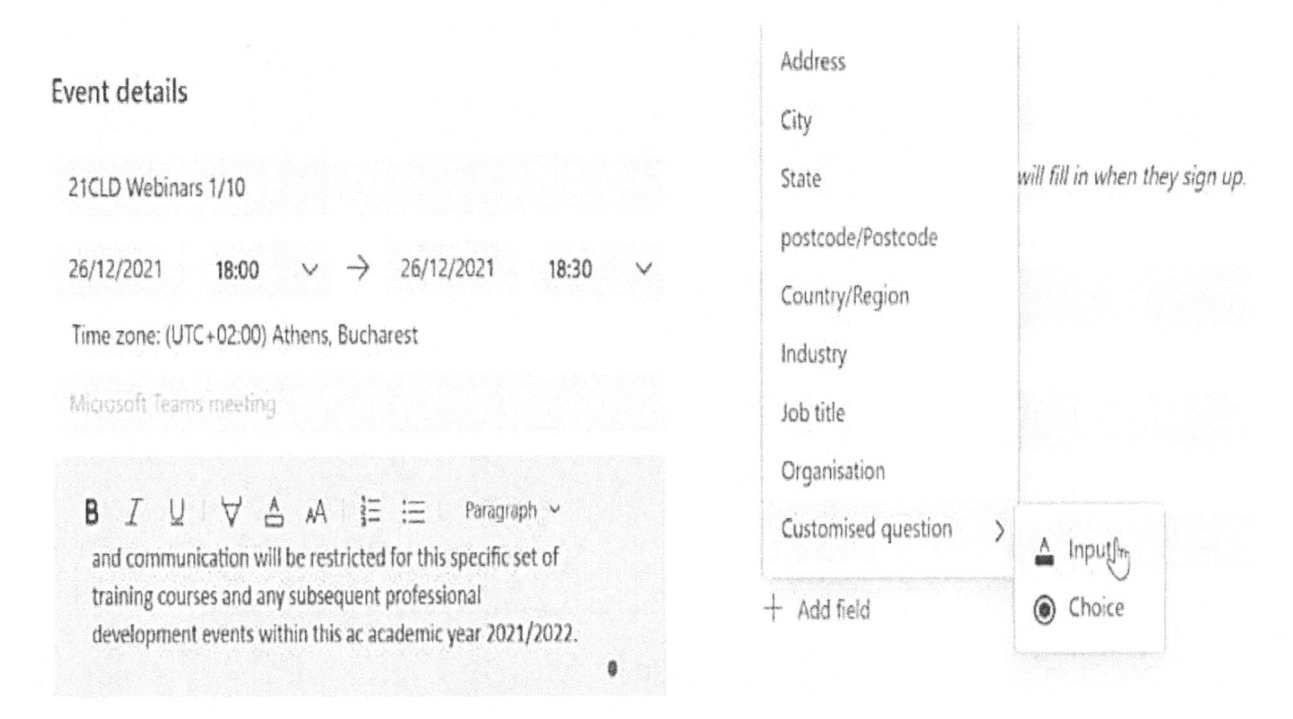

Once you've done this, this is the setup of the registration form; nothing else. This is what the attendees or the people are going to receive when they click on the link that you send them. The next action is to save this and as soon as you do that it gives you the option to view this in your browser to see what it looks like. So, if you click on that, you can see what the people that are going to want to attend this webinar are going to see when they click on the link. When you're satisfied with this preview, you can simply close this, and now you can go back to the setup.

Please note that even after you've sent this Webinar, you can go back and modify the registration process. So, if you realize you've done something wrong it's not a big issue; you can go back and modify it and it won't affect anything.

So once you're satisfied with your webinar setup, you can simply click on **"Send"**, and as soon as you do that it's now scheduled for this webinar here. If you open this up you can customize the registration form again, if that's something you want to do. You can copy the registration link and send this to people and they will be able to log in. It will be a good idea to shorten that URL using a **Bitly** or some other kind of URL shortener.

When someone registers with the link, what that's going to do now is to send a confirmation and the person will receive an email confirming the registration for the webinar. If they click on that, it's got the link so they can join the event and they can add this to their calendars and that will save the attendees having to go back through their backlog of emails to go and find the email and find that link.

If attendees go to their calendars and click on the webinar, they can just click on **"Yes"** to accept and indicate that they will be attending. So, although they've registered, they're going to confirm that they will be attending, and when they double-click on that, they can join the event and when they join this event they're joining as attendees.

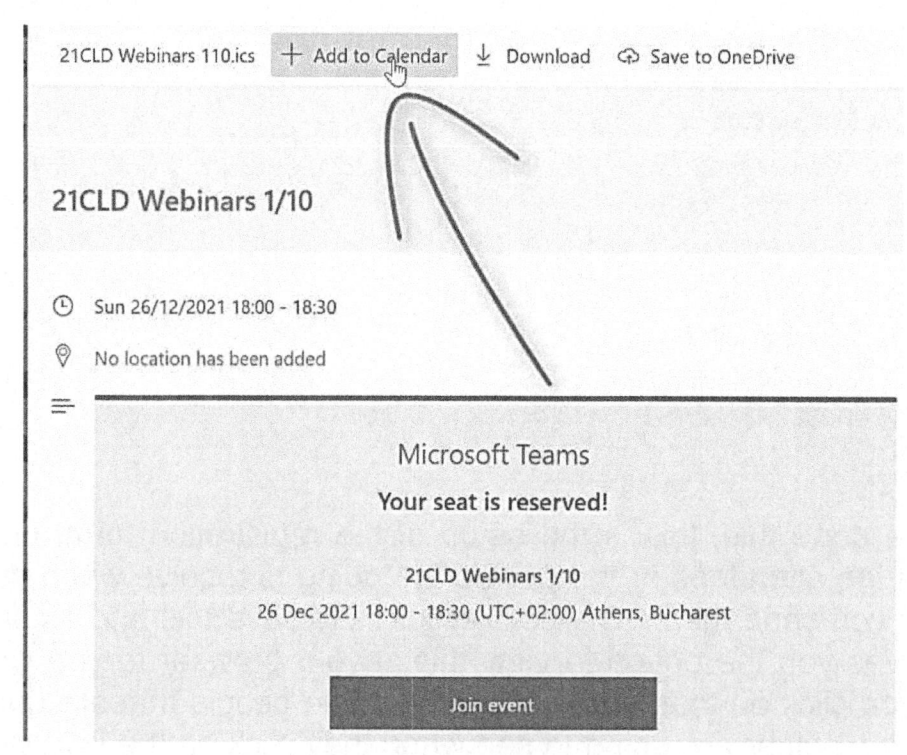

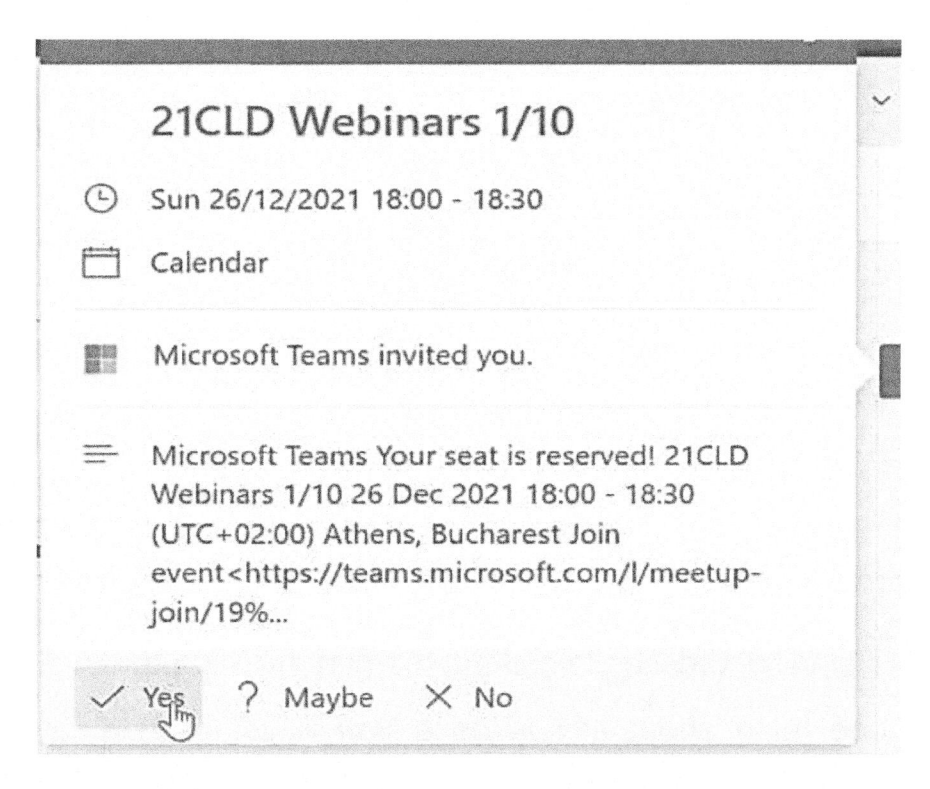

The experience of joining as an attendee for a webinar is the same as a team's meeting and the meeting options have been set so that all attendees wait in the lobby. So as an organizer, you can admit the attendees.

The only difference is that for attendees, automatically the settings for "**Allow mic**" and "**Allow camera**" are disabled straight away, so as an organizer, you don't need to go and change this in the meeting options or to think about it beforehand. Webinars have already got those settings as default, and this is useful because you're expecting in a webinar, more people will be attending and if you've forgotten to set that setting you don't want to go and disable every single person one by one or to go make everyone an attendee so that you can then go and disable microphones and cameras.

Apart from that, there aren't many differences; it's the same as any other meeting and you can just treat it the same way.

The webinar is that you have a good idea of how many people will be attending that webinar because of the registration process. After the webinar is over, you can go to the scheduled webinar, open it up and you can go to the "**Registration**" and see how many people have registered for this webinar, so clicking on that will download the file. If you go to the downloaded file, this will open up an Excel Sheet that shows you the people that have applied for this. So before the webinar, you know exactly how many people are interested in joining this webinar.

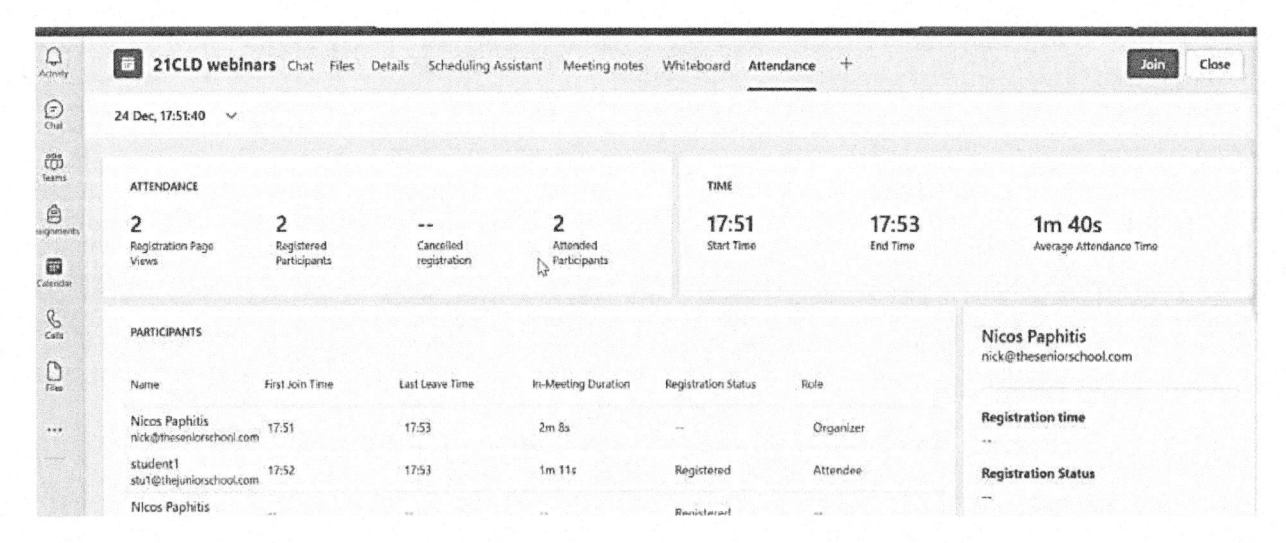

The other good thing is you've got a list of the email addresses so you can contact them in the future providing that they've agreed to be contacted and you can use these email addresses to contact them about the future webinars.

The other good thing about this is once you have finished, even after the webinar you can use the Attendance module and that will show you who attended the webinar. You can see the duration that they were connected for and some other information as well.

We're going to look at Microsoft Teams' Live events next.

Live Events

Back in your Microsoft Teams Calendar, you can **set up a live event**. This one's the easiest to set up, as there are very few settings, however, it's the hardest one to orchestrate at the time when the Live event runs.

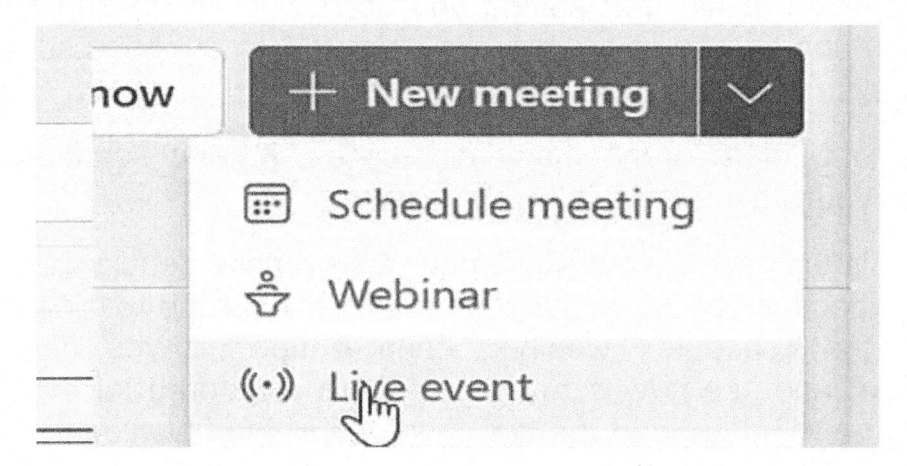

The first thing you're going to do is you're going to add the title and schedule the date and the time. The time itself and the date is not important, as such it's only so that it books it inside your calendar. What you're going to give your attendees is going to be a link and that link is going to be live from the time that you start the live event on your end.

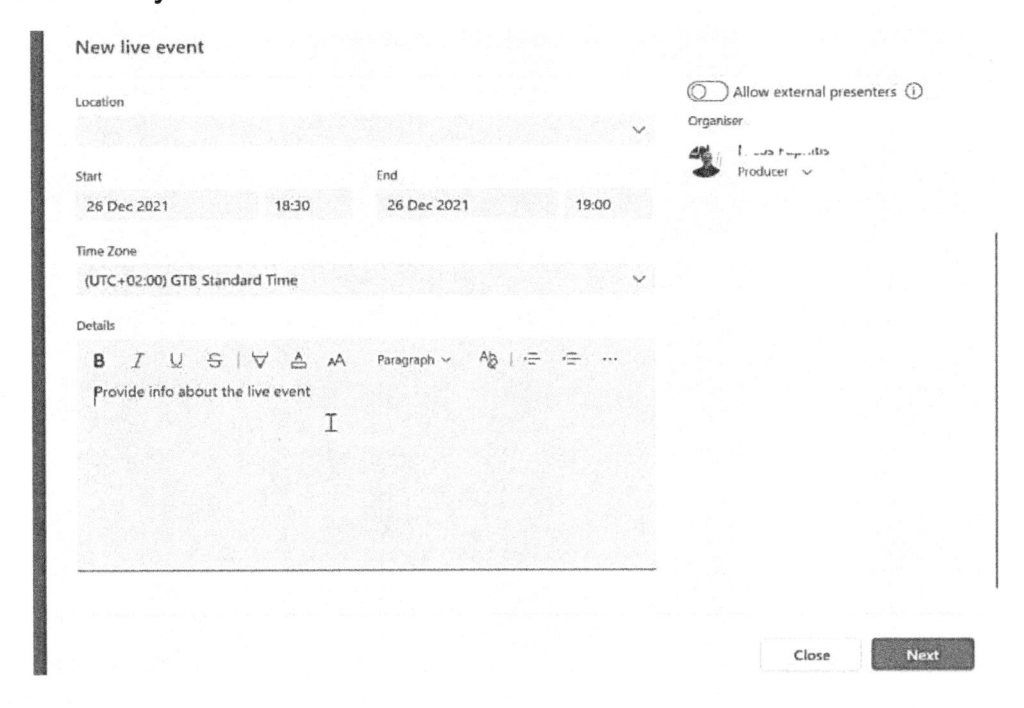

If you want other people to present during this live event you can add them if they are part of your organization, and if you want people from outside the organization to present then you're going to "**Allow external presenters**" and that they will be able to join the event, however, you would have to make them a presenter during the time of the event.

To make things easier for Admins, you can create presenter accounts and you simply give your external presenters one of these presenter accounts and that gives them access directly to this event without them or you having to worry about whether they're going to be able to connect as a guest and you don't have to worry about making them a presenter because you've already made the account a Presenter Account.

You can add some details about the live event and click on **"Next"**.

Next, you have a few settings for you to work with. You can choose to add people from different groups, so this will be different teams that you have or groups which are set up in your Office 365 Tenant or you can make it organization-wide for only people which are in your organization and they have to sign in to their accounts or you can make it a public event where people can join using the link as guests and it will be open up to everybody including people your organization and guests as well. Make your choice and scroll down.

New live event

You plan to use another tool to share content. Learn more

Event options

☐ Recording available to producers and presenters
☐ Recording available to attendees ⓘ
☑ Captions
   Spoken language English (United States) ⌄
   Translate to Greek (Greece) ⌄
☑ Attendee engagement report
☑ Q&A

Support

Give attendees access to support info for your organisation.
URL
https://support.office.com/home/contact

[Close] [Back] [**Schedule**]

Next, you've got how you will produce your live event, and that's default by Teams unless you've got some other external app devices and this is going to be grayed out.

There are other options you can look at as well. You can choose to make the recording available to producers and presenters, and attendees as well.

If you want different captions, you can add captions as the spoken language and translate too. So, when the language is being spoken, you can translate it into up to six different languages and you can just choose the languages that you're going to allow this to translate and create subtitles for, and depending on the culture of the school or your company make sure to be thoughtful and choose the six most common languages.

If you want to open up the **Q&A**, to allow questions and answers you can also do this during the live event. So, you can have that disabled here and you can enable it later on. With this, you've got the option to moderate a question that is asked by an attendee and then presenters and the organizer of the event can make those questions and answers public or not because in a live event attendee cannot open their microphone and cameras and you can't allow them to either. The whole point of the event it's a one-way thing; it's from the presenters to the audience.

Once you're done, you simply click on **"Schedule"** and then you get the attendee link. This is the link that you're going to give to all the attendees; you can share this by putting it on social media or just sending it to the people who are going to be interested in joining this event.

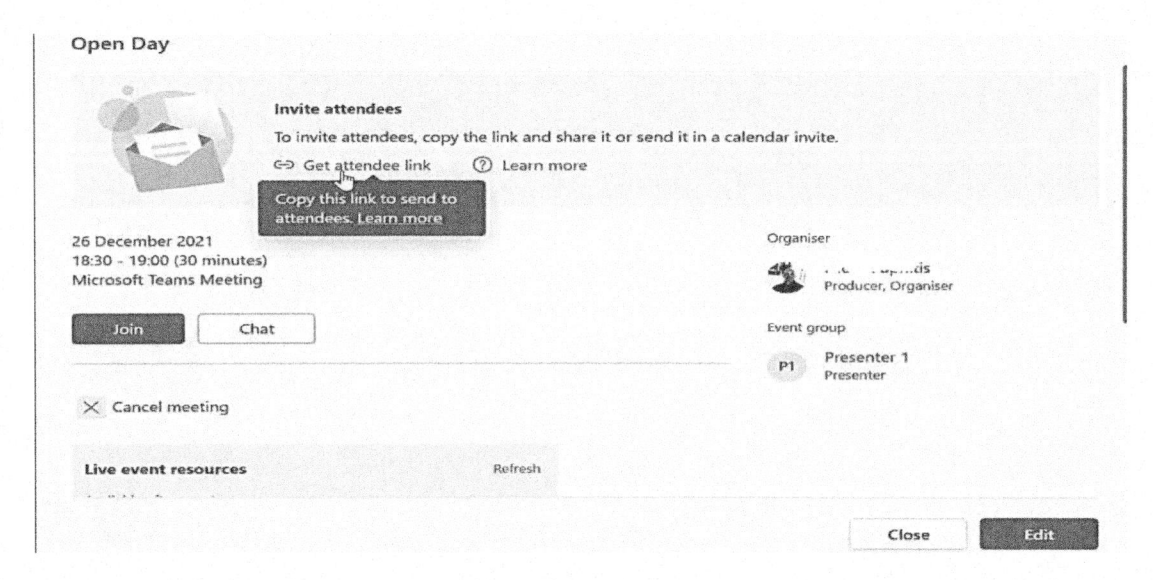

If you scroll down here, it's got **"Join live event"**. Only the presenters get this.

If you are an attendee and you are invited to a live event, you can watch the live event either by using the Teams App or using the web instead. Whether you are logged into an account or not, if you are looking into an account then your name and your account will be visible because you're logged in with your account and if you're not then you can just give a default name. So, you can either sign in with your Office 365 account or join anonymously.

When the event does start, this will open up and you will see the presenters and whatever the organizer or whoever your production manager is, and the event feeds through to the private event; that's what the attendees will see.

Summary

So, let's do a quick review of what we've covered today and look at some numbers. The table below covers the basics and the differences between the three types of meetings or events.

	Meetings	Webinar	Live Event
Attendees	1000 up to 10,000 view only Soon 20,000 view only	1000 up to 10,000 view only Soon 20,000 view only	10,000 with capabilities for a Q&A
Attendee microphone /camera	Microphone /Camera can be disabled (which prevents attendees from enabling)	Microphone /Camera can be disabled (which prevents attendees from enabling)	Disabled for attendees
Breakout rooms	Yes	Yes	Not available
Registration	No	Yes	No
Attendance Report	Yes (if scheduled through Outlook)	Yes	Yes (if public will display anonymous for guests)

First of all, let's have a look at meetings. Meetings and webinars are very very similar. The only difference that you're going to see here is that there is no registration process for scheduled meetings, whereas you do have a registration process for a webinar. So that's good if you want to know or have a good idea of how many people are going to be attending.

Meetings are quite useful and easy to set up, there's no registration form to complete or set up, and this can be used within the company and have some external people join in, and mostly done from a channel.

However, if you do want to have a registration process so you have a good idea of who's going to be attending, the webinar is the way to go. You can **have up to 1,000 people join either a meeting or a webinar**; remember they're very similar apart from the registration process. You can control the microphone and the camera of the attendees whereas with the webinar it's automatically done by default.

With the scheduled meeting, you're going to have to go to the meeting options and just make sure that nobody is a presenter apart from you and then you can disable the camera, microphone and control those for the attendees later during the meeting.

The other thing with webinar meetings is that you do not have an attendance report for meetings unless you schedule the meeting through Outlook, whereas with the webinar it's automatic. Another fact here is that **you can have meetings scheduled for multiple teams channels, only if you do that through Outlook**.

So, you get up to 1,000 people who can be attendees. These attendees can use their microphones and cameras if you allow them. You can get up to **10,000** with views only and soon that will go up to about **20,000** in march 2022. What does **"view only"** mean? Well, once your account reaches a thousand the maximum for the meeting or the webinar, anyone else who attends will only be able to attend and view only; they won't have access to a microphone and they won't have access to their camera so they can't enable these and that will allow you to go up to ten thousand. To enable this feature, your **Tenant administrator** will have to enable this through **PowerShell**. This is not something that is turned on automatically; the Tenant admin has to enable this through PowerShell.

Live events allow up to **10,000** people, with the ability of Q&A. There are no microphones and cameras. It is a one-way process from presenters to audience, disabled for attendees so there's no way of enabling them. There are no breakout rooms for live events because these are not able to interact whereas with meetings and webinars you can have breakout rooms. You don't have a registration process; however, you do get an attendance report and with that attendance report if it's a public live event and somebody has joined anonymously then it's going to say anonymous user or guest or something like that and it says the time that they logged in and the time that they've locked out of the event.

So based on this data here and everything covered in this chapter, you should be able to decide what is best for you.

Chapter 6: Focus On Private Channels

Inthischapter, you will see how you can set up a Private Channel in Microsoft Teams.

Why would you ever want to set up a Private Channel in Microsoft Teams and what does that even mean?

What It Means

By default, when you set up a team in Microsoft Teams, the channels that you create are public, meaning that anyone who's part of that team can see those channels. Well, let's say that you're a manager at a company and you want to have a private channel with other managers so you could discuss employee performance or you're a teacher and you're teaching a class with another teacher and you want to discuss between teachers and you don't want your students to see it. Whatever your reason, Microsoft Team supports Private Channels and you'll see how you can set it up not only that, you'll also see what it looks like for people who have access to that channel and people who don't have access to it.

If you already have a team set up and you also have a few different channels set up, these channels are available to anyone who's part of this team.

Creating a Private Channel

To **create a new Private Channel** what you're going to do is to click on the ellipses next to the team's name and go down to **"Add channel"**.

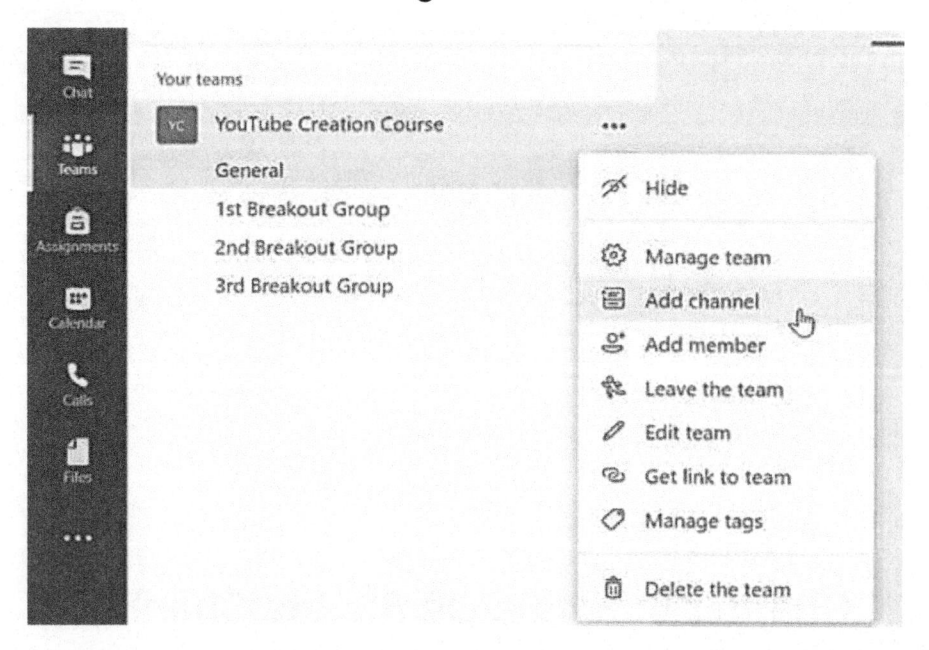

Once you click on that, it'll tell you that you could create a channel for the team that you have and you can proceed to enter the details of this channel.

You'll see under privacy that by default the setting is **"Standard"**, so it says **"accessible to everyone on the team"**. What you're going to do is to click on this drop-down and change it to **"Private"** so it's **"Accessible only to a specific group of people within the team"**. Go ahead and click on **"Next"**

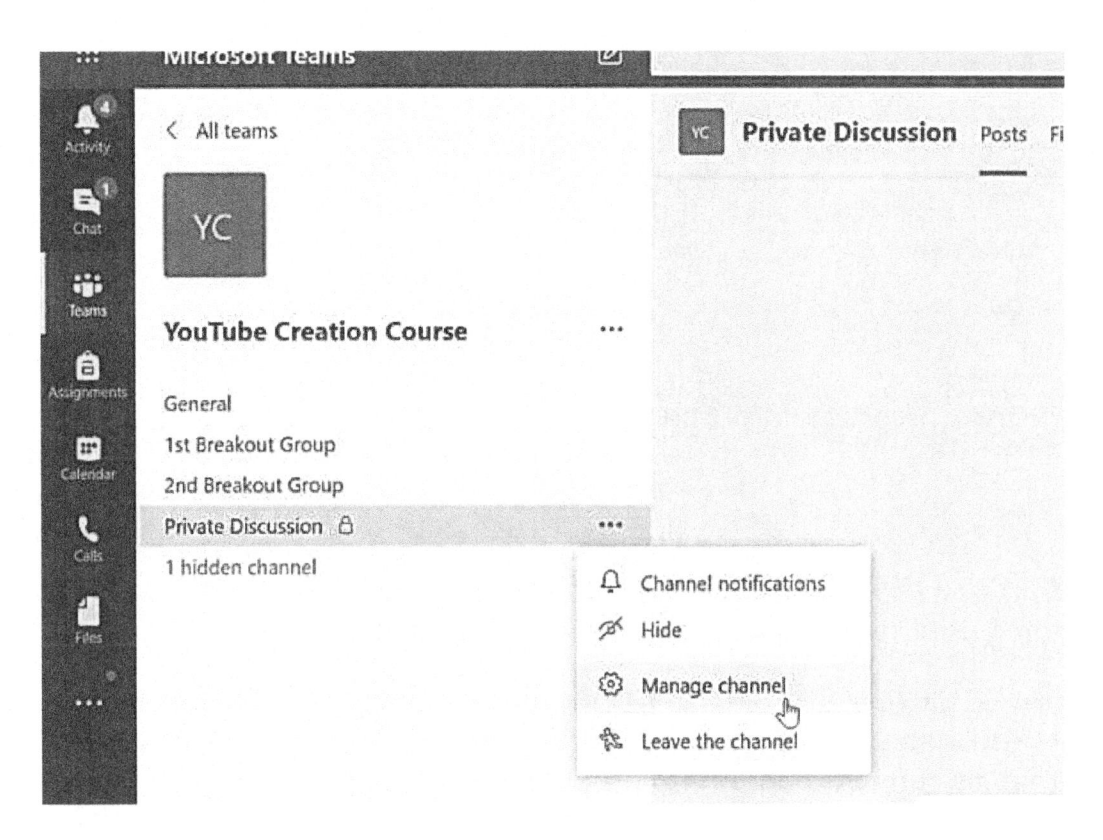

Now that it's created your channel, what you need to do is to add members to it. When you add members, you could either **set them as members** or as **owners**.

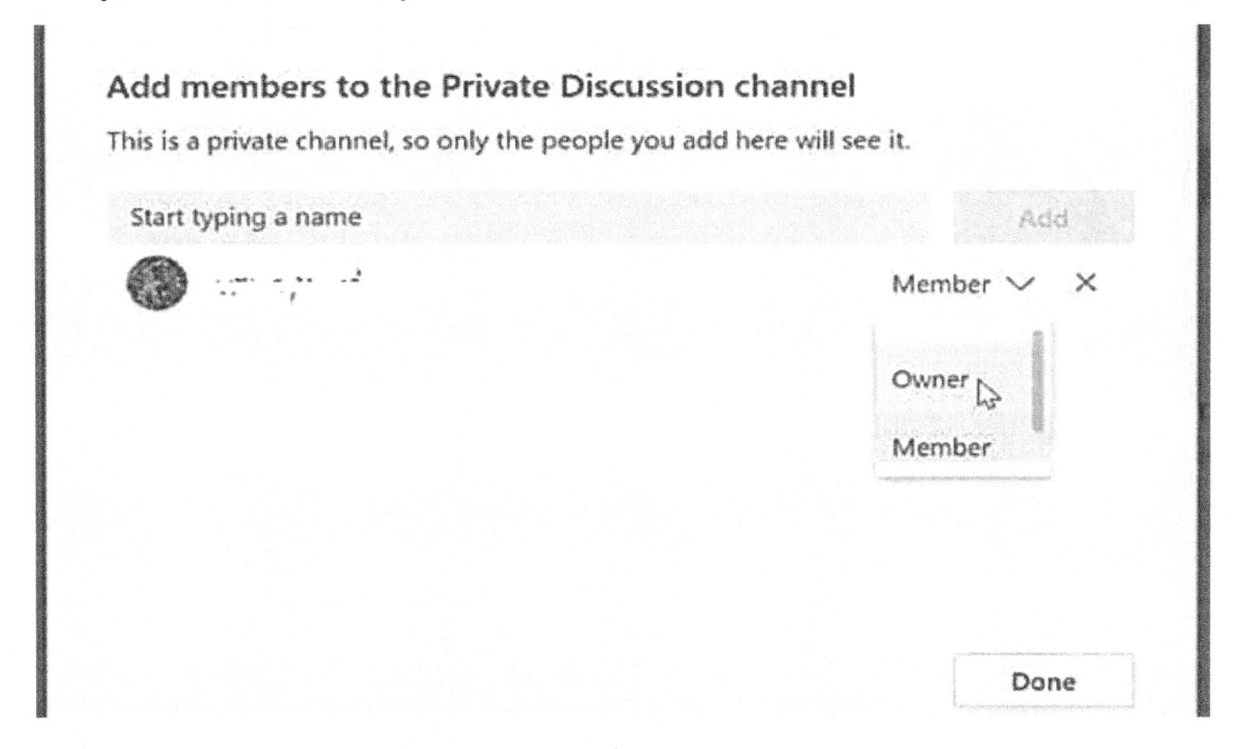

If a user is an Owner, the user could go in and **add other people** to this private channel, however, if you just set that user as a member, you are the only one who can add or remove people from this channel.

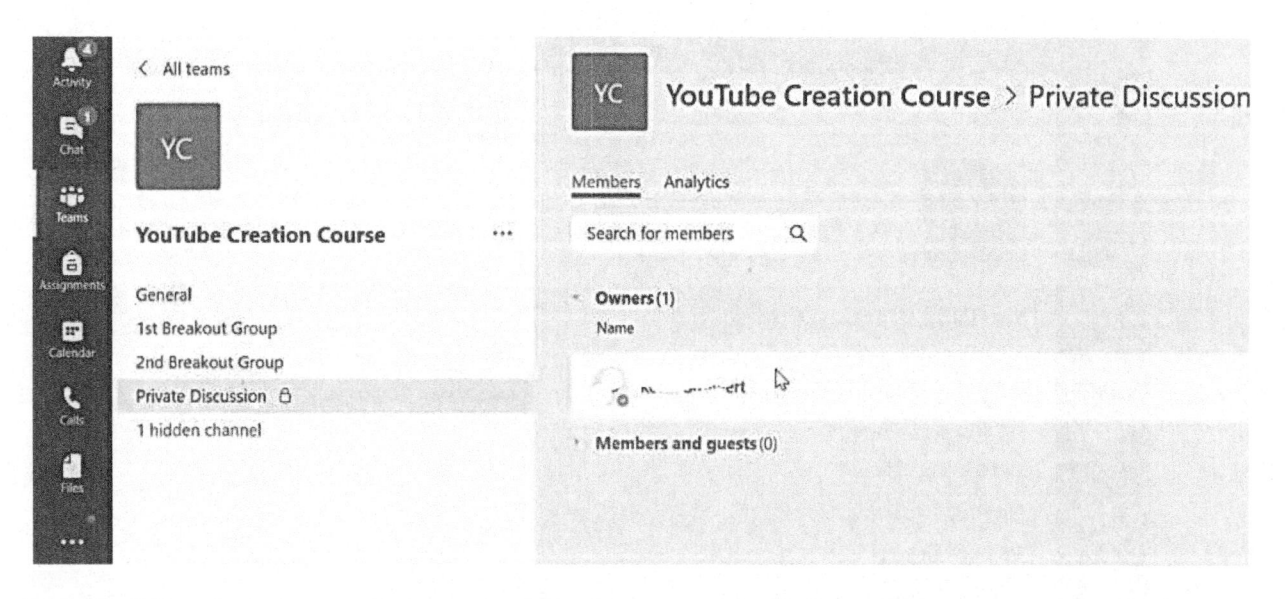

After adding your members, go ahead now and click on **"Done"**.

In the users' view, you'll see that they have access to the private discussion channel. You'll see that there's this **lock icon** next to the channel name, which means that it's a private channel and only certain individuals have access to this channel.

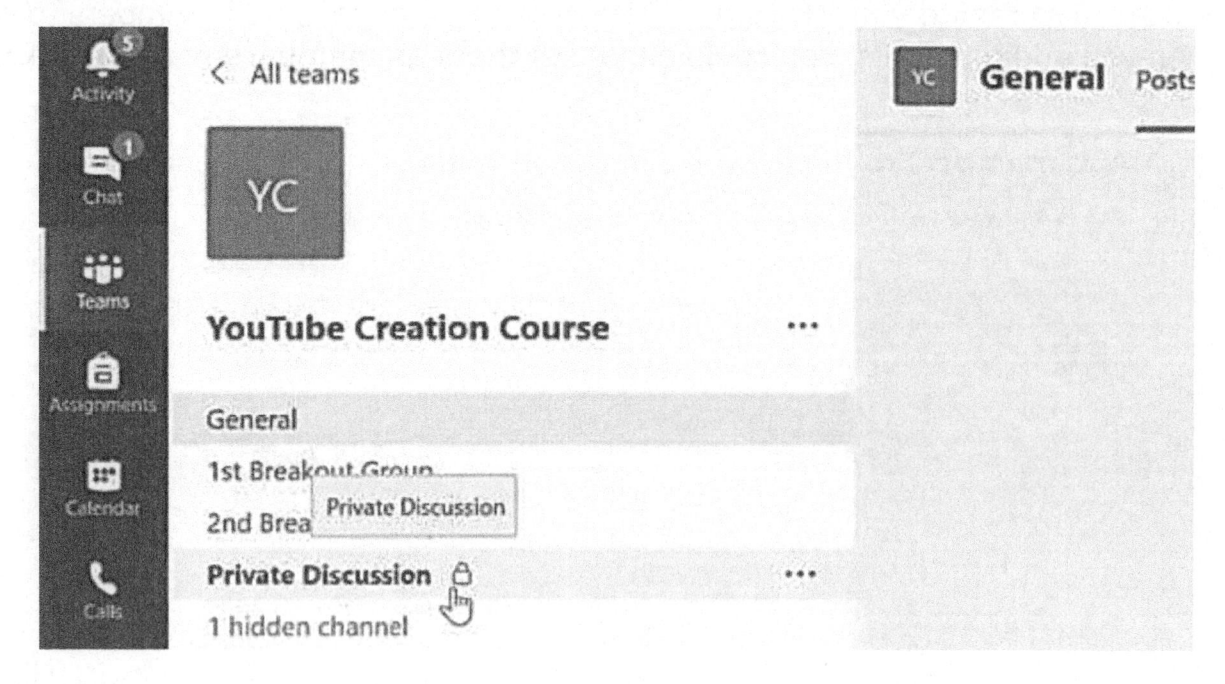

Within the member's view if you hover over the channel and you click on the ellipses, one thing you'll see is the member can manage the channel but when they go to manage the channel, they are unable to add additional people. This is because you set them as members.

If you're logged in as someone who is not a member of this private channel, if you click on your teams, it'll show all of the different channels that you have access to, but there is no private discussion channel; so, you cannot see the Private channel.

This is a quick example of how you can set up your private channel especially if you want to have a discussion that's outside of the general visibility of the broader team; a private channel is a way to go.

Summary

In this chapter, you learned the following:

- The basics of a private channel, including its features
- The distinguishing factors between public and private channels
- How to create a private channel for your organization.

Chapter 7: Designing With Teams Templates

In this chapter, we are looking at administering templates in Microsoft Teams and we will discuss what they are, how they work, and more importantly what they can do for you.

Over the last few years, when you've created a team in Microsoft Teams you could create just a blank team or you could create a team from another group. In recent months we've started seeing more and more templates and these are pre-created with different channels and applications for different scenarios. So for example you might be working in a medical setting like a hospital or you might be working in an IT department and need something for incident response or finance in a bank. There now seems to be templates for everyone, but how do you create and administer them in the admin center? and how do they work?

We are going to go deep into these and answer these questions. In doing so, we'd take a look at the templates from the perspectives of the Admin Center for Microsoft Teams and the other one is the Teams client

From the end-user perspective

Here you can see a selection of teams along with a couple of channels. To create a new team, you just come down to the left-hand side and you say you want to either join or create a team. When you create the team here you've got a choice; you can either choose to create a team or join a team with a code and that means you've got an invite code.

If you're wondering how to get an invite code, well, if you just click on the "**more options**" menu of a team as an administrator, you can see "**get a link to the team**" and that would be the invite code there.

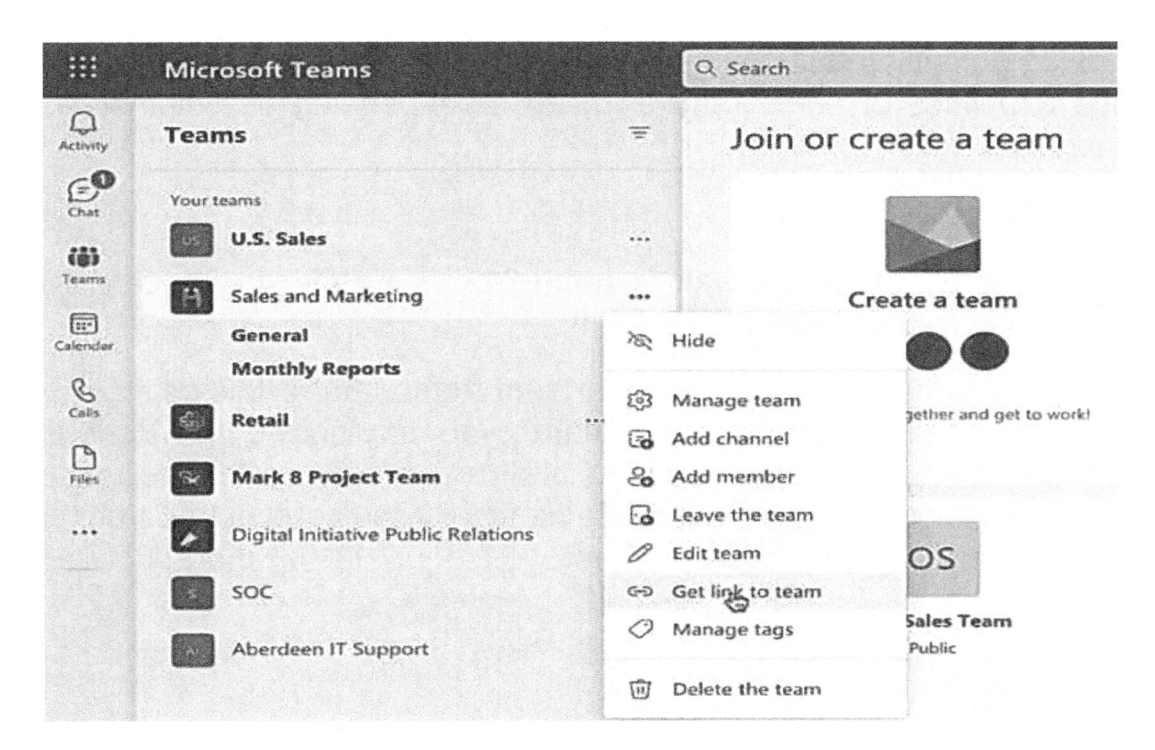

Also, if you go into the "**Manage team**" and go into settings, then you can see that you also can **generate an invite code** and you'll just give that to a user and they would then be able to create that team.

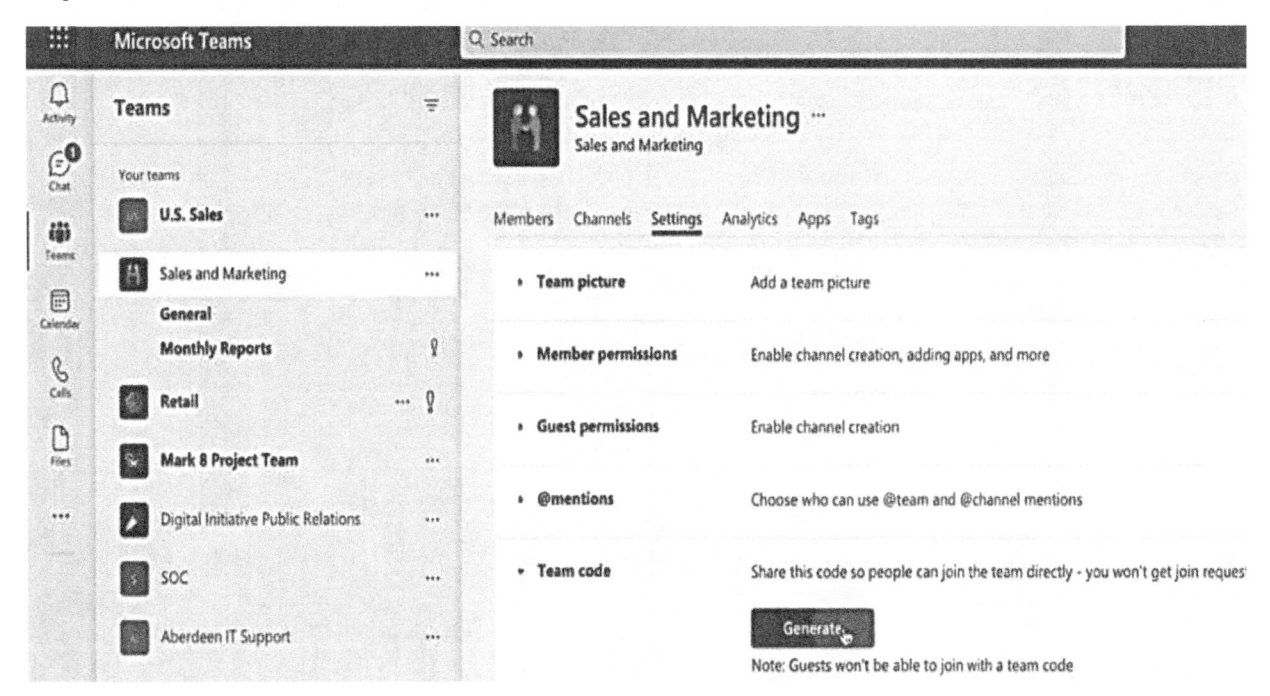

Please note that when you create a team you also create a Microsoft 365 group and vice versa, but what we're looking at here is to create a team from a template. So you have some options to work with, and depending on the templates that you have some of these are premium templates; which means depending on the plan that you have with Microsoft 365 you may see some or all of these templates or some maybe not at all depending on whether you're a home user.

Creating A New Team

To create a team, you can **create a team from scratch**, or you can **create a team from a group or an existing team**.

So for example, if you want to create a team from either a Microsoft 365 group or an existing Team, if you chose a **"Team"**, you may not be able to do that for some of the teams because it's either they are private or they've got private content in them and for some, you'll be able to take the content that's not private; this means you're not taking the content, you're just taking the structure of the team.

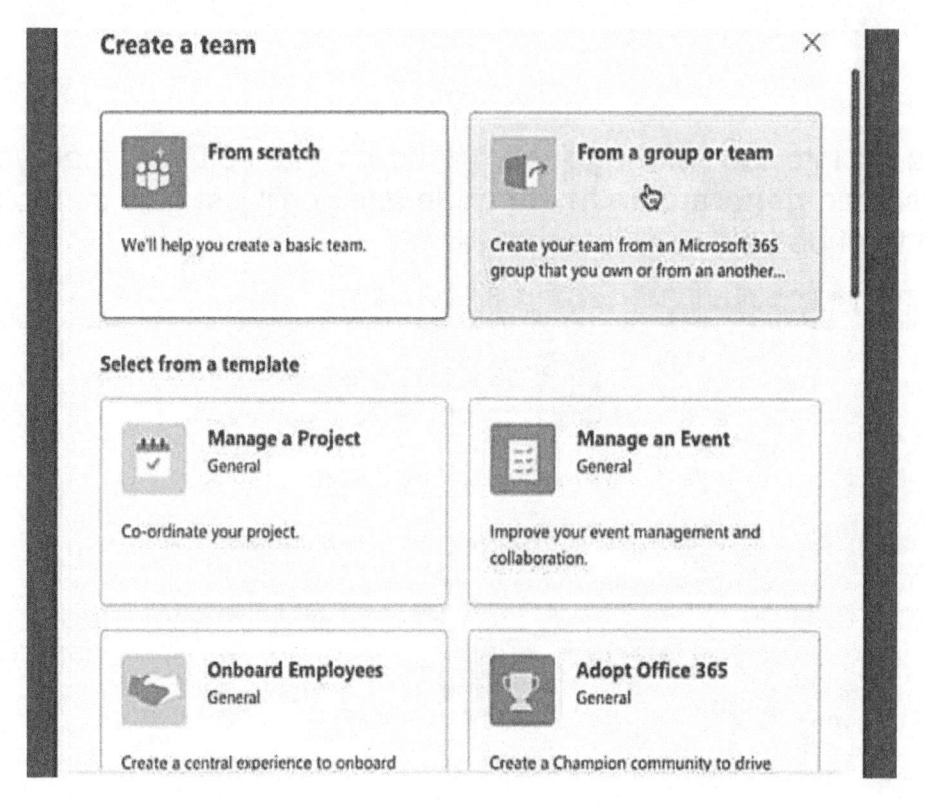

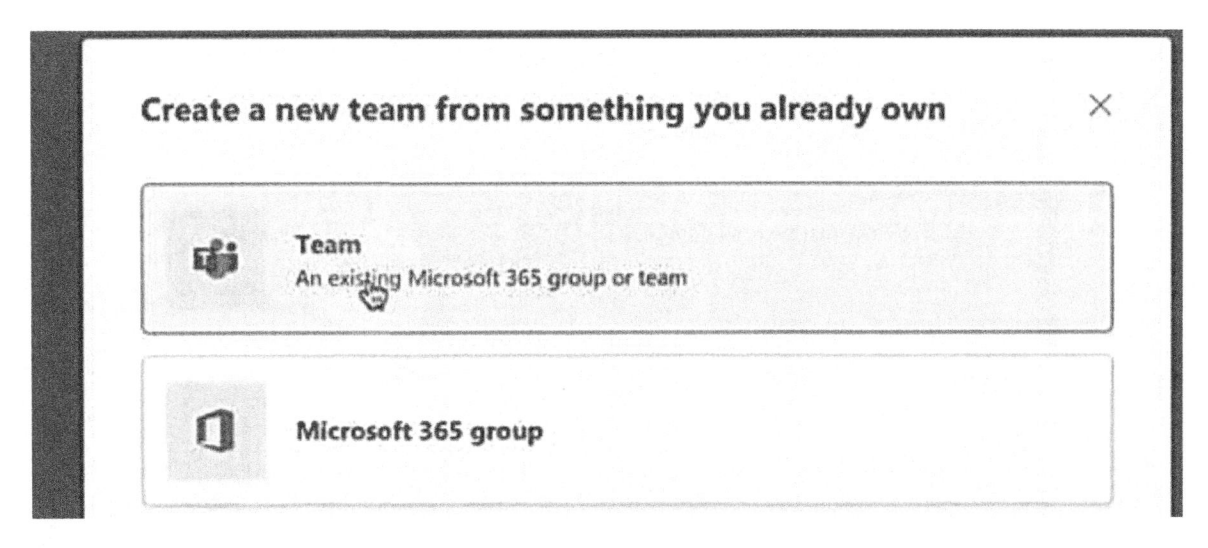

So, if you click on a team, you can see it asking what you want to include from the original team. This could be the tabs, the team settings, you can even bring the members across if you want to, and that's if you're an owner by the way, and you can also bring any apps as well.

In terms of privacy, only team owners can add members or you can go with a public option, which anyone in your organization can join; you can then go ahead and create that team.

As mentioned earlier, you can create a team from something existing or you can go ahead and create a team from one of the available templates. These templates are available, depending on the type of business that you are, for example, Event management, Project management, maybe something in HR, Incident Response (this is a government template), Crisis Management for a financial organization, you've got a Manager Store and Healthcare, among others. You can see that there is something for everyone here.

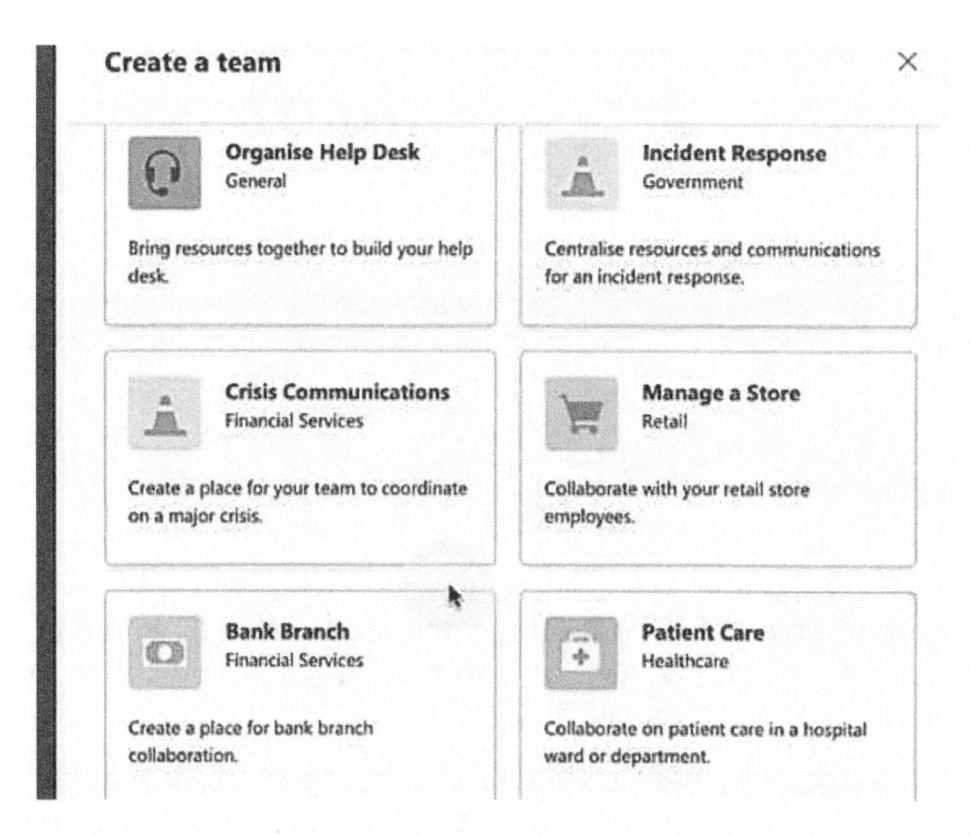

After choosing your template, you get about four **default channels** and you can see that you get some **default apps** as well.

Remember that Microsoft Teams includes not just Microsoft apps but also third-party apps as well, and that's one of the powerful things about Microsoft Teams.

So, you're going to click on "**Nex**t" and you're going to choose if this is going to be a private team or a public team. Well, for this demo you can make it a public team.

Next, you're to give your team a name and add a description so people know what this team is about. You can customize the channels if you want to, so if you want to rename or edit them, you can do that from here. Now go ahead and click on "**Create**" and it creates that team for you.

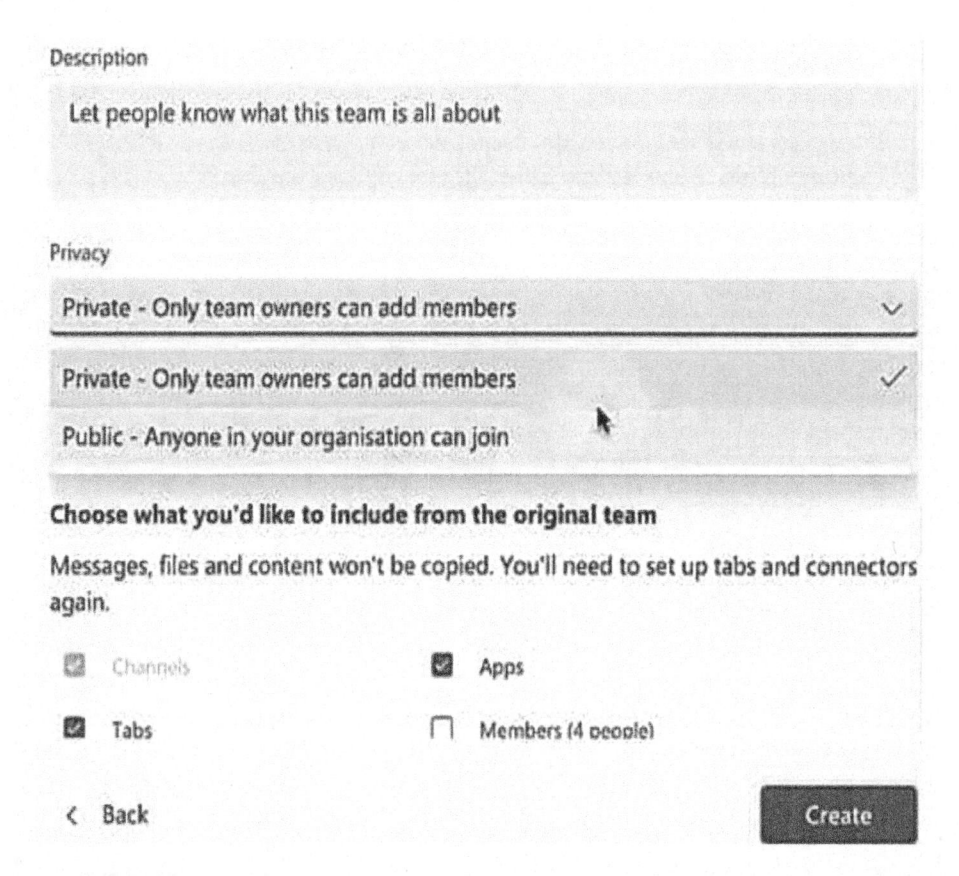

So the team is now created, and now you can see that your team has been added.

The next thing that you would want to do is to manage the team and when we talk about managing the team, you can see that because you created the team you are the owner of that team. To proceed, you can start adding some members to your team. After adding your members in here, click on **"Close"** and the rest of course is history.

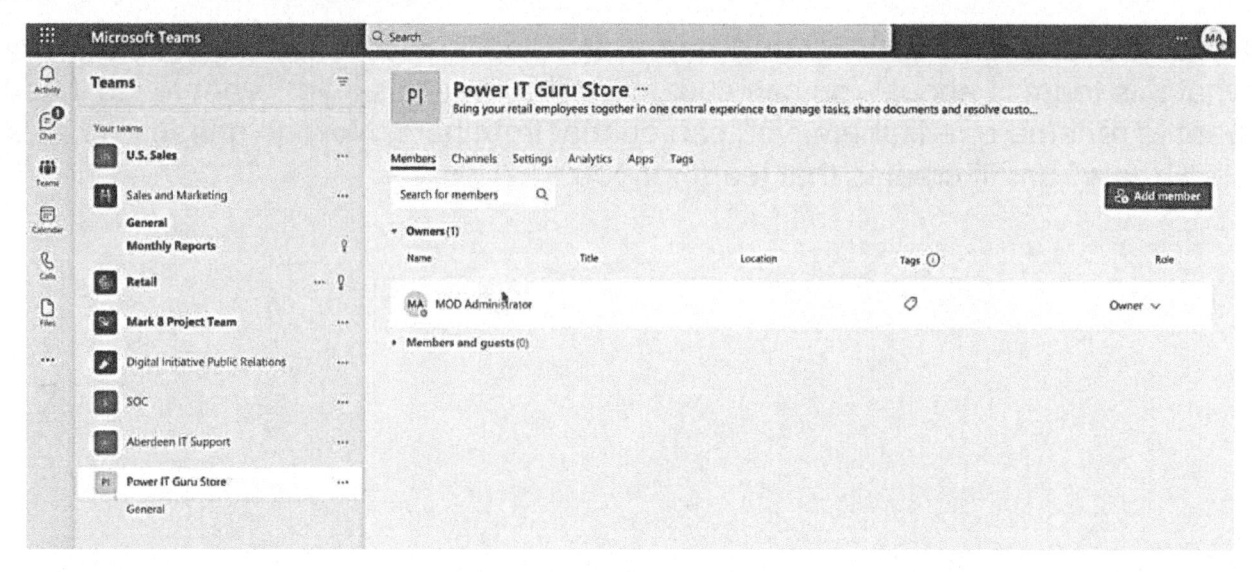

Once the team is created, you can create multiple channels and there you go. So that's what it means to create a team from a basic template. These templates are nice and they're completely customizable. Remember that this is from the end user's perspective.

What about the admin's perspective?

From The Admin's Perspective

For this, you need to come into the Microsoft 365 admin center and you go down into Microsoft Teams.

Just before you go there, flip over into **"Teams & groups"**, then **"Active teams & groups"** and locate the team you just created.

You can see that it's created a Microsoft 365 group for that Team, if you click onto the group here, which is quite important that you do, and click on **"Members"**, it shows you all the members, but if you go into **"Settings"**, this is important; if you want the team to be contactable externally, then allow external senders to email this group, send copies of group emails, and you can change the privacy here as well.

Now the one thing that you cannot change is once it becomes a team, that's it. Essentially a team is an extended Microsoft 365 group. It is extended because you can use third-party products here as well.

Administering the team templates

In your admin center, you're going to click on the drop-down arrow for Teams and in here you're going to come into **"Teams templates"**. Here is a complete list and this is useful because you get a description of exactly what the team is, you can see who published the team template (now there are hundreds of templates out there and there are quite several third-party providers who are also providing these templates), it shows you how many channels, how many apps the team has got, and also when it was last modified. So, you can see that you've got the same templates here and you may be wondering if it is easy to create a template here.

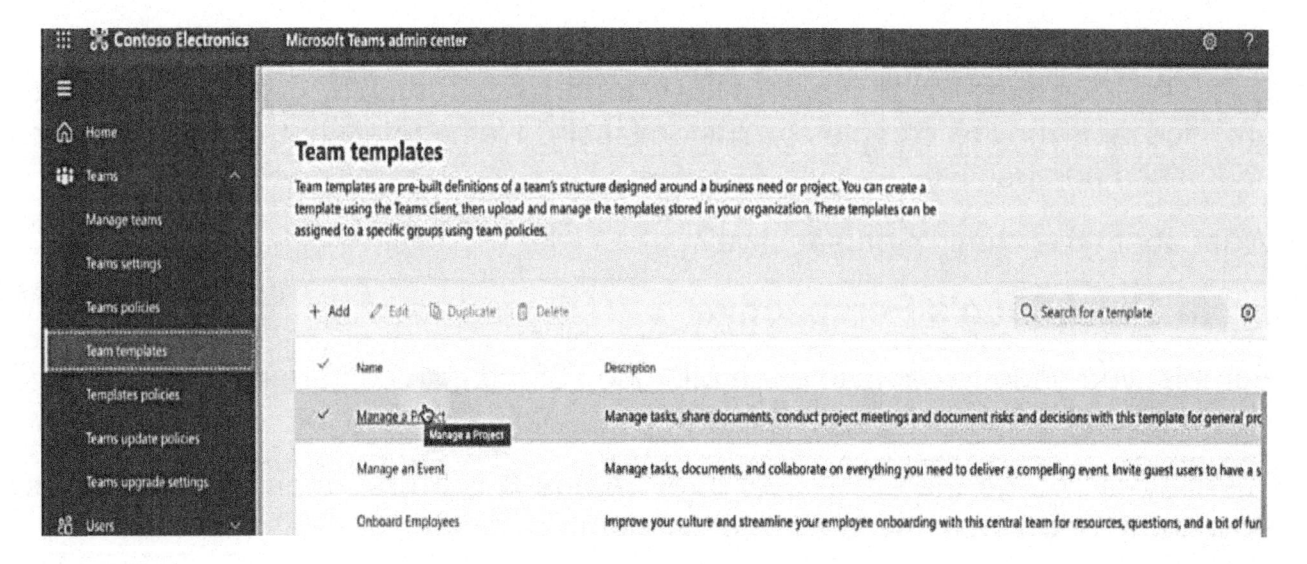

Click on the "**Add**" button, and just as you saw in Microsoft Teams, you can create a new template, use an existing template or start with an existing template.

You can go ahead and create a new template. Give it a name, put a little description in here and you can specify the locale; if your demo tenant is in the US, you would need to use a US-based tenant. Click on "**Next**" to proceed. Note that if you try and click on next and you don't have a description you need to go ahead and put that in before you proceed.

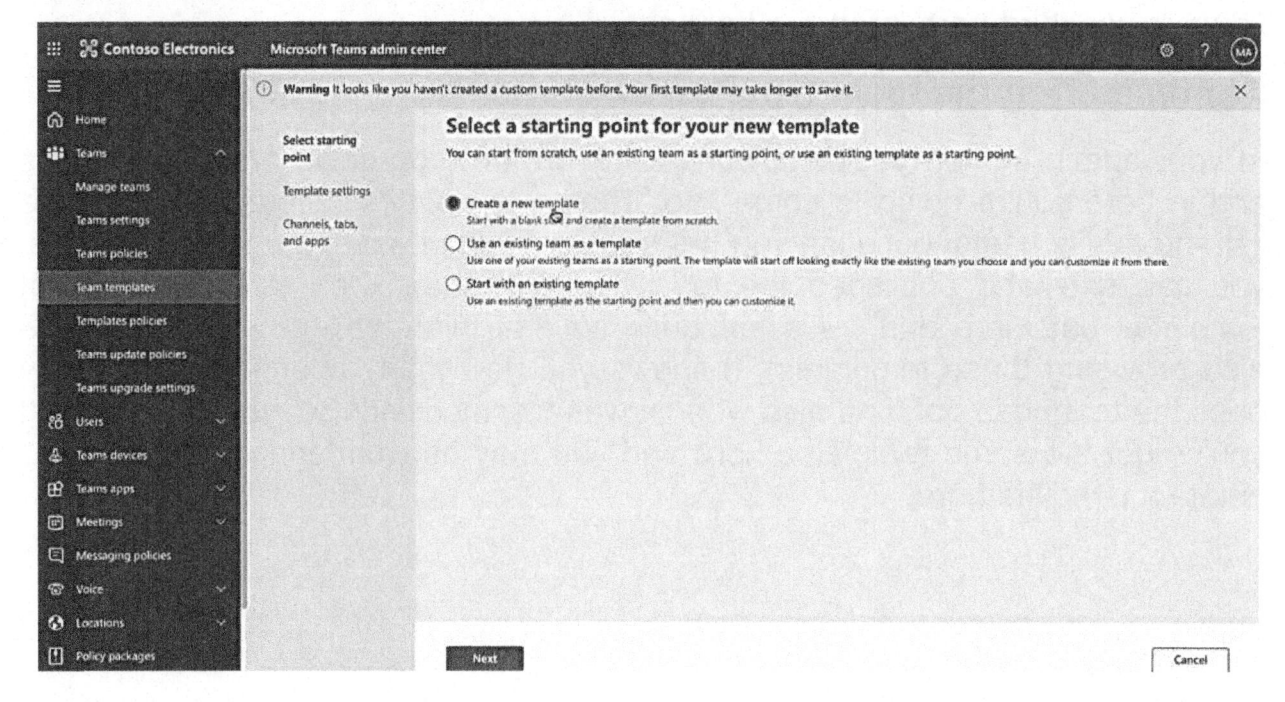

Now, you're going to enter how many channels you want. So, you're going to click on "**Add**" and enter the details for the channel(s). You're just going to apply that and it will add that channel to the template.

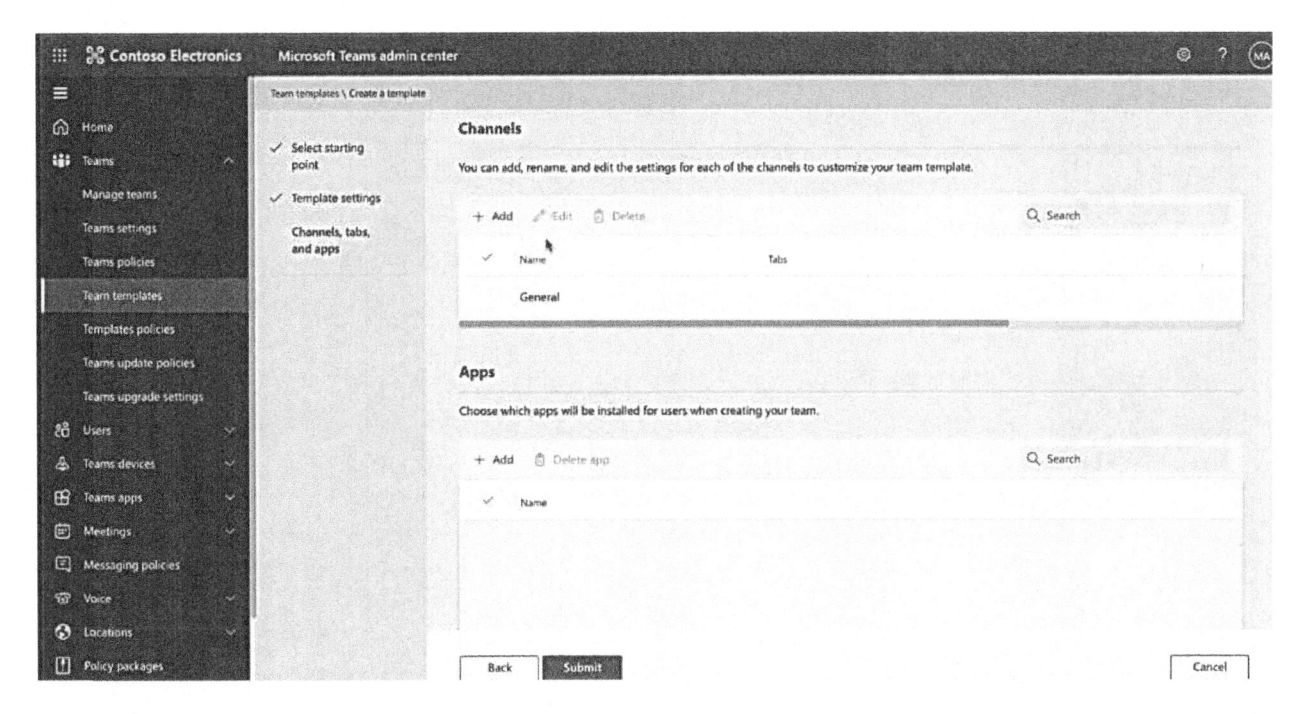

You can also add in apps as well if I want to. So, you can bring in an app by simply typing the name of the app. Any app that's grayed out shows me that the app is already in there, so you get that by default but if there are any third-party ones then, of course, you would go ahead and add those.

So, you go ahead, click on **"Submit"** and you can see that you've now created this template here. Any templates that you create will go straight to the top of the list and this is very similar to other Microsoft products.

So that's typically how you create the templates. If you go back to one of the other templates here you can see that this tells you a little bit about the template; you can see you've got a nice description in here, the number of channels and apps, and each template has its unique ID here. It shows me which channels have got which apps applied to them, so a little bit of planning is often useful here. You can go into the apps; it shows you which apps are in here and you can click onto them to get more detail on them too.

The next thing then in your journey of administering templates is something called **"Template policies"**. There is a global policy that contains pretty much all of the templates there but you might want to create your template policy and then assign that policy along with those templates to your users.

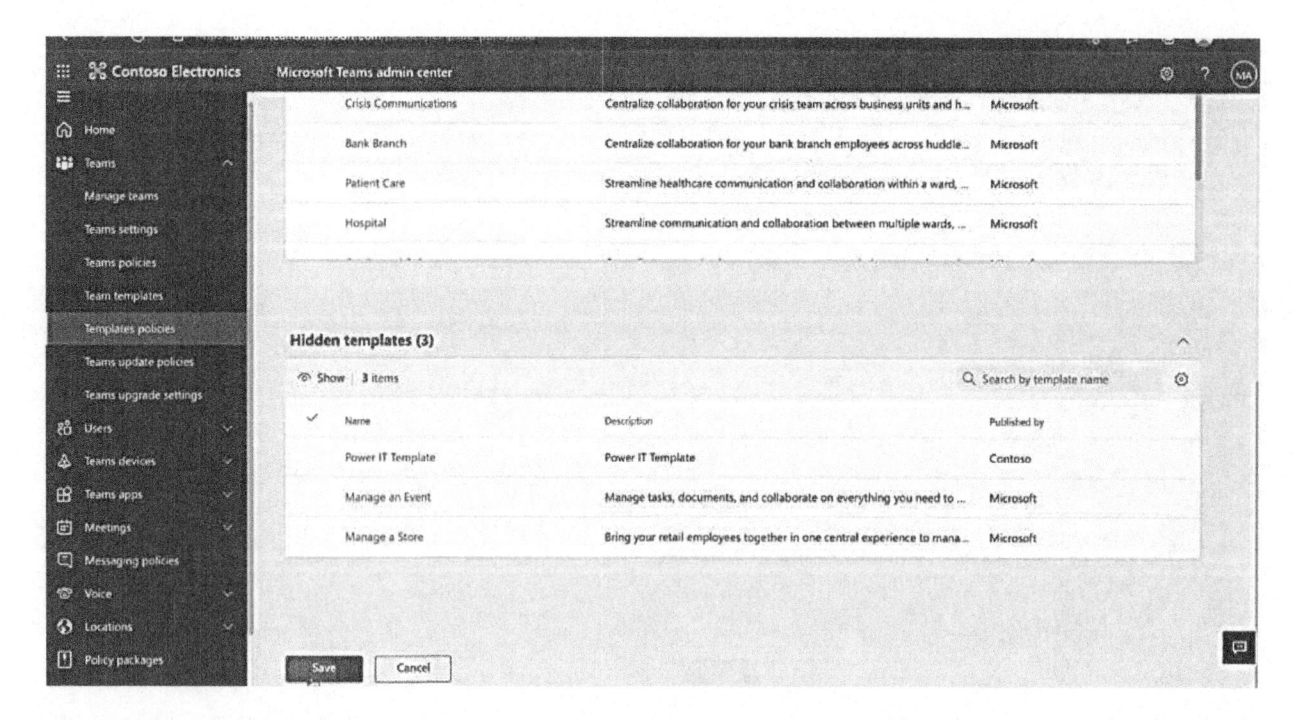

What you can do is to go ahead and add a Template policy. You can decide which templates you want to show and hide. Notice that you're not deleting the template; all you're doing is you're just hiding that specific template here. Again, you can put in a description, and once you've done that you can scroll down and see that it gives you a list of those hidden templates there. So, you click on **"Save"** and now that this is selected, you can decide if you want to assign this template to any particular user.

When you search for names in teams you need to search a minimum of three characters. When the users now log into teams, these templates will be the only two templates that they see and it shows you here which templates have been distributed and how many users have been applied there.

The other thing that we have here is **"Teams update policies"** and if you go into the default settings here, this means how often you want Teams to be updated. This used to be in organizational-wide settings but it's worth mentioning here because if you enable the **"Office preview"** you're going to get new features updated including Teams templates.

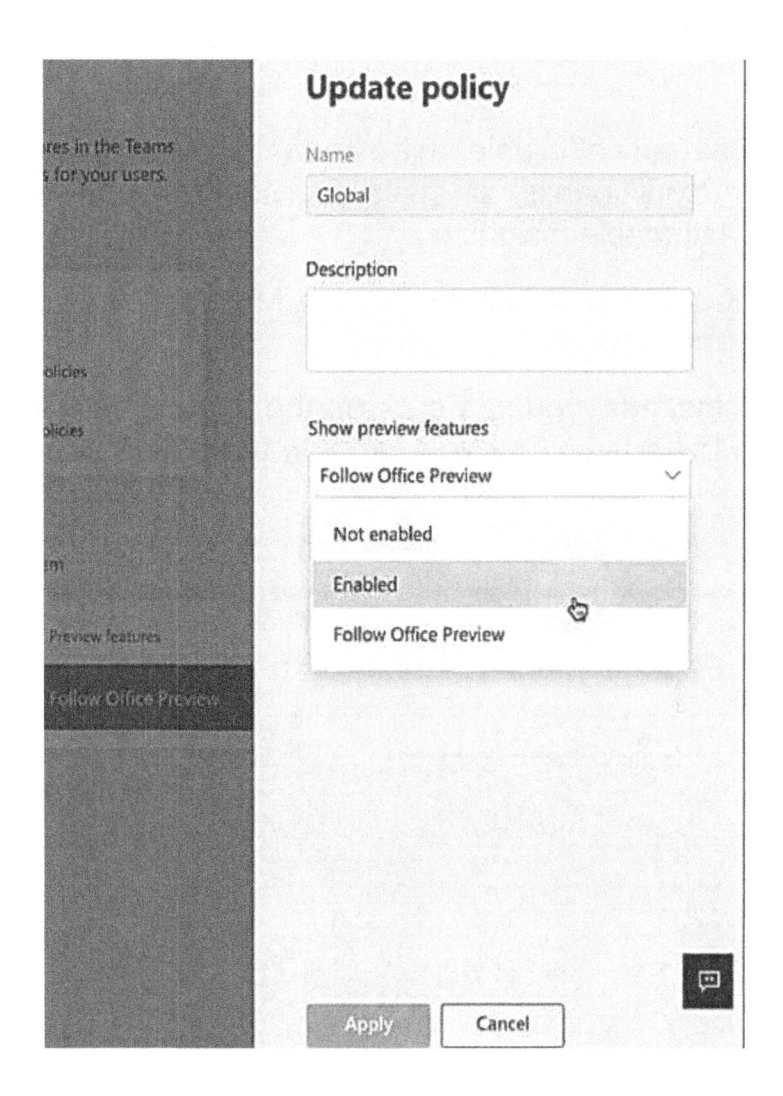

Summary

In this chapter, the main focus was on Teams and this was explained from the end-user and administrative perspectives.

We went further to explain how to create a new Team from scratch and use templates.

Chapter 8: Leveraging Microsoft Viva

Recently, Microsoft announced a new employee experience platform called Microsoft viva and this embraces four models which are Connections, Learning, Topics, and Insights.

We will look at these models one after the other by knowing what they are, what they do, and how useful they can be to you.

Viva Insights

This is a new app already available in the Team Store. The main goal of this app is to build better work habits. It gives individuals, managers, and leaders personalized and actionable insights.

To get started, you need to install this app in Microsoft teams and it is already available in the Teams app store.

To install the Viva Insights, you can click on the three dots in the left navigation pane here, and in the search box you can just type **"Insights"** and this app will show up.

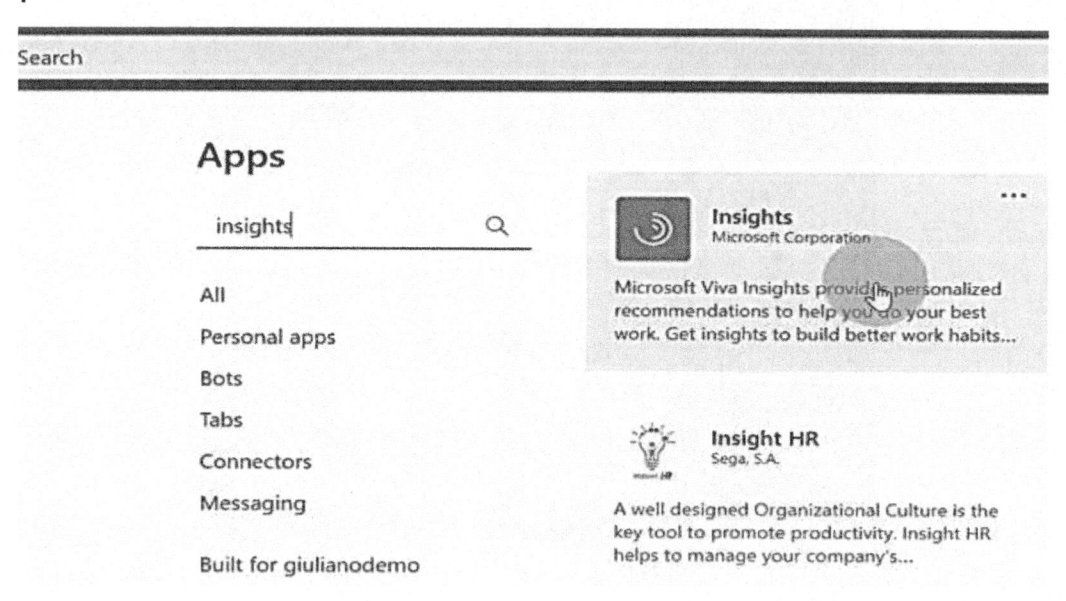

You can even click on more apps or the Apps icon below, this will open the Teams' app store and here you can search for insights and there you go. Please note that Microsoft Viva Insights is a personal app; this means that it will be hosted on the left navigation pane in Microsoft Teams. Now click on **"Add"** to install this application.

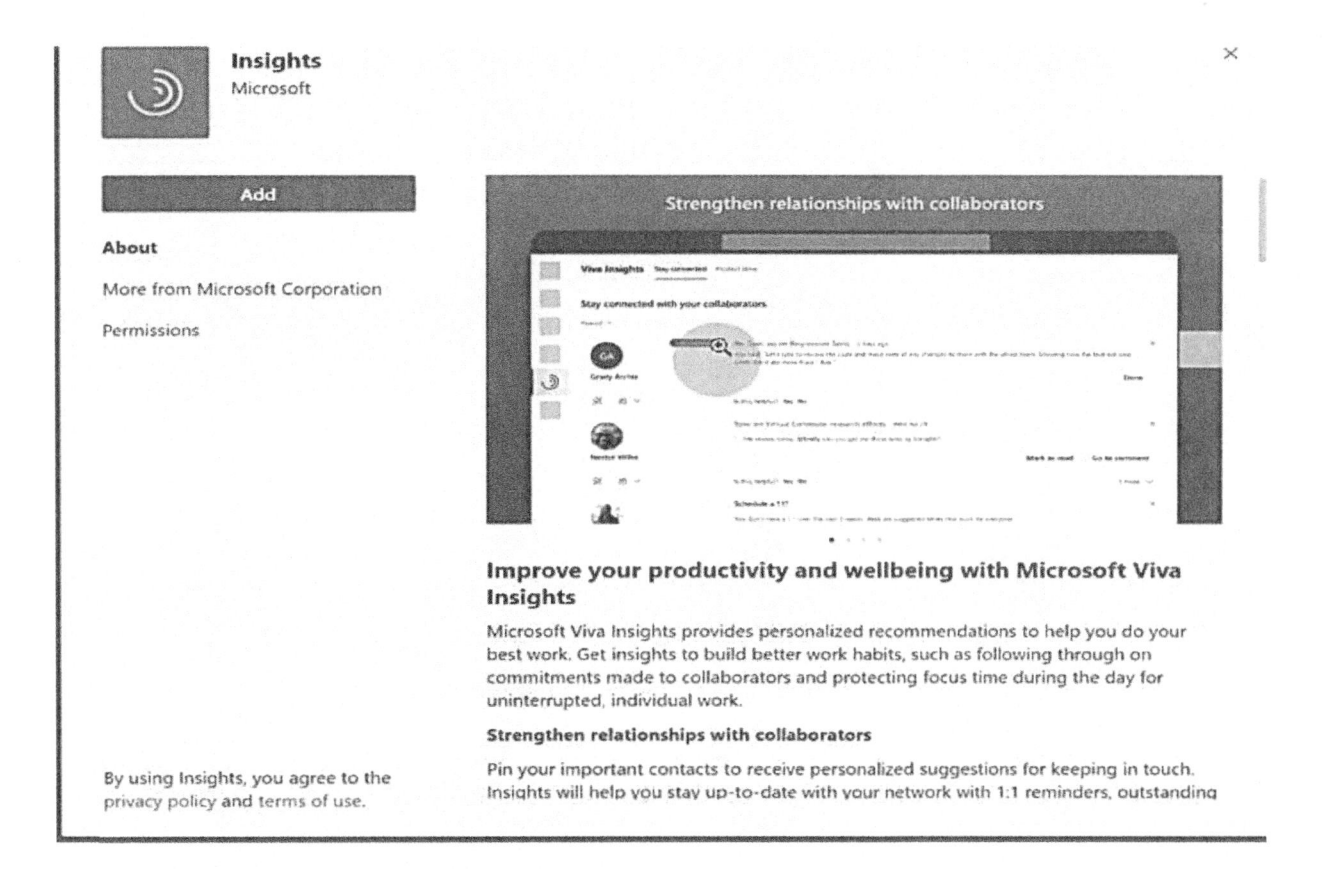

In the personal view of viva insights, you have on two tabs at the top: **"Stay connected"** and **"Product time"**.

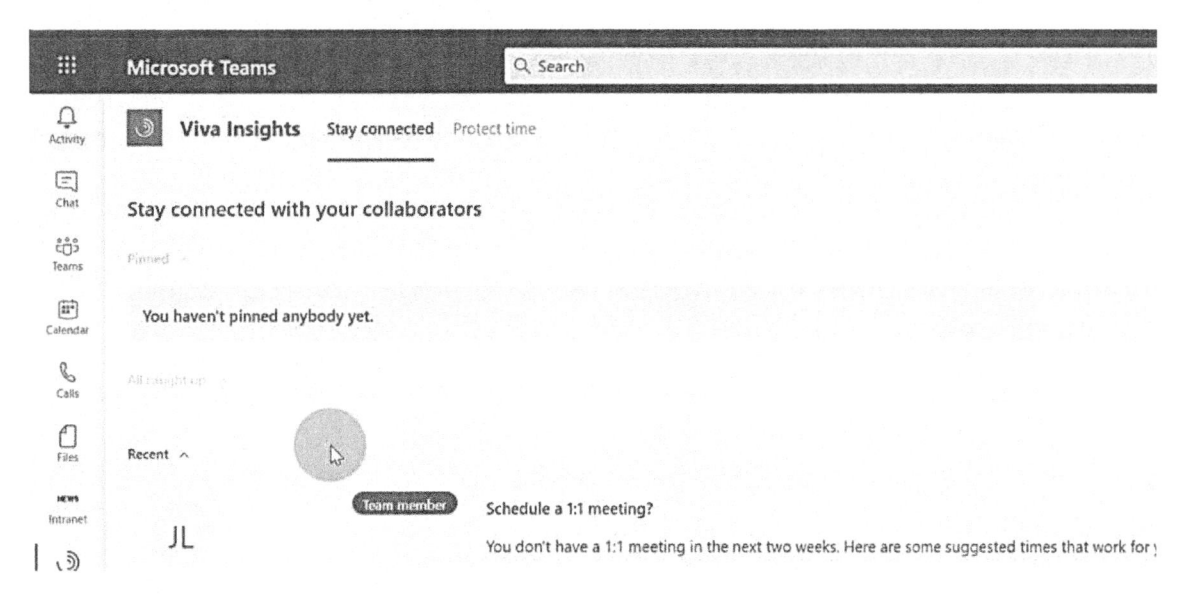

Under the **"Stay connected"** tab, you have two sections, the **"Pinned information"** and below that, you have **"Recent"**.

The main goal of this tab is to improve the collaboration with your colleagues and your teammates.

You can schedule a one-to-one meeting, and use the suggested times which could work for you and your teammate. So you can easily check a time slot, or open the calendar and then send an invitation to your teammate to stay closer to improve your collaboration and to speed up your projects.

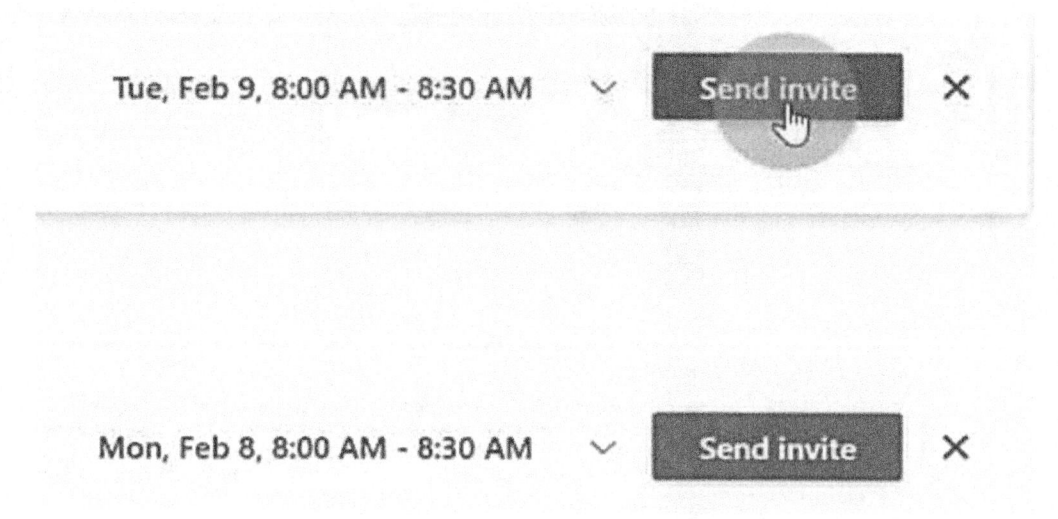

You can pin this information or choose to get a reminder every two weeks, or monthly or not.

After pinning a suggestion, it appears on the Pinned section. This is good if you have a lot of suggestions and you want to follow up with three or four suggestions that are very relevant and important to you.

After sending an invitation, your teammates receive the invitation via email, clicking on this email they can decide to accept the invitation to have a one-to-one chat with you or not.

However, if they accept the invitation, you will see the meeting scheduled in your calendar and if you open it, it'll appear as a reminder for your one-to-one chat with your teammate.

In the "**Recent**" section you can also collect information related to the invitations. If you've got an invitation from your teammate and you haven't provided an answer, click on the drop-down where you can provide an answer by clicking on **accept** or **decline**.

Product Time helps you to **schedule Focus time**. Every time that you need to stay focused on a project, or if you have an idea and you need time to develop this idea to build something new, or if you have some sort of training, or you need to have some time to learn new technology, what you should do is to open the calendar in Outlook and book your time.

There are several time slots with options that help you to book time on your calendar. Click on any of the options that work for you, and click on **"Book time"**.

You can expand the option to show all available times and you get to see other days as well.

If you made some mistake, you can click on the button **"Remove slot"** and this will be automatically removed from your calendar.

After booking a slot, if you click now on your calendar you can see that the time slot is booked, so your status will be "do not disturb" and this way you can stay more focused on your idea.

Please note that to have the full capabilities of this app, a workplace analytics license is required.

To get a Workplace Analytics, first of all, you need an Enterprise agreement with Microsoft, then you need to have an Office 365 product that contains either Exchange Online Plan 1 or Exchange Online Plan 2, then you can assign the Workplace Analytics to your managers and leaders and the full capabilities of the Insights app will be available.

Viva Learning

Microsoft Viva Learning is an application inside Microsoft Teams that creates a central hub for learning where people can **discover**, **share**, **recommend** and **learn** from content across their organization.

There's a free and also a paid version of Viva Learning. To get Viva Learning, simply search for it in the Apps section and it will be added to the left pane in your Teams app.

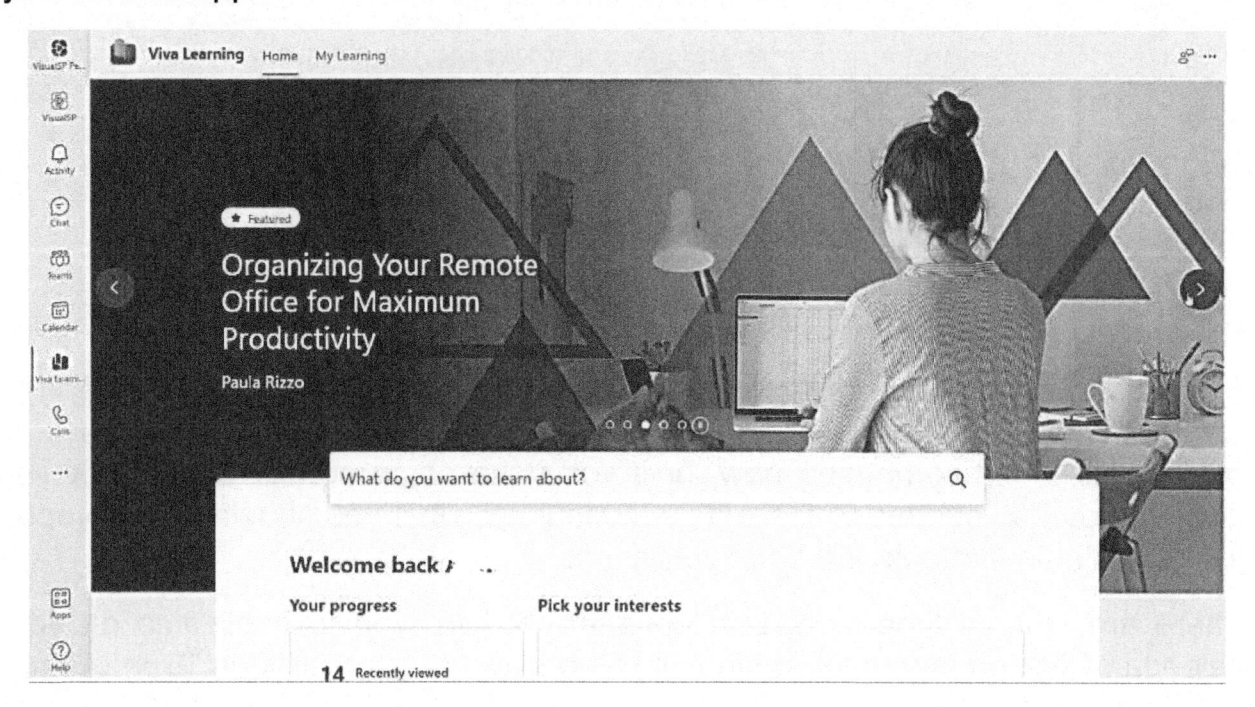

Now let's go through the interface of Viva Learning.

To get started, you enter Viva Learning by clicking on the Viva Learning icon in the left rail on Teams, and once you enter, you'll see a hero image carousel that shows you the featured and trending content. For the paid version you can control what's going to be featured in the trending, but for the free version, you cannot.

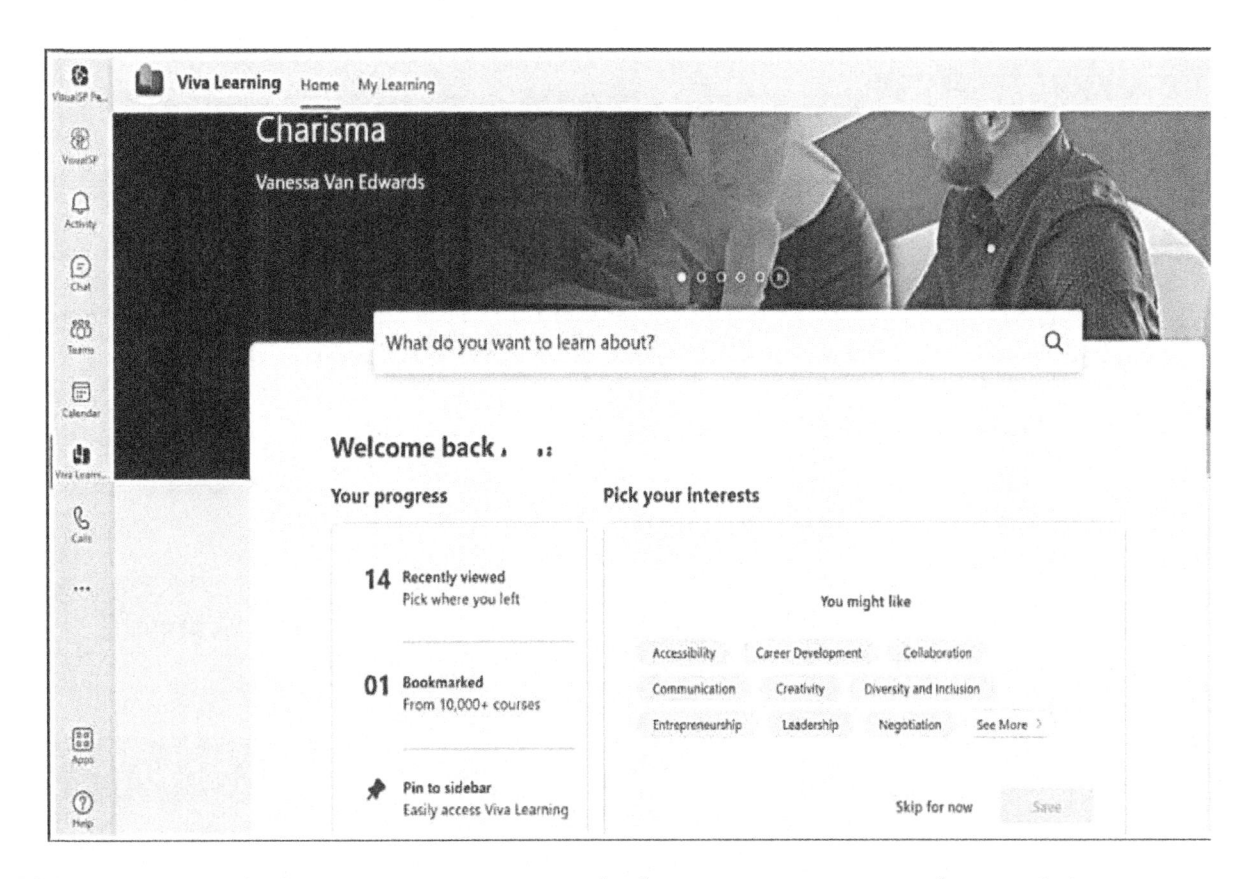

With the search box, you can search for courses, you also get to see your progress so far, and an invite to pick your interests. You can click on "**see more**" to see all the different interests that are available, you can go ahead and search for interest or you can pick one.

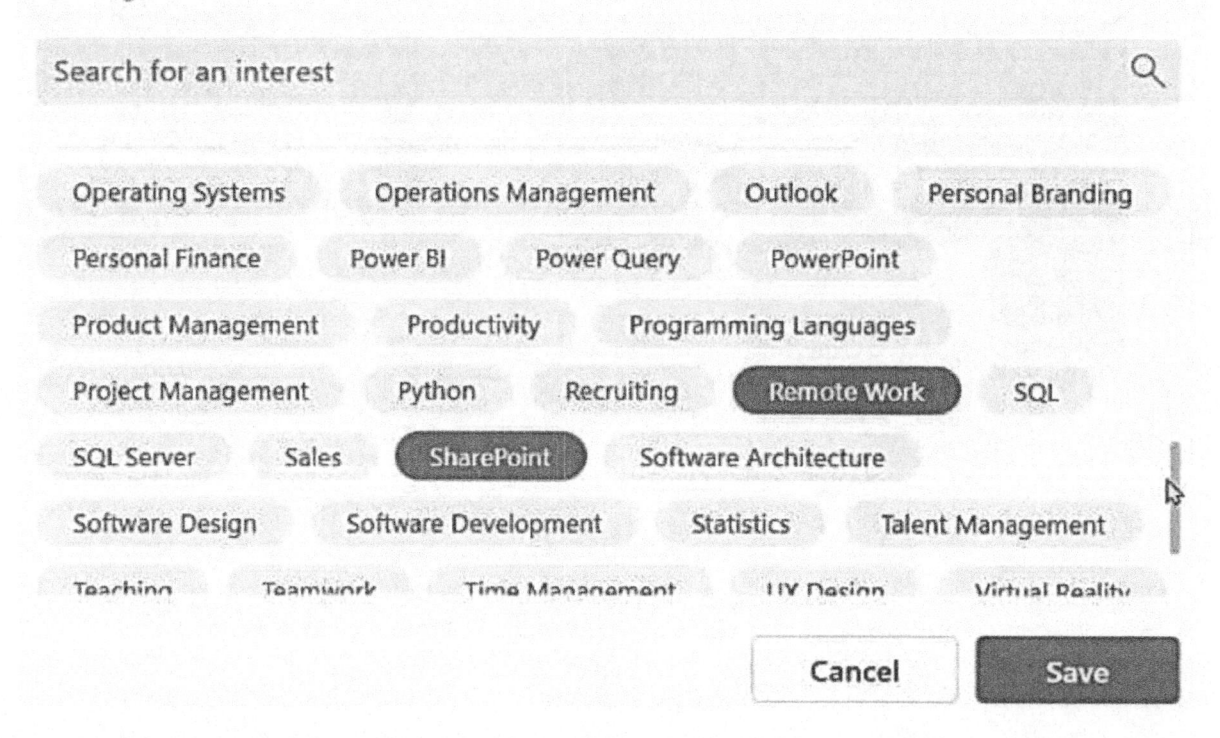

After picking all your interests, go ahead and click on "**Save**". Based on your interests it'll show you recommended courses and if you want to see all, it shows you all the courses based on the interest that you've chosen.

Back on the home page as you scroll down there is a section for browsing courses with your interests, providers, and duration tabs. Within "**your interests**", it has roles corresponding to each of the interests that you pick.

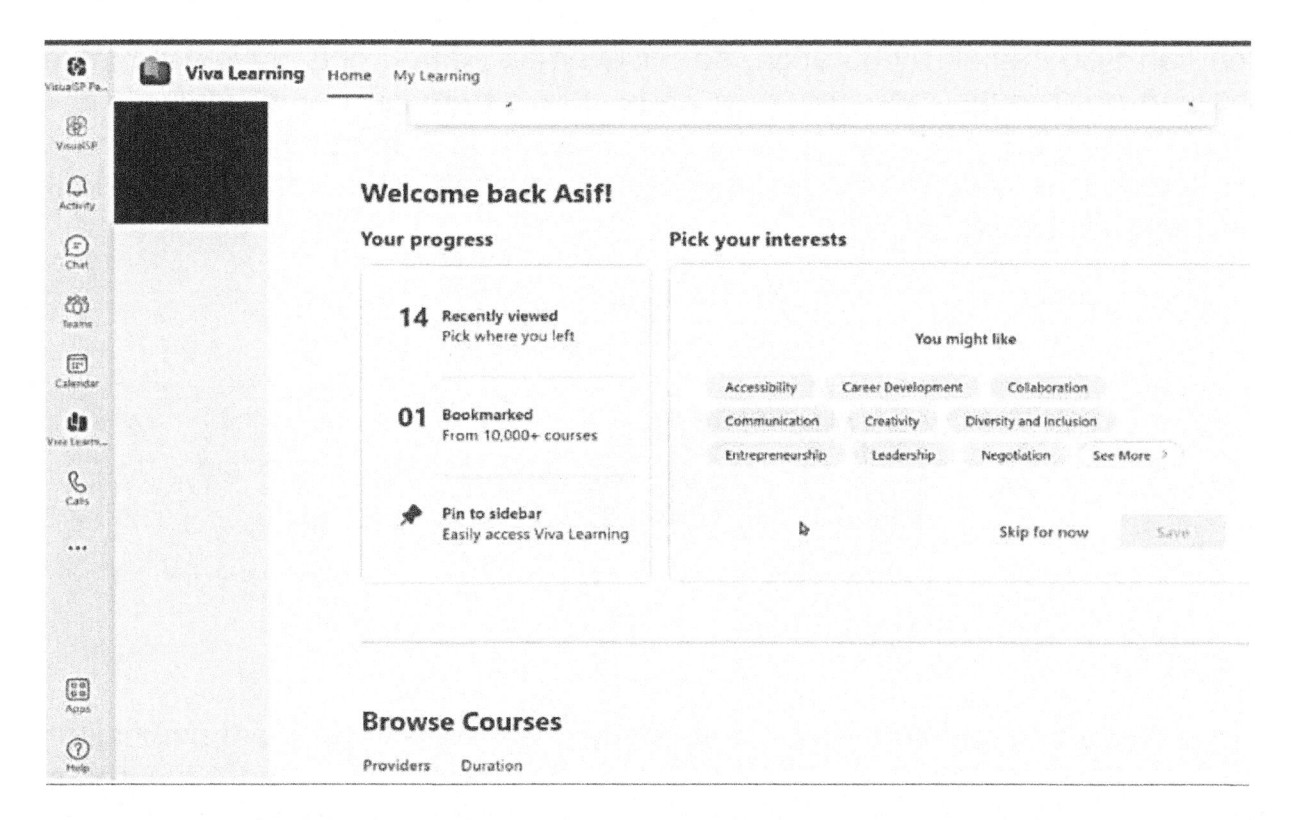

The Providers tab shows all the different content providers that you already have set up like LinkedIn Learning, Microsoft 365 Training, Microsoft Learn, Coursera, among others. Keep in mind that to provide these courses you need to have organization-level subscriptions to each of these, and you also will need a Viva Learning Premium License.

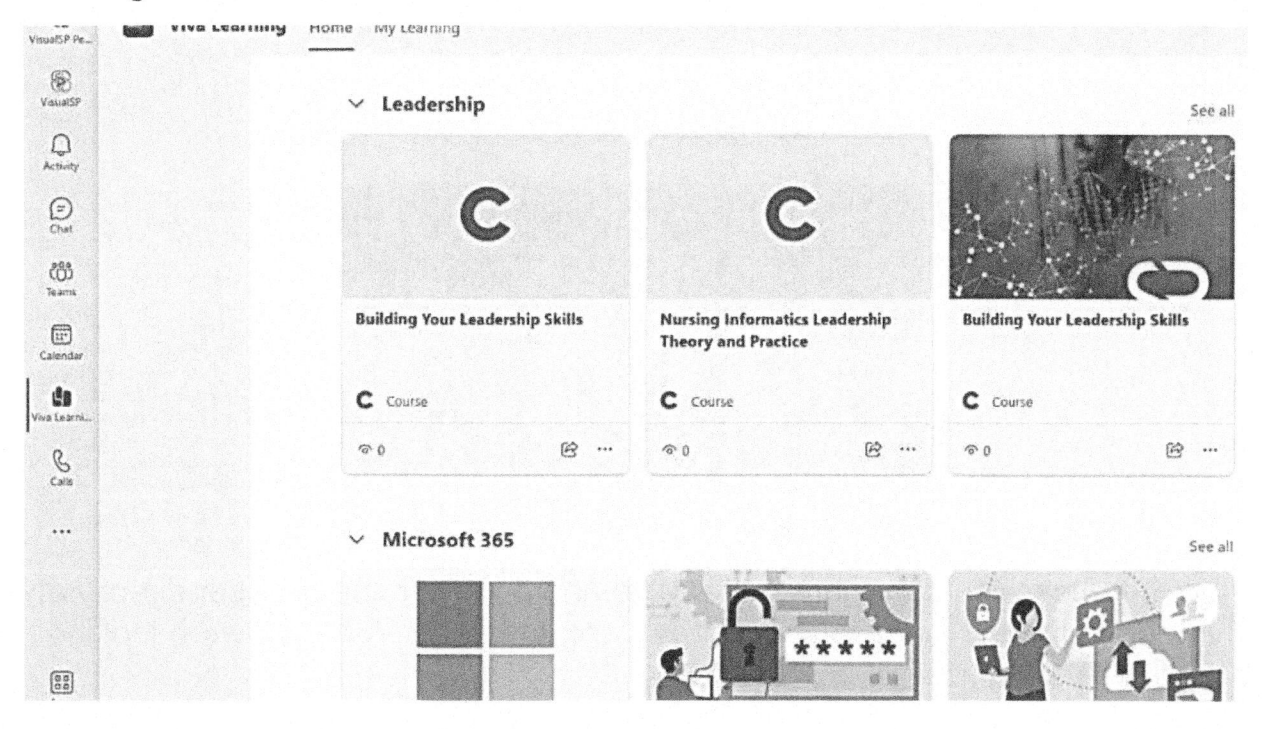

You can also search by duration, so for example, if you only have 10 minutes, you can go through those courses under this **category**, if you have 10 to 45 minutes or you are looking for courses that are from 45mins to 2 hours, you will find them under their respective categories and whatever is not defined is in the uncategorized category.

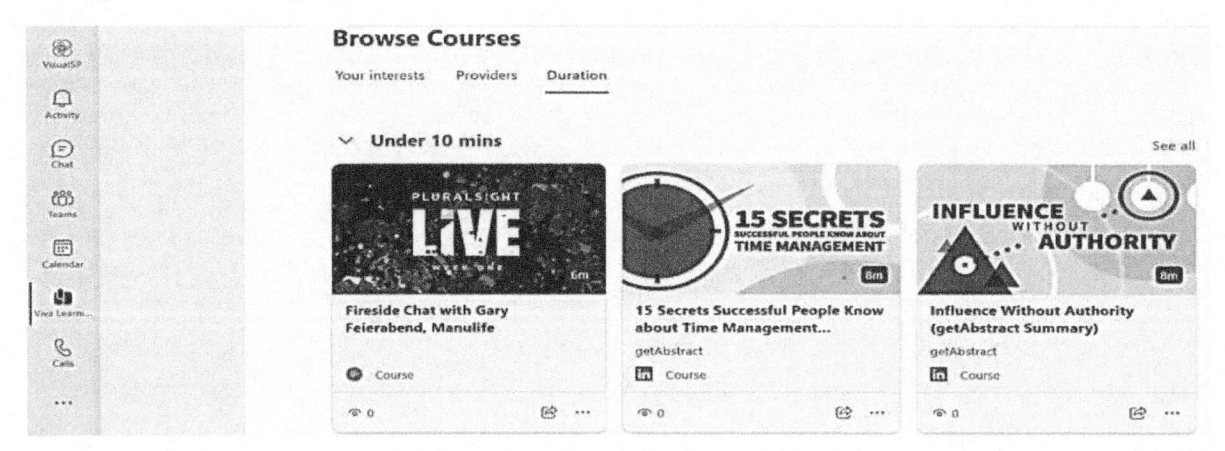

If you find a course and click on it, it opens it up, shows you the thumbnail, the content provider, author, the duration, and some information about the course. When you go to the course, it brings up the player directly within Teams and the player has the same features as it would have when you're in the browser as well. You can go to different chapters; you can also bookmark this course so you can easily return to it.

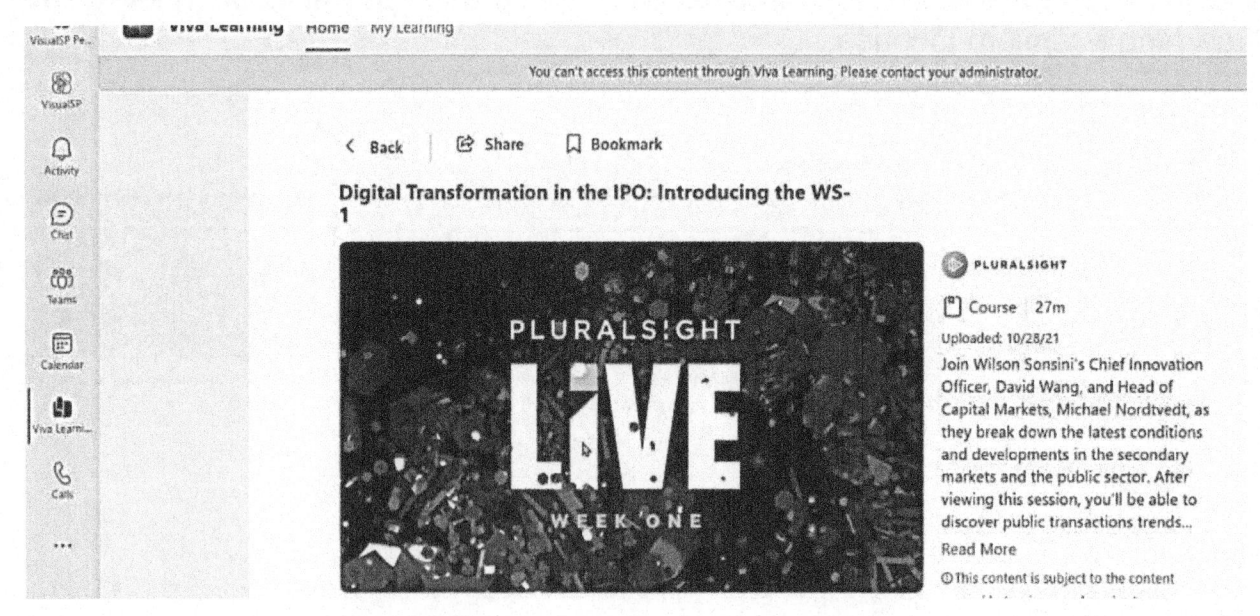

From this view, you can share with others and open it in the browser directly and if you open it up in the browser, it shows you the same view you were looking at before within Teams.

Back in Teams, if you click **"Share"**, it allows you to share directly with Teams or copy the link. If you copy the link, you can send it through email or chat message. If you choose to share in Teams, it gives you a dialog box where you can directly put in the name of a person or a team of people to share it with.

Below that, it shows you related courses coming from other places and also more courses from the content provider you have used.

Keep in mind that these are not all free courses, they're just related courses, so you still would need access to it.

Back in the home tab in Viva Learning, if you go to the Providers' Section and you can click on a provider such as Microsoft Learn to see the experience. if you click on a course in here and it shows a globe icon, this means that it's only available in the browser. So if you click on it, it opens up the browser, takes you to the course and then you can go ahead and take the course, but you have to take it in the browser because it's not available in Teams. What I'm saying here is that all the information and courses on Microsoft Learn as well as Microsoft 365 Training are available on the web for free and are just being brought in to Microsoft Teams and being exposed to you and your users.

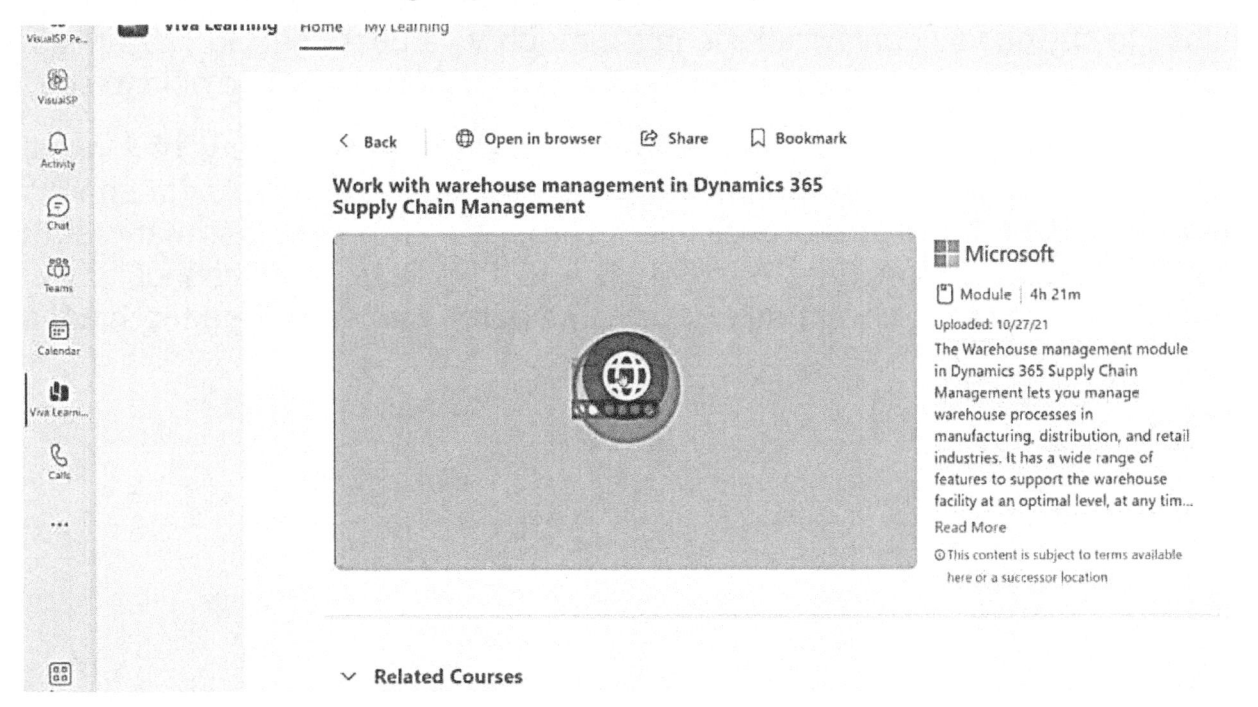

Back in the Providers section, let's look at the premium providers and the experience there. So you've got **Coursera, edX**, and **Pluralsight**; if you go to one of these and click on one of them when you get to the course you will see that there is no play button or globe circle and it's telling you that you don't have access to it, you need to talk to your administrator to get access to it. For this to work, you need an organizational-wide license.

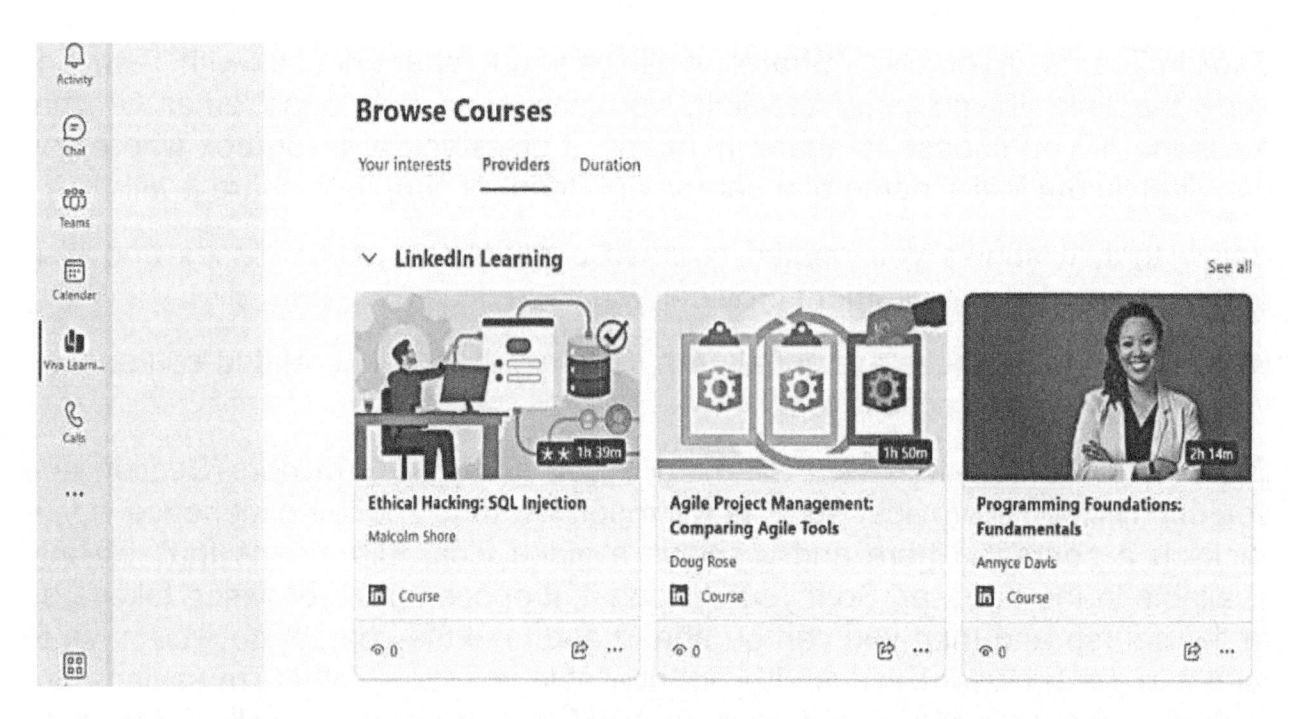

We'll check out one more provider, so once again from the home page, if you go to Providers, this time around go to another well-known entity called Coursera and if you click on one of the courses you'll get the same no play button and a message saying you cannot access this through Viva Learning. So you'll need a Viva Learning Premium License and the license for Coursera to be able to see it.

Now let's look at some LinkedIn courses. There's a big library of LinkedIn Learning as we all know but when you go to Providers, go to LinkedIn Learning there are about 125 courses available for free which means that many of the courses that you'll see here are not available for free. You cannot have a personal license for LinkedIn and get access here; you would need to have an organizational license.

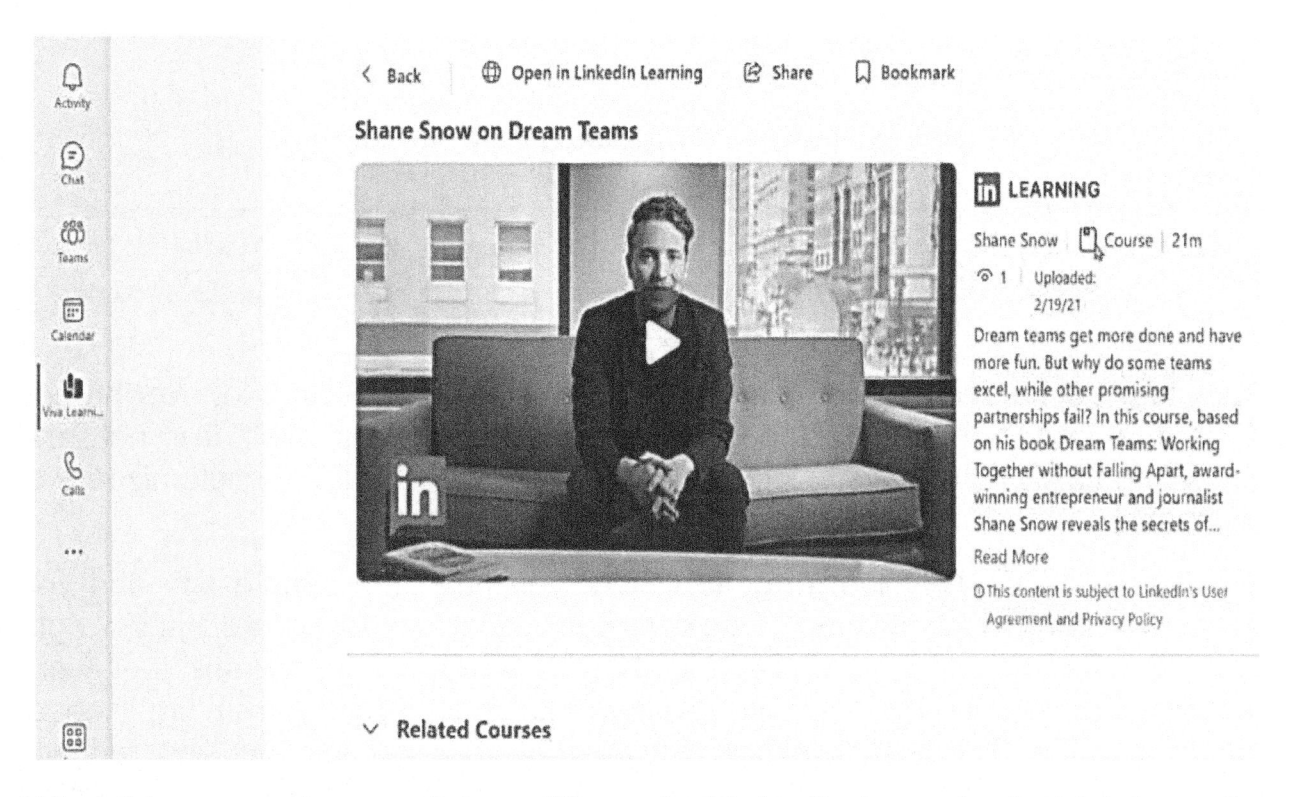

What this means is you click on **"Open in LinkedIn Learning"** which is on the web you do have access to it as an individual user, but you don't have access to it through your organization and that's why you cannot see it in teams but you can see it in the browser.

Back in Microsoft Teams, you can also go into a particular team, click on the plus sign to add a tab, and choose Viva learning for that tab. Here you would have to identify courses that you want to see in that tab. After selecting courses for this tab click on **"Save"** and it will push those courses right here in this tab. Once again just because they're showing up here doesn't mean you have access to them so make sure you have access to them before you put them on a tab.

Another experience is when you're in **"Posts"**, let's say if you start a new conversation or participate in a conversation there's a Viva Learning icon you can click on and then you can search for a course right there. If you find something that you're looking for and you want to share, click on it, type in your message, click on Send, and now it's been posted to this channel, and it works the same way in chats as well.

Back to the Viva learning app, another question that comes up a lot over here is if the icon and the viva learning wording are customizable. Well, it is not, and according to Microsoft, this brand will remain the same and not customizable or brandable.

If you click on the **"My learning"** tab, here you have the search box and you have four tabs which include **"Bookmarked"** where courses are shown right here, the "recommended to you" tab that shows you any courses that were recommended to you but that also requires the Viva Learning Premium license, the next tab is **"Recently viewed"** which is all the courses that you recently viewed, and the last one is **"Completed"** which also requires Viva Learning Premium and an LMS integration for this to show any courses that you have completed.

Setting Up Viva Learning

Another question being asked is how to set up Viva Learning.

To do that you must first be an administrator, then go to Microsoft 365 admin center, go into **"Org settings"** and in here you look for Viva Learning, click on it and this is where it shows you what Viva Learning is and what content sources you can provide.

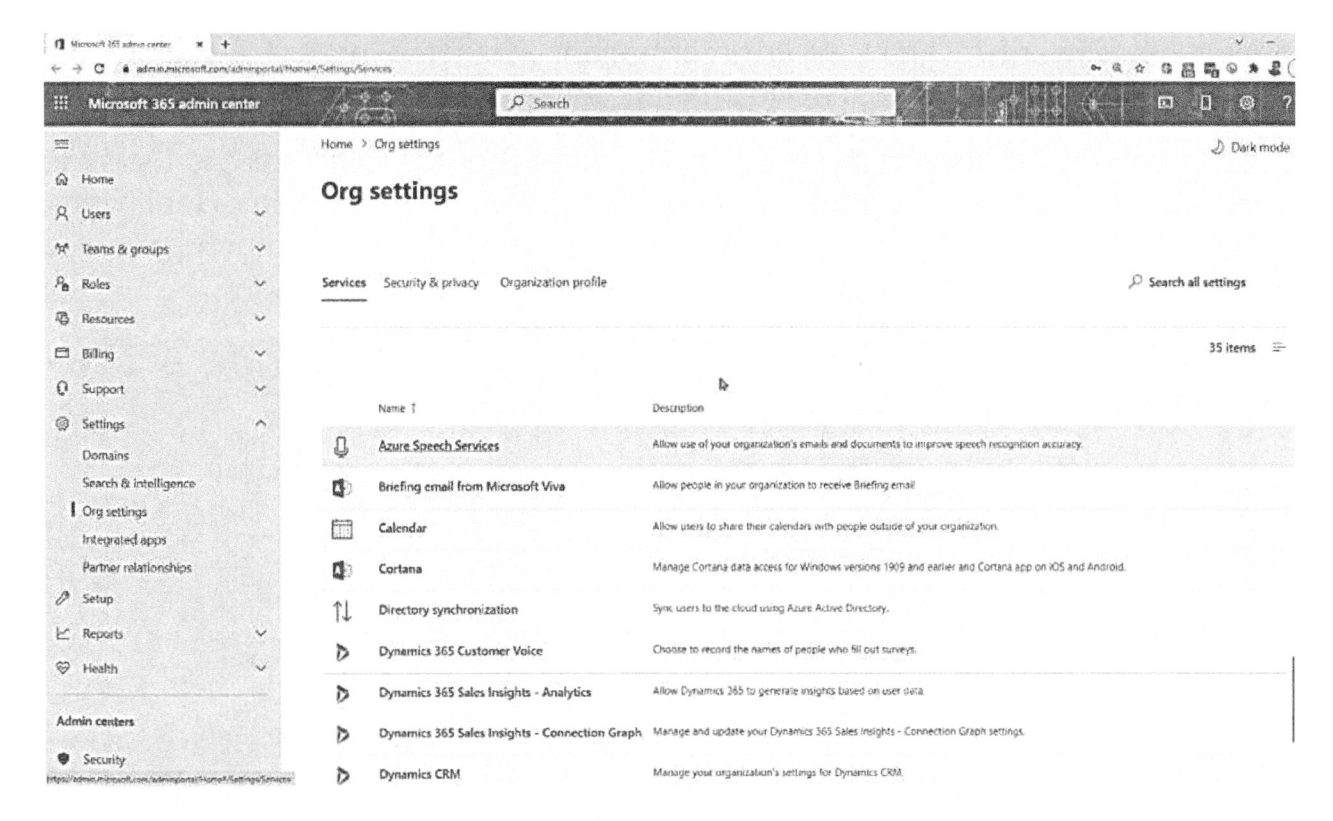

This is the way that you can provide the custom content that you have created to users in your organization and also, if you want to, you can purchase Viva Learning premium which provides you a way to integrate with other content providers like these and also integrate with your LMS.

Now you can decide if Viva Learning is the right solution for your organization. It may or may not be depending on your needs.

Viva Topics

Here we shall be discussing what Viva Topics is, how to set it up and how to create Viva Topics.

For any organization, knowledge is a key Factor and Viva Topics helps connect to knowledge and experts. According to statistics, people spend about an hour a day for up to 7 weeks in a year searching for or creating information. Viva topics come up with a solution over here.

It turns the content into knowledge using Microsoft 365, Graph, and AI. it organizes the content into topic pages and this content is easily discoverable from other Microsoft 365 products like Office and Microsoft Office products.

Consider an example of an employee onboarding process. When an employee joins an organization, everything is new for them. When they are assigned to a project, they want to know more information about the project including the Knowledge experts for that specific project. Viva Topics can come in to help.

It is not only limited to the employee onboarding process. Viva Topics is useful to other areas such as Science, Space, Education, Construction, Healthcare, Finance, and lots more. To understand the Viva Topics more thoroughly, you need to be familiar with the term **Topic Center**.

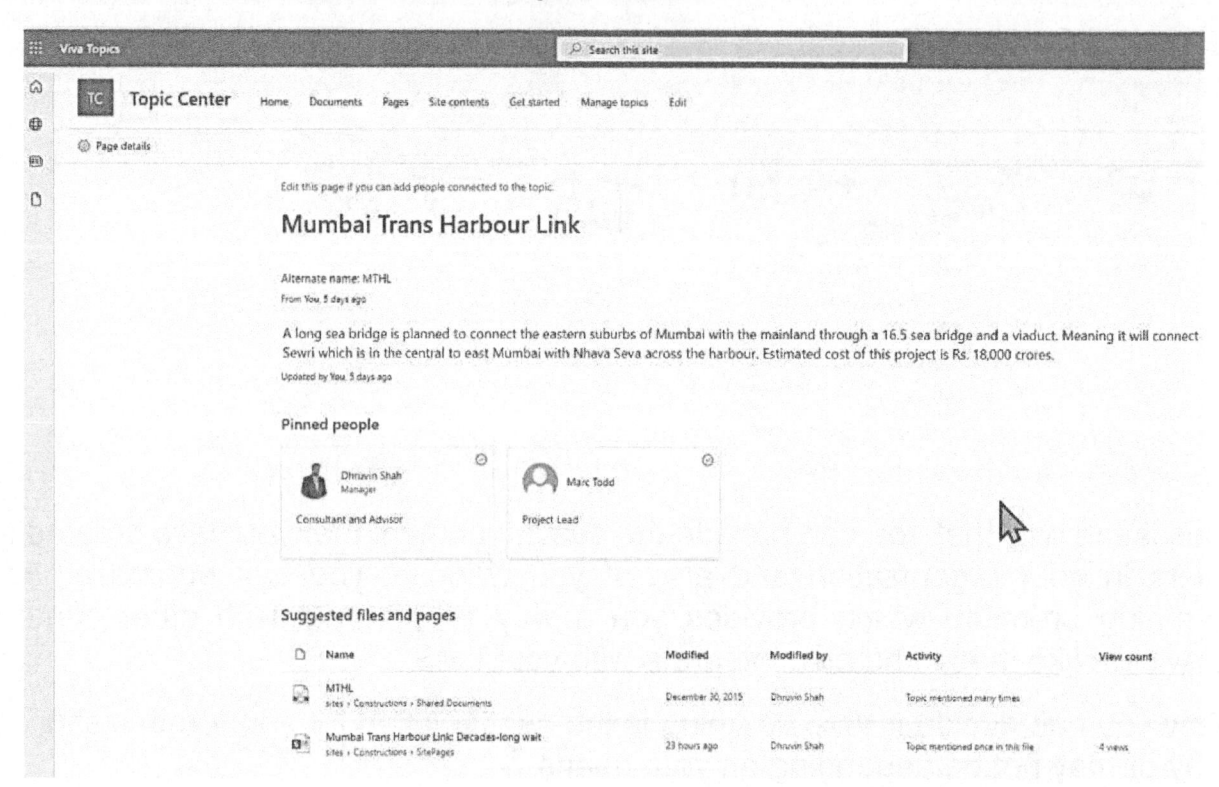

The Topic center is a centralized place in your tenant where all the topics you have are stored. If you need detailed information about a particular topic, simply click on it and you'll be able to get all the detailed information about the project, connected people, the different files and pages that are useful for that particular project, and anything sites for that Project.

Setting up Topic Center for an organization

To set up Viva Topics you need to activate the license for Viva. To activate the trial license, you need to visit the Viva product page, click on "**see pricing**" and you'll be able to see the pricing for Viva Topics. Click on "**Free Trial**" and when you do that you will see the signup form for Viva Topics Activation; you need to provide the organization's email address and fill in the other information. After doing this successfully you are good to activate Viva Topic for the organization. By default, it comes up with 25 trial licenses and a 30-days free trial.

After activating the trial, the second important step is that you need to set up a Topic Center for your organization and as I explained earlier Topic Center is a centralized place where all the topics from your tenant will be stored and the **knowledge Manager** can manage those topics.

To set up Topic Center for the first time, go to Microsoft 365 Admin Center and click on "**Setup**", you will see an option to "**Connect people to knowledge**". Click on that and you will see the option to get started. Once you open that it will show you the **guided procedure.** There are about four to five stages here and you need to pass these stages for your topic center to be set up.

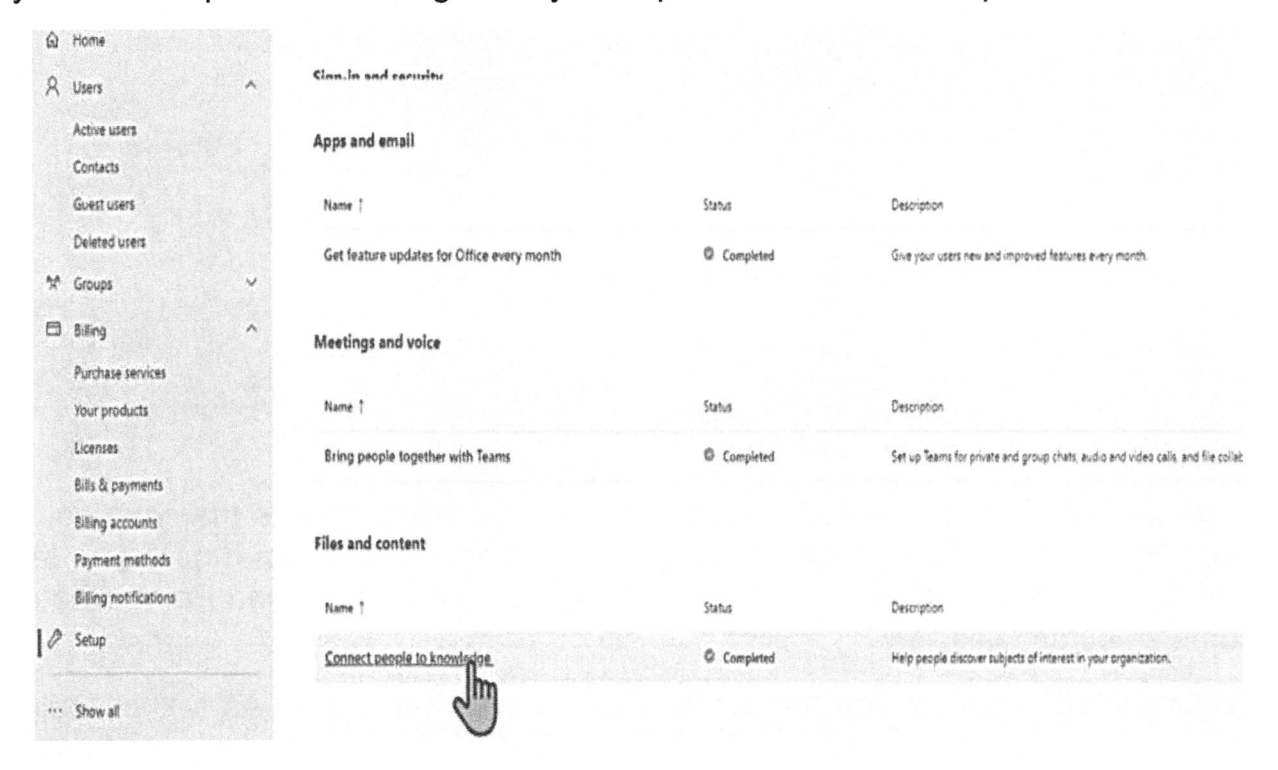

After setting up the Topic Center, you will see the "**Manage**" icon from here. Some of the things you can manage during the setup procedure are **Topic discovery**, **Topic visibility**, **Topic permission,** and the **Topic Center**.

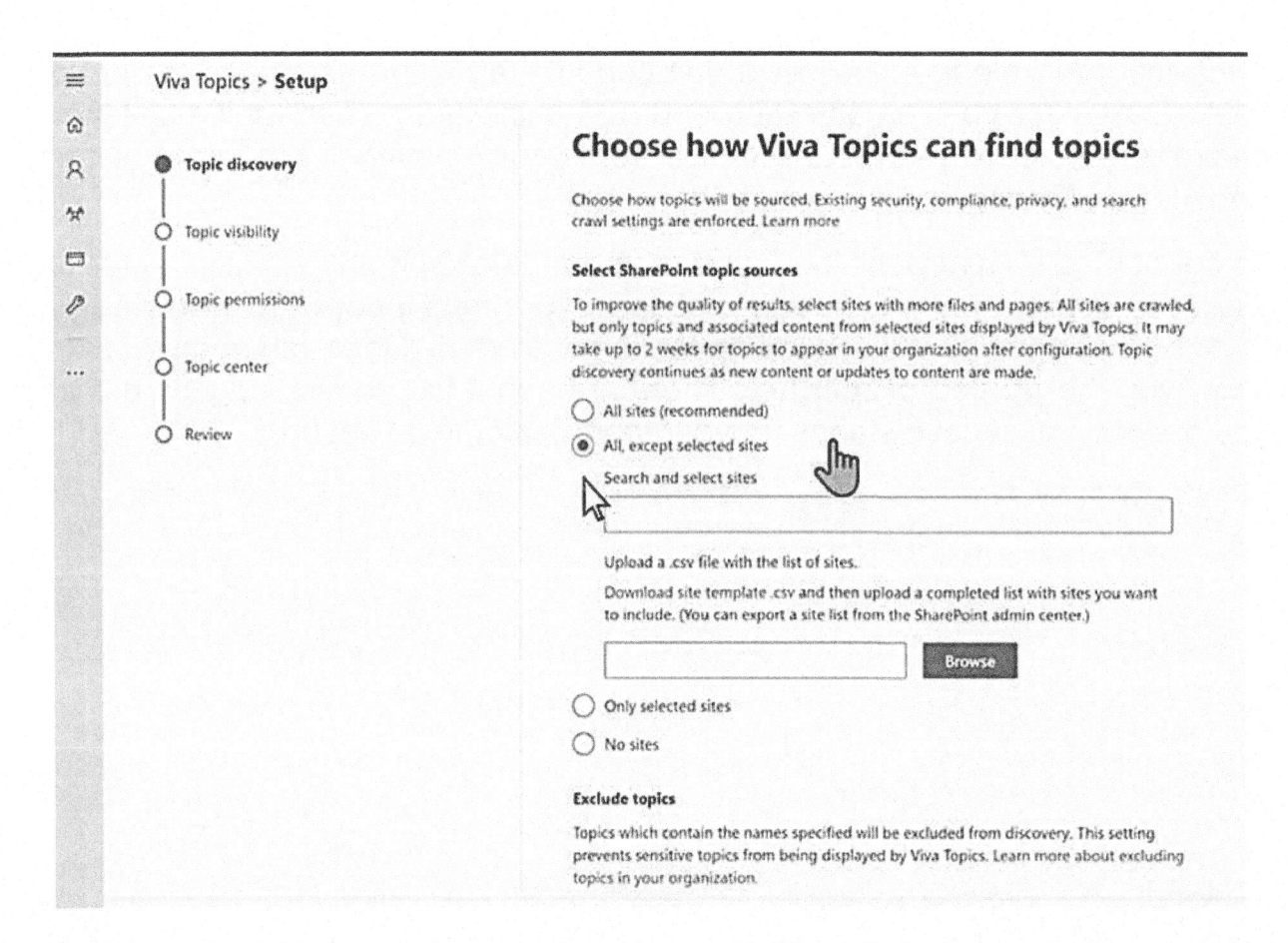

In your organization, you have quite a several SharePoint sites that you would want to discover knowledge or craft topics from; the **Topic discovery** tab enables you to select if you want to grab topics from all the SharePoint sites or some selected sites.

Topic visibility allows you to decide who can see the topics. As a knowledge manager, if you have assigned a topic, you can decide if it is to be seen to only those who have been assigned the topics or you may want to specify the topic search for specific people or groups. If any of this applies then you need to select the corresponding option.

The next step is **Topic permissions** and here you get to choose who can create and edit topics. Mostly the knowledge manager can create and edit topics so you need to specify that in the option provided. You can also choose who can manage the topics.

The last tab is the **Topic center** and here you need to provide a name for your Topic Center. You also get to see the site address that would lead to the homepage of your Topic Center, and here you can see the different topics that have been created by users.

When you go to the Topic Center for the first time, you need to click on "**Manage topics**" and here, there are four different tabs which include "**Suggested**", "**Confirmed**", "**Published**" and "**Removed**".

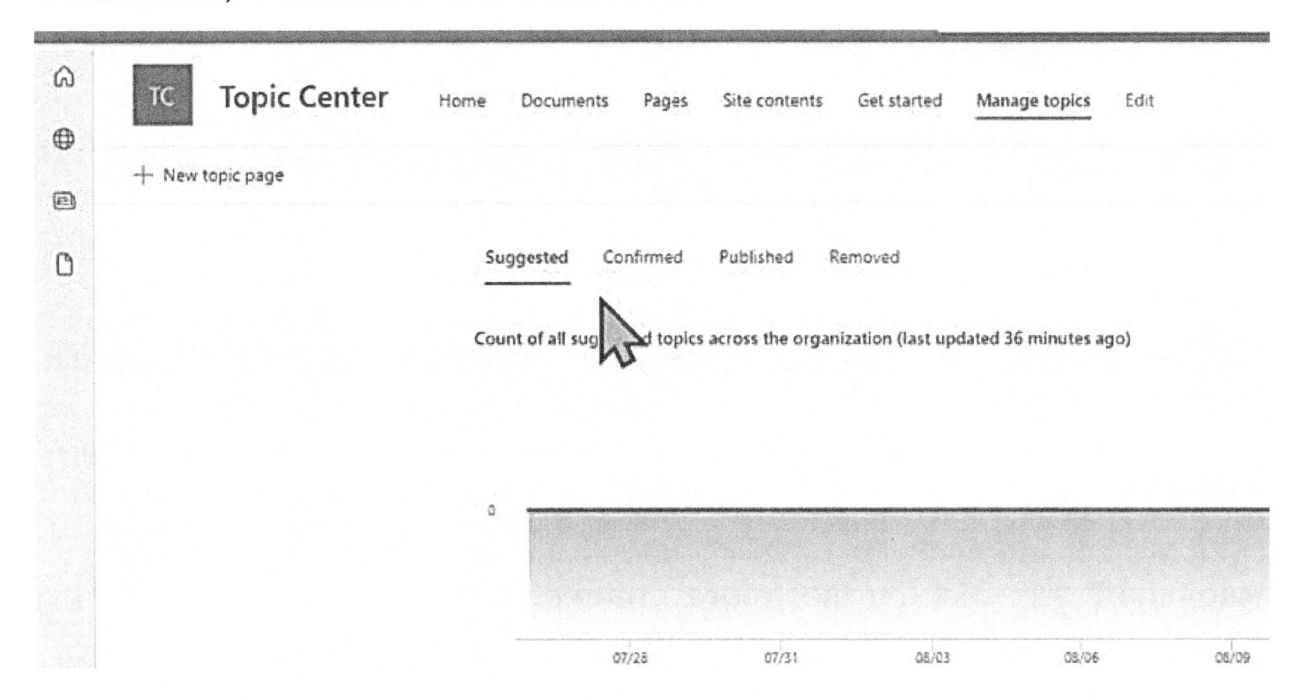

Under the "**Suggested**" tab, you get to see the suggested topics in your organization and it uses **AI technology, Microsoft 365,** and **Graph**. It will show you all the suggested topics from all your sites and provide you with a quality scroll. It also provides **impressions**, tells you **when the information was discovered,** and suggests people who are associated with that particular topic. Please note that **you get to see suggested topics only to which you have access**.

Creating a new topic page

To create a new topic page for an organization, under the "**Manage topic**" tab in your Topic Center, click on the plus button to **add a new topic page** and it will bring up a window for you to create your new topic page. You get to fill in the details of this topic page and when you are done click on "**Publish**".

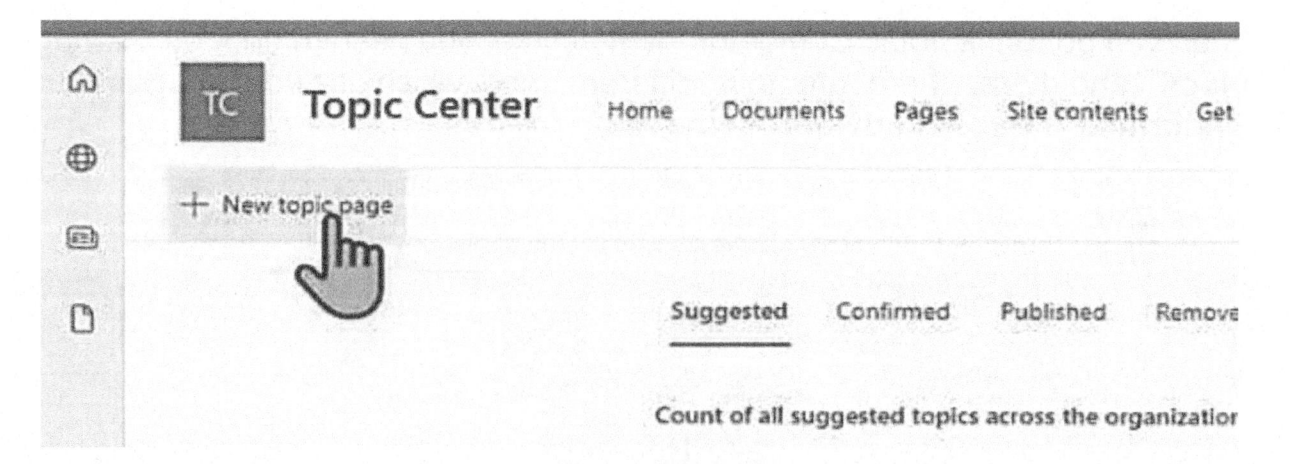

To confirm if your topic has been published, go back to the Topic Center, and under the home page, click on the **"Published"** section and you can now see your newly published topic, although this could take up to 24 hours before it appears here.

If you are not satisfied with a published topic, simply select the topic under your **"Published"** tab, click on the **"more options"** menu and from here you can **review**, **edit**, **republish** and **remove** that topic entirely.

The removed topic will appear under the **"Removed"** section.

Viva Connections

Viva Connections is one of the new Viva apps and services in Microsoft Teams. It integrates your SharePoint internet with Teams, so you can get access to both in one place. The Viva Connections app on the Team's app bar will be used to open up your SharePoint intranet.

In this section, you will see what SharePoint and Teams connections look like and also how Viva Connections will work with the new SharePoint app bar and its global navigation.

First, please note that the configuration for the things that you're about to see is mainly done by an administrator. Some of the setups have to be done with a PowerShell script, so typical users of Teams and SharePoint without administrative access can't do it. So for this first look, you'll see what can be done and what the benefits are, and later we'll look at the part for administrators with all of the details.

The image below shows how the Viva Connections app looks in Teams.

Your administrator can package up your SharePoint Homesite as a Teams app. That process requires admin and script access, but once your admin has created the app, they can make sure that everybody sees it in the app bar in Teams. They can also control the position of the app and add a custom icon.

So if you've packaged up your SharePoint Homesite as an app and given it a name, you can now have the app at the top of your Team's app bar.

When you use this app, it's like your SharePoint site is running straight out of Teams, so rather than open a browser to access the intranet you can use it here instead. All these items on the page work as you'd expect, so for example you can use the menu and you can open up pages, and if your homesite is also the app site you'll see the app site menu at the top as well.

So the Teams' app will honor any of the app site setups that you may have made. You can also see some icons over there at the top right corner and they allow you to follow the site, get a link, refresh the page, and also open up the site in a browser.

You can also use the global navigation which is configured here in Teams as well. If you press the app button here, it opens up a menu that shows you your navigation, your site, and news.

You can also use the search box to find things in SharePoint as well as Teams. If you type a keyword here it will offer to look for the results in Teams but also in the app which is your SharePoint site and if you choose the app it will open a browser and show you the results.

Setting Up Viva Connections

This is strictly for administrators and it's going to show you how to set it up and configure it so it's ready to use by everybody in your organization. The goal of this section is to set up Viva Connections and you're going to do that in five steps.

The first thing you need to do is set up the SharePoint home site and next, you enable the global navigation so you prepare the SharePoint site ready for adding to the Teams app. The third step is to create the Team's app and we do that by running a script that Microsoft has provided and then we upload the app into the Team's catalog, then you distribute the app by pinning it to the left-hand rail in the Teams app.

There are some prerequisites you're going to need to do all of these things. First of all, is to be at least a SharePoint administrator. You can do it if you're a global administrator as well and you're going to need to be able to download and install the PowerShell module for SharePoint so you can run commandlets, you need to download the Viva Connection setup script, and finally, you'll need to be able to access the Teams' administration center and be able to upload apps into the catalog there and configure them too.

Setting up the SharePoint Homesite

To do that, you create a communication site and give it a name; you could use a team site if you want to. and you can see in the settings menu that you are an owner of this site and in this Tenant, you have the global administrator role.

To set up the SharePoint home site you're going to use **visual studio** code to run your PowerShell. You can use your favorite IDE but you must run it as an administrator or have the rights to install the SharePoint PowerShell module once it's running. So once you have it running you need to do three things.

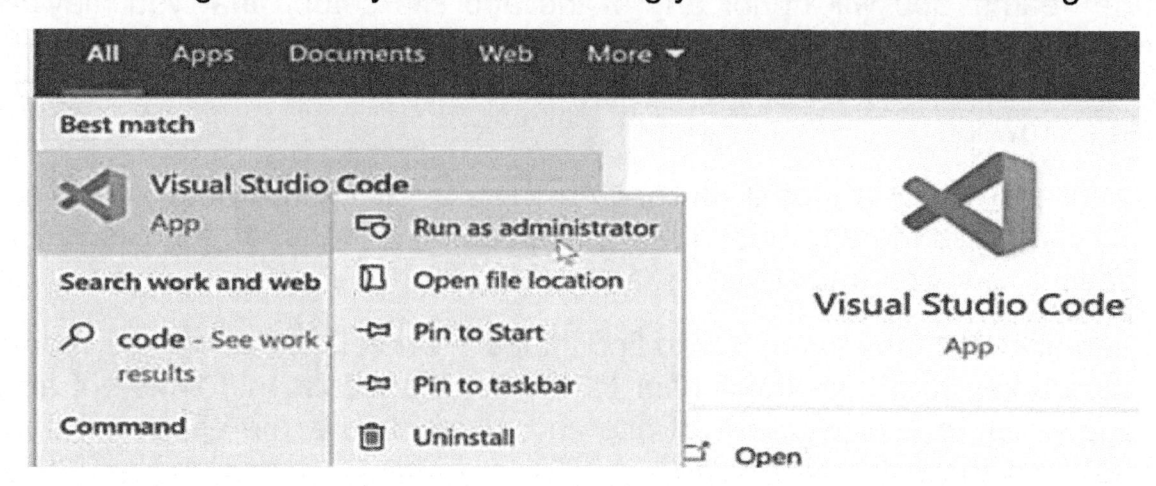

First of all, install the PowerShell module. You could do that with the command "**Install-PowerShell-Module**" with the name "**Microsoft.Online.Sharepoint.PowerShell**".

The next line is "**connect-SPOService**". So, this connects you to office 365 and you'll be asked to authenticate when you do that and you'll log in with the user that has either SharePoint administrator role or global administrator. Once you've connected to the service you should be able to run the SharePoint PowerShell command link, so you could do something like a "**get command with spo**" because they all start with "SPO" just to see that they're available or you could run something like "**get sposite**". As long as you get a return and it shows you some sites then you know it's worked okay and you're ready to go.

The last thing you need to do is set up the home site. To do that, just grab the URL of the site, so just copy that from the address bar and then in PowerShell, you want to run "**set-SPOHomesite**" with a parameter of "**-HomeSiteUrl**" and then paste in that URL and run it. When you do that, it prompts you to confirm it's okay and you just say yes and now you've set the home site.

Enabling The Global Navigation

You do that from the home site that you just configured. Go back to your site, go to the settings menu and you should see a **"global navigation"** link in that settings menu. You only see that on the home site you won't see that anywhere else; sometimes it takes 5 or 10 minutes to kick in so if you don't see it immediately don't worry, keep refreshing it, come back to it after five or ten minutes and it should be there.

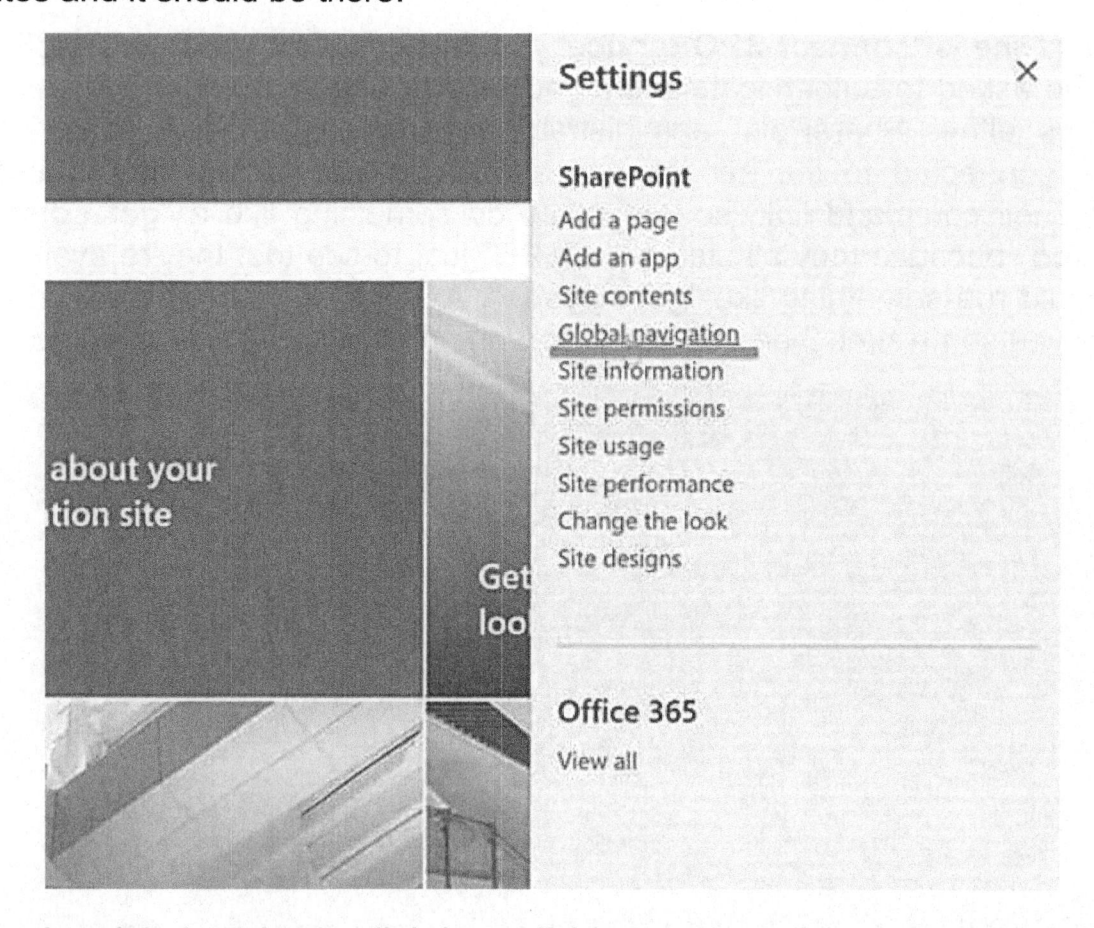

When the global navigation link is available you can click on it which will take you to the settings panel then you can toggle on the navigation here and that will enable it, then you can choose the source of the navigation which should be the Homesite navigation and then press **"save"**.

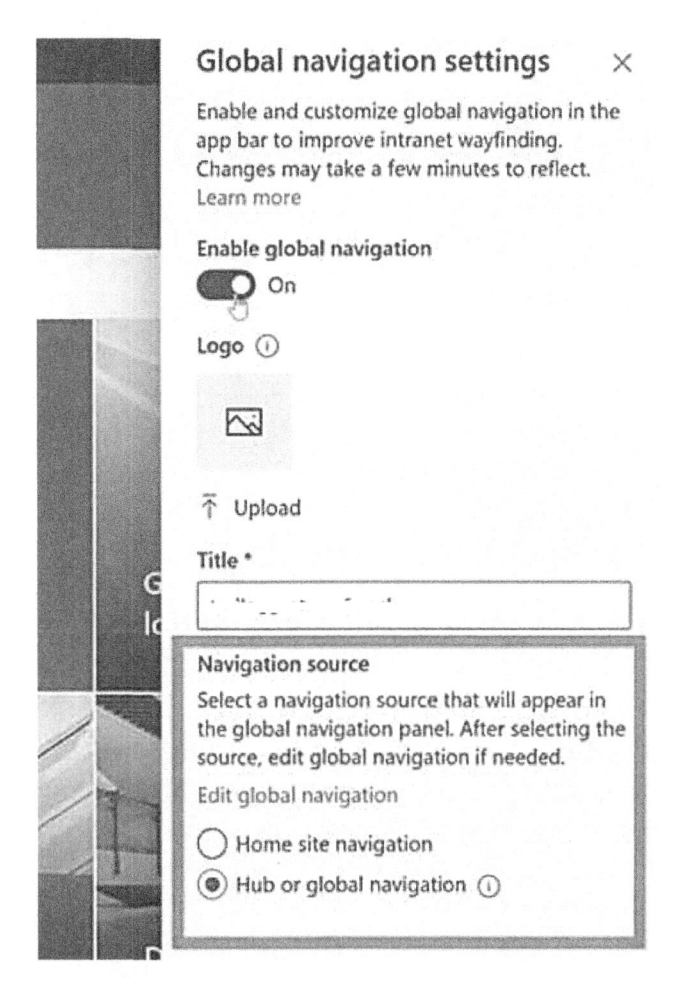

What this does is it changes the behavior of the home button on the SharePoint app bar so now when you press on it you'll see that global navigation pop out on the left-hand side and you can also see that it's using the links from your home site, so things like home documents pages and so on. Now, that will also be seen in Teams once you've created the app and uploaded it into the Teams admin center.

The last thing you can do here and this is an optional step is to add an icon for the SharePoint app bar that will replace the home button you can see in the top left. To do that just go back into global settings, hit the upload button in the logo section, go find yourself an icon preferably a square image file, open the file, save the settings, and you should see that the home button is replaced with the icons that you set.

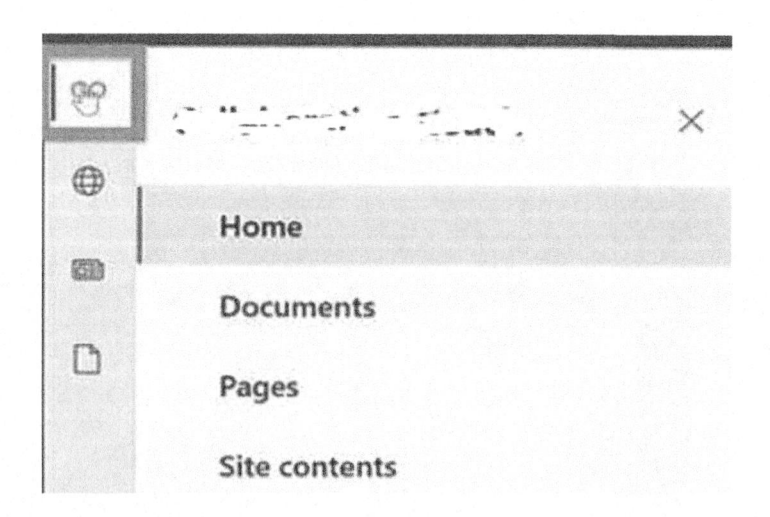

Creating the app for Viva Connections

To do that you need PowerShell access and you need the Viva Connections setup script which is available from Microsoft. So once you've downloaded that there are some other prerequisites that you need to consider. Remember what you're doing here is creating a Teams app and every Teams' app needs a bunch of information that will display in the Teams app catalog. So, the things that you see in this **list below** are the things that are required to do this properly.

Pre-requisites

- Short description (80 characters)
- Long description (4000 characters)
- Privacy policy
- Company website
- Terms of use
- Company name
- 2 PNG icons 192x192 and 32x32 pixels

It is not recommended that you do this in production without a test, so run through a test first so you can get it right. You're going to need a **short and a long description**, a **link to a privacy polic**y, the **company website**, and **terms of use page**, obviously the **company name**, and **two icons are very specific sizes**; they have to be of a certain size so you may need to speak to someone who manages your images for you. It uses these icons in the Teams app itself and the app catalog.

So you're going to run the Viva Connection script from Visual Studio code, and you're going to run it without debugging. The first thing it asks you for is the site

URL, so that is the URL of the home site that you created earlier.

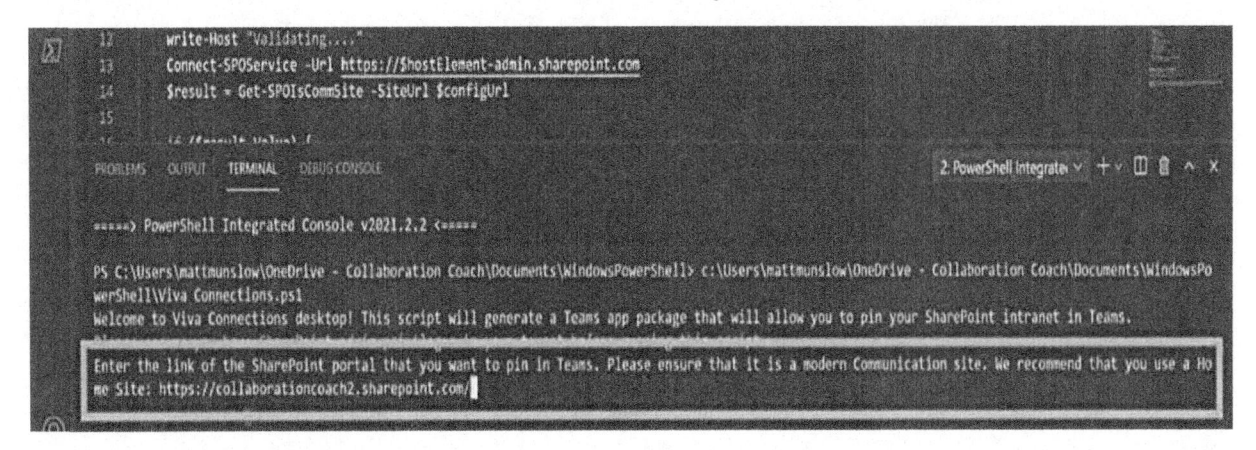

It will ask you to validate, so you're going to log in just to prove that you have permission to do this, so you need a SharePoint administrator or global administrator.

Then it will ask you how you want the app to be named and this will appear in the app rail in the Teams app; you need to keep it nice and short otherwise it won't fit on the rail.

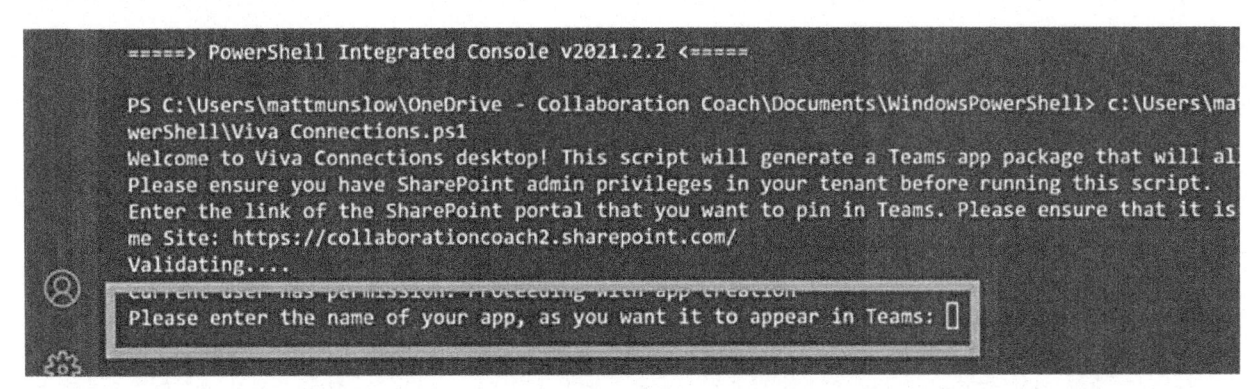

Now you're going to add a short description and this is what appears in the catalog and a longer description also will appear in the catalog.

You've got to **provide a privacy policy**; now if you don't have one you can just hit enter and it will use the Microsoft privacy policy, and the same with the terms, so if you've got a terms page on your website you can use it here otherwise you can just hit enter and it will use the Microsoft policy.

Next, you will be asked the organization name and then finally, the URL of your company's site.

After that, you will be asked to pick up the icons that it's going to use in the app itself and the catalog. The first one is the bigger one of the two and then it would ask for the second one which is 32x32. After this, it does the configuration and creates a zip file which it puts in the desktop folder of the user that you're working with. If you go to file explorer and go to the desktop, here you can see a zip file with the name of the app that you chose and now that's ready to upload into the Teams app catalog.

Uploading the app to the catalog

To do this you need access to the Teams' admin center and when you're in the Team's admin center you go to "**Manage apps**", and the first thing you should check is whether **Org-wide app settings** have third-party apps allowed on that should be on by default but just check in case.

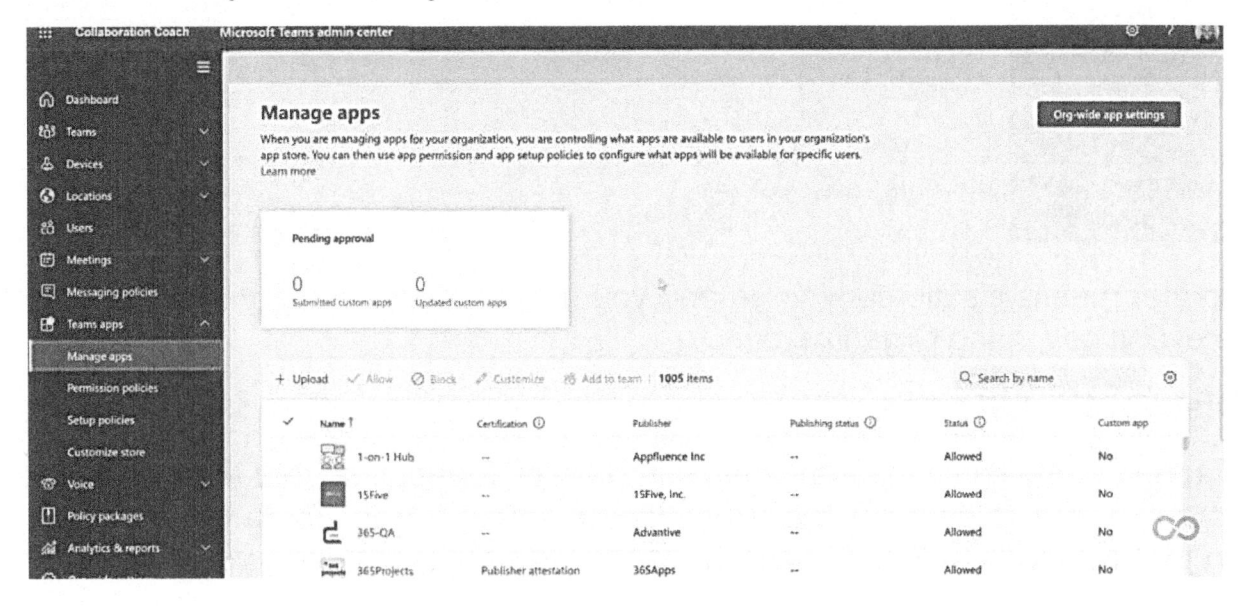

Then you go to the upload button, select a file, and then you find the zip file that you created in the previous step. Open that and if it uploads correctly, you should see a green bar at the top saying "**Added comments to the list**", also to check it's there if you just go to the search bar and type the name of your app you should see it listed there.

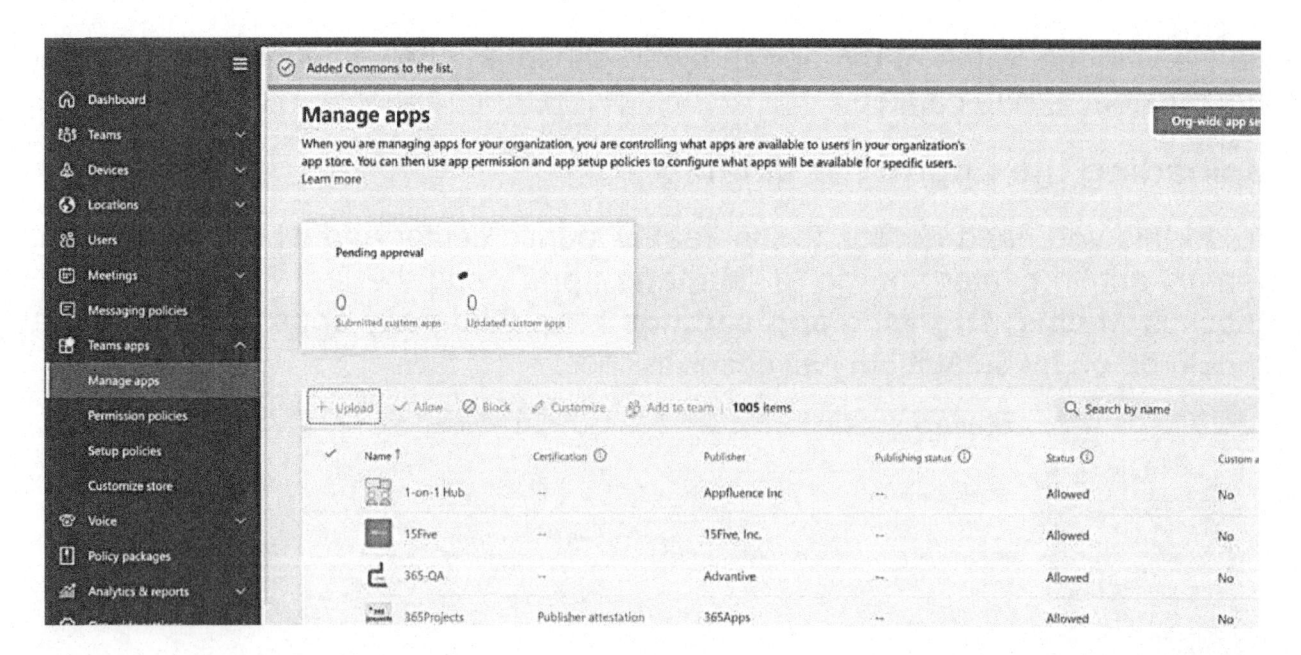

So that means it's all ready to go and you can configure it and make it available to everybody in the Organization.

Distributing the app

You do that by changing the global setup policy for apps so that everybody sees your new app at the top of the rail on their team's desktop. To do that we need to go to the "**setup policies**" **section** of manage apps and then you need to edit the global policy.

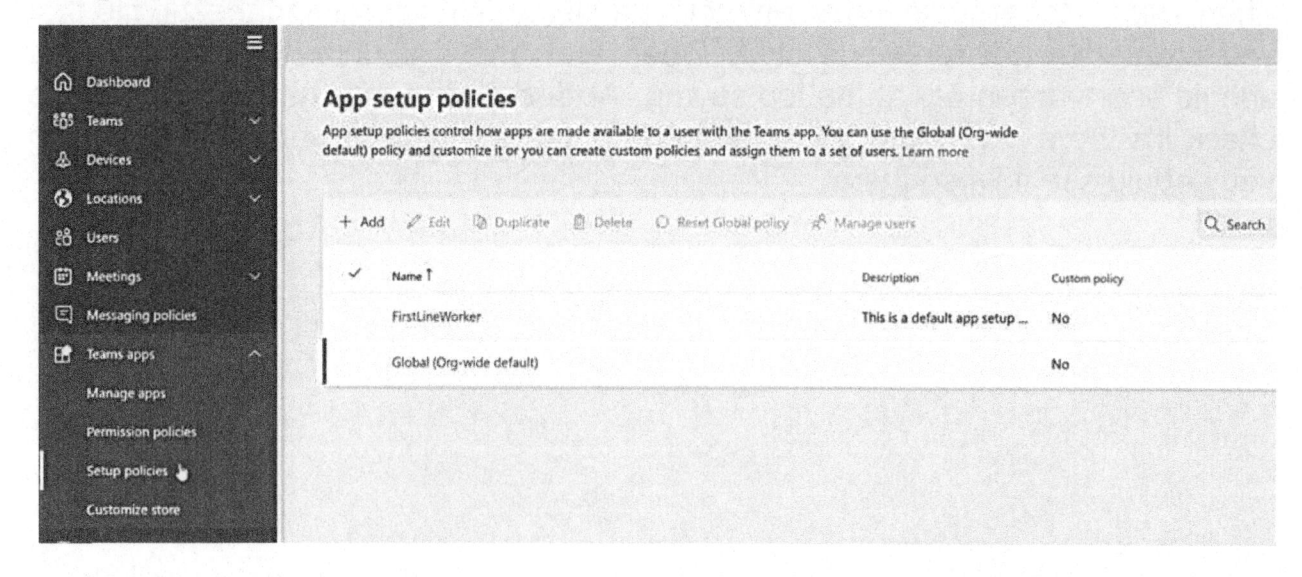

You go to the pinned app section and choose "**Add apps**", then search for the name that you used for your app, click "**Add**" and then click "**Add**" again.

Add pinned apps

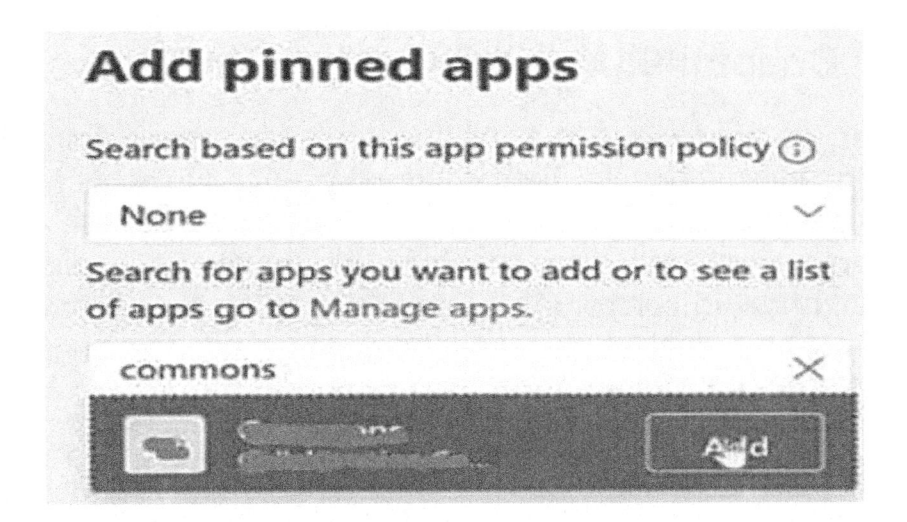

Search based on this app permission policy ⓘ

None ⌄

Search for apps you want to add or to see a list of apps go to Manage apps.

commons ✕

[Add]

Now you should see your new app at the bottom of the list and you can select it and move up to the top using the move up button and then save the policy.

You should see a green **"success"** banner at the top meaning that your app should start to show up in people's teams. So the outcome of all that work was that you should now have an app for your company intranet. This might not take effect straight away so you might not see it immediately but over the next day or so as people log in and out of teams it will appear, and what you will have in your tenant is this app, and when you click on it you can see you've got your app site, with your news pages and so on, and when you press the comments button again you can see you've got your organization's global navigation. This means that you can move between sites and you can see news and so on, all from inside of Teams. You will also notice that when you go back to the app, you've got some icons over here that allow you to follow the site and you've got links that you can open in the browser as well. It's just a good way of embedding your company's intranet using Viva Connections.

Summary

With the recent announcement of the new Microsoft Employee Experience Platform called Viva, this chapter is equipped with details to get you familiar with this platform.

It covered the four models of this platform which are Insights, Topics, Learning, and Connections.

We went further to explain how to set these up as an administrator and how to utilize them as team members for maximum productivity.

Chapter 9: Maximizing Apps In Teams

In this chapter, we are looking at Apps in Teams and we are going to talk about some common applications in Teams, identify suitable applications for your users in your organization, recognize common attributes of successful application deployment, will also see how to deploy an application to your environment and how to control those applications for your users. Lastly, we're going to talk a great deal about security and compliance considerations for Teams.

Before we go further, let's look at some common Myths of using applications in Teams

Some Common Myths About Using Apps in Teams

The following questions are being asked all the time by customers when we're talking about Teams and applications.

- **Allowing third-party apps will create licensing headaches**

A majority of the applications used in Teams are free or leverage existing enterprise licenses. You should focus on the line of business applications your users are already using and make sure you allow that in Teams for these users.

- **Apps will access all my confidential files and conversation**

Apps can only access files that you explicitly send to that service, and they can only read messages when the app is explicitly mentioned in a message. So, in a Teams and channel construct, when you're conversing with a bot, the bot will only see messages and files, which you send to it.

- **Apps will access all my personal information and send spam**

Application developers get access to very basic personal information about the user who is logging into their service. They have to be able to identify that user, but sending any sort of spam violates your application store policies and will result in the application being taken down.

- **It is inconvenient to uninstall an app after setting it up**

Users can uninstall an app personally with two clicks and administrators can control an application for a user with two clicks. As we proceed, you will see how this is done.

Apps Background

You should be familiar with the core workloads of Teams which are Chat, Meetings, and Calling capabilities. This is how we communicate within our environment.

We've been using Office 365 applications, both to Teams and historically with Skype for Business to collaborate. We can collaborate in various file types, co-author documents, share documents and files, internally and externally with the organization.

Using these powerful productivity tools is a great way to work better together. Putting this together using an extensive platform, at the center of it we communicate (chat, meetings and calling internally and

externally to our organization), we collaborate using all these file types as parts of the Office 365 ecosystem, and we extend on that, do more with these applications which are close to 500 applications, including third-party applications available in Teams; this is how we get more work done by connecting all our systems and processes.

The application you're using can appear in a Team and Channel construct, right when it is needed. When you're collaborating with people, you can mention that application and contact cards appear, but the concept here is that we're using these applications in the context of where they are needed right within Teams, and if the user's already using a line of business application within your organization, they should be able to use it in Teams as well. No need to contact switch, leave the application, go to a browser or desktop application; if that is an application Add-In for Teams, it should be allowed for the users to use.

Categories of Teams Apps

First, we have the **Microsoft applications**. These are Microsoft-developed applications, parts of the Office 365 ecosystem and there are about 45 of them.

Next, we have the **third-party applications**, which have been developed for Teams and they are close to 500 of them by now.

Lastly, there are **custom applications** an organization could develop. These include Processes apps, Productivity apps, Employee Services apps, Approvals, and Workflows apps. To build these applications you can use the Microsoft Power Platform; these are low-code, no-code solutions using the power tools that we have. These tools include Power BI for dashboarding capabilities, Power Apps for drag and drop, building applications for the enterprise, and Power Automate to automate workflows in the environment.

We also have application templates for creating your custom apps, you can access them at "**aka. ms/TeamsAppTemplates**", and there are about 20 of them. The most popular are Company Communicator and FAQ Plus. Every organization has an FAQ survey in the environment; it can be HR, or IT related.

Also, users who are using Teams can interact with these applications, these FAQs in a Bot format, where you ask questions and get answers. If you need to get some help with some drivers for your laptop, an **IT FAQ** can help you locate those. You can ask an **HR Bot** about tax information, modifying, how to update some type of information, whatever it is, you control and provide the contents of the FAQ for these applications.

These are also low-code, no-code type of solutions, with these templates published for you to use. You can build an application from scratch using bots, tabs, or message extensions. You can use the Microsoft Graph identity framework and build all sorts of applications required in your line of business.

Publishing An Application

An application can be published to the **Store**. If you are in an organization that develops applications for customers, you could publish that application to your Microsoft store and all customers can take advantage of it.

You could write an application just for your **tenant** and publish it for your organization; application templates would be a good example of that.

You can publish an application to a **Team** for testing purposes or specific functions and If a group of users needs to have access to a specific application, you give them access.

Discovering Applications

In the Team's interface, you can access the application from the left rail, and on the left pane of the Teams apps, you can look at the type of applications here. These include Personal apps, Bots, Tabs, Connectors, and messages extensions. You can look at the categories of applications that have been organized conveniently for everybody.

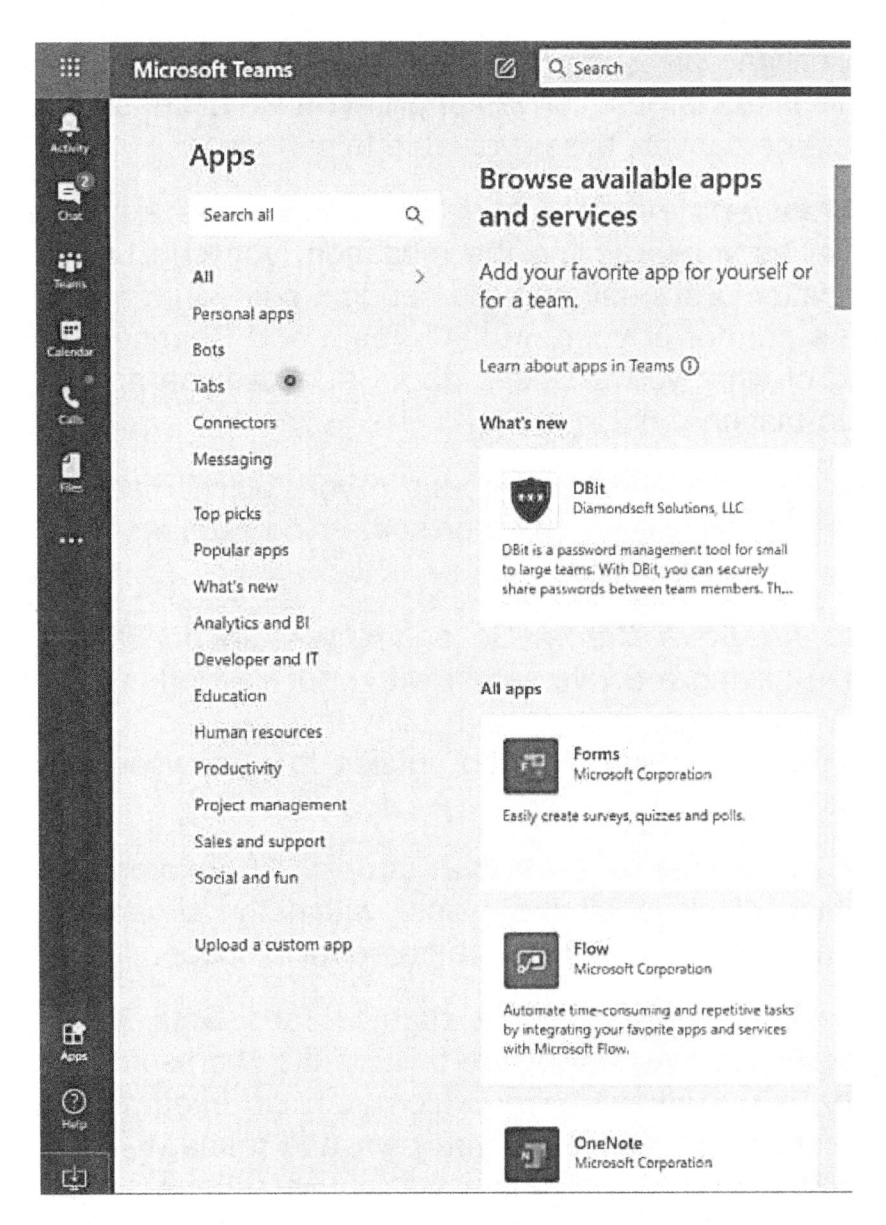

On the right side, you have some apps displayed and in each of these little tiles, you get information about the application, consisting of the name of the app, the creation provider, and a little description about the app. You can install the application from here.

Extensibility points and capabilities of these applications

Bots. These help users get tasks done conversationally. So, you're in a Teams client in your chat window, and you start a conversation with the bot. You can ask the bot about tasks for the day and the bot looks at all the lists of tasks you have access to and gives you a list of tasks assigned to you for the day. This is a simple conversational item, and you get the information to the user as they need it.

Tabs. An application can appear in Team and Channel construct as a pinned application. This is the largest canvas application we have, so for an application that requires a large canvas, this is valuable to surface it.

Messaging extensions. An application can show up as a message extension. This means that as you're writing the message, you can bring up information from that application. Let's say you are sending some information or asking for feedback from a partner of yours in their Team and Channel, they immediately get the context of what you're talking about because the application will insert the relevant information.

Activity Feed. An application can appear in your activity feed. It can send you messages when something happens or something requires your attention, just like any other activity notification.

There are also ***Adaptive Cards***. So again, you are in Teams and Channel construct, you're having a conversation with your co-workers, you can bring in the information that is relevant for that conversation and they can act upon it right there; no need to copy a link, go outside to a browser to authenticate on another tab and act on that message.

An application can have a ***personal scope***. An example is the Planner application, which displays all the plans, within the organizations you have access to and you are in on, or it can be personal in scope.

So all of these immersive experiences such as Tabs, Bots, Message extension, Adaptive Cards, and Activity feeds, are built on the Microsoft back-end platform. Microsoft Graph is our identity layer which you can integrate with your line of business applications, as you do it, you own and manage. You can also build applications on Microsoft AI, which is power conversations with intelligence, pre-built, and custom models. With it, you can analyze data and get that right into your application in Teams.

Now you know how to discover applications and the capabilities of these apps, let's look at managing these applications.

Managing Apps

In the Teams Admin Center, there is a dedicated section here for managing these applications. If you go to "**Manage apps**" under "**Teams apps**", you get a list of all applications available for your users. You can also control the app status by either blocking or allowing them. Here, you also get to see if they are custom applications or not, you can look at the certifications of these applications and find out more about the application and its capabilities.

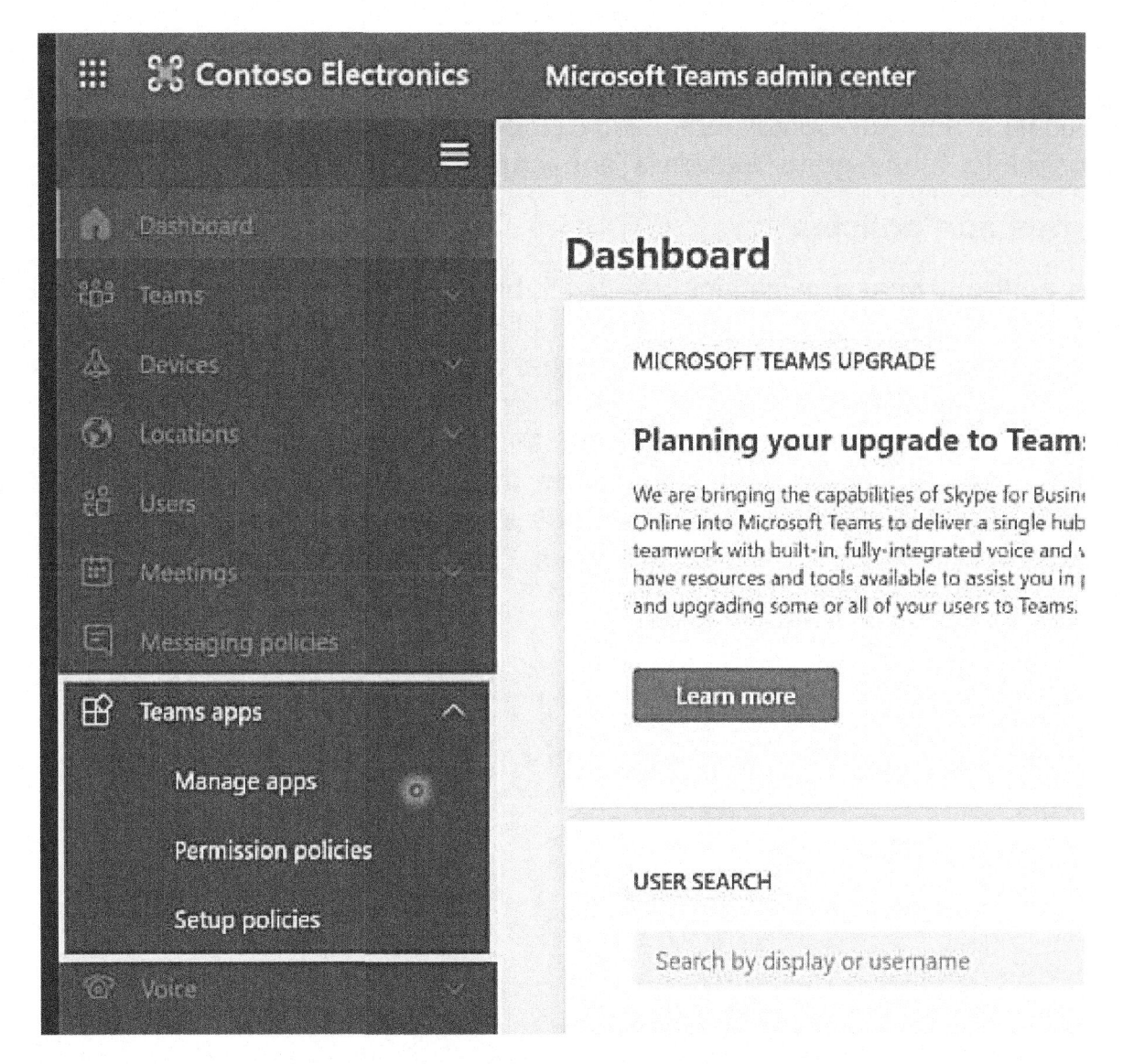

You can also control the applications organization-wide. This is a handy approach to control applications. Here you get to choose what happens to the third-party applications in your organization, although you can use Permission policies to control applications as well, and it leaves you with enough room to experiment and test out applications that you may want your users to use in the future.

Microsoft 354 Publisher Attestation is developer-provided security, data handling, and compliance information across 90 vectors, in a consistent format, in a single location. You can look up this information and analyze it for your organization.

You can also build trust further by certifying an application, and some applications are certified by Microsoft. So you do Pen testing to check for Application security, you look at the Operational security of the application via

Patching, Malware management, Vulnerability scans, and Risk management items. You also look at Data Handling Security and Privacy for that particular application and the Compliance Claim Checks that your application may have. To check for these, go to "**aka. ms/TeamsAppCertification**".

Permission policies

This controls what applications are available to individuals or groups of users. There is always a global policy that applies to the users, or you can create custom policies, and a policy controls what applications a user will see. Looking from the Global Policy point of view or any policy you custom, you have to consider the app categories which are Microsoft apps, Third-party apps, and Tenant applications; and the capabilities include to "**Allow all apps**", "**Allow specific apps and block others**", "**Block specific apps and allow others**", or "Block all applications", of a certain type. This is a much easier way to control applications for a user.

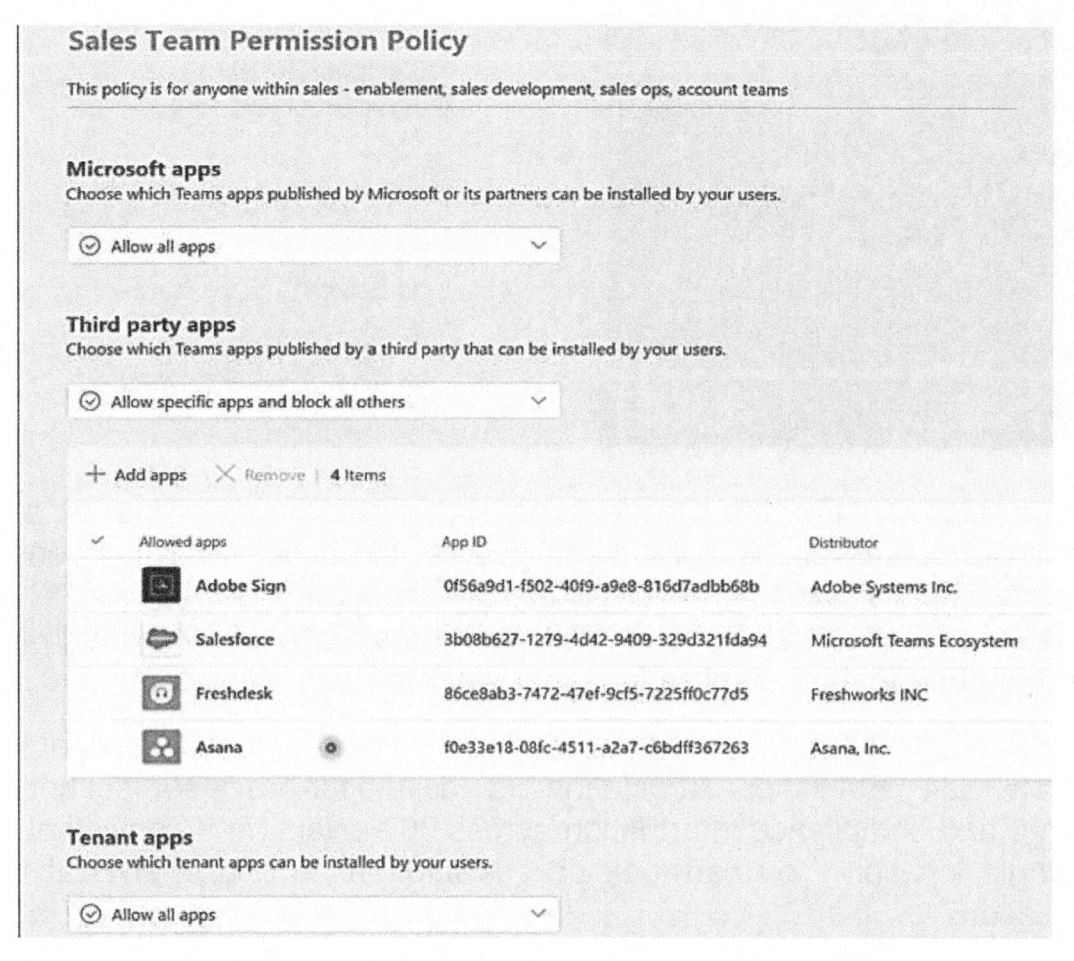

Sales Team Permission Policy

This policy is for anyone within sales - enablement, sales development, sales ops, account teams

Microsoft apps
Choose which Teams apps published by Microsoft or its partners can be installed by your users.

⊘ Allow all apps

Third party apps
Choose which Teams apps published by a third party that can be installed by your users.

⊘ Allow specific apps and block all others

+ Add apps   × Remove | 4 Items

	Allowed apps	App ID	Distributor
	Adobe Sign	0f56a9d1-f502-40f9-a9e8-816d7adbb68b	Adobe Systems Inc.
	Salesforce	3b08b627-1279-4d42-9409-329d321fda94	Microsoft Teams Ecosystem
	Freshdesk	86ce8ab3-7472-47ef-9cf5-7225ff0c77d5	Freshworks INC
	Asana	f0e33e18-08fc-4511-a2a7-c6bdff367263	Asana, Inc.

Tenant apps
Choose which tenant apps can be installed by your users.

⊘ Allow all apps

For example, there is the Sales Team permission policy for anyone within sales, such as sales development, sales operations, and account teams. Here, you allow Microsoft Office 365 applications for these users, but on the third-party application pane, you only allow them these four applications, Adobe Sign in, Salesforce, Freshdesk, and Asana. This is because they may use these applications on a day-to-day basis in their line of business.

Then you can manage the users and add them to this list. That's it. You create an application permission policy, assign it to the users, and those are the applications they will have access to.

Apps Policy Precedence

First, you start with Org-wide application settings, next you have the Custom permission policies which is how you control what applications a user has access to, and lastly, the global or the Default permission policy which applies to the user. There is no other policy that specifically applies to them.

Setup policies

So you control the applications your users have access to with permission policies, but with set up policies, you can surface those applications to be more visible for your users, right under that left side in Teams.

So, clicking on the **"Setup policies"**, you can add an application to your policy and when the user logs in to Teams, this application appears to them. They don't need to install anything on their desktop via the web or their mobile device. Just by assigning this application to them, it will appear on all the devices they log into Teams with.

Another example here is Adobe Sign In and Seismic pinned to the left rail for the user. It appears to them on a mobile device based on their state and It goes to the overflow for the users. If it doesn't fit on the

screen, it can be seen in the **"more options"** menu. The idea here is you assign the policy to the users, they get the application and it appears to them in their client without installing anything else. They have access to it and they can utilize it.

Also, in the Teams Admin Center, under Usage reports, you can look at what applications your users are using. Let's say you have the default policy where all applications are enabled and allowed for the users, you can look at what they have installed, what type of application it is, the user activity, how many users are using it, and how many active teams are using it. So, you do get some reports which you can also download and analyze in Excel.

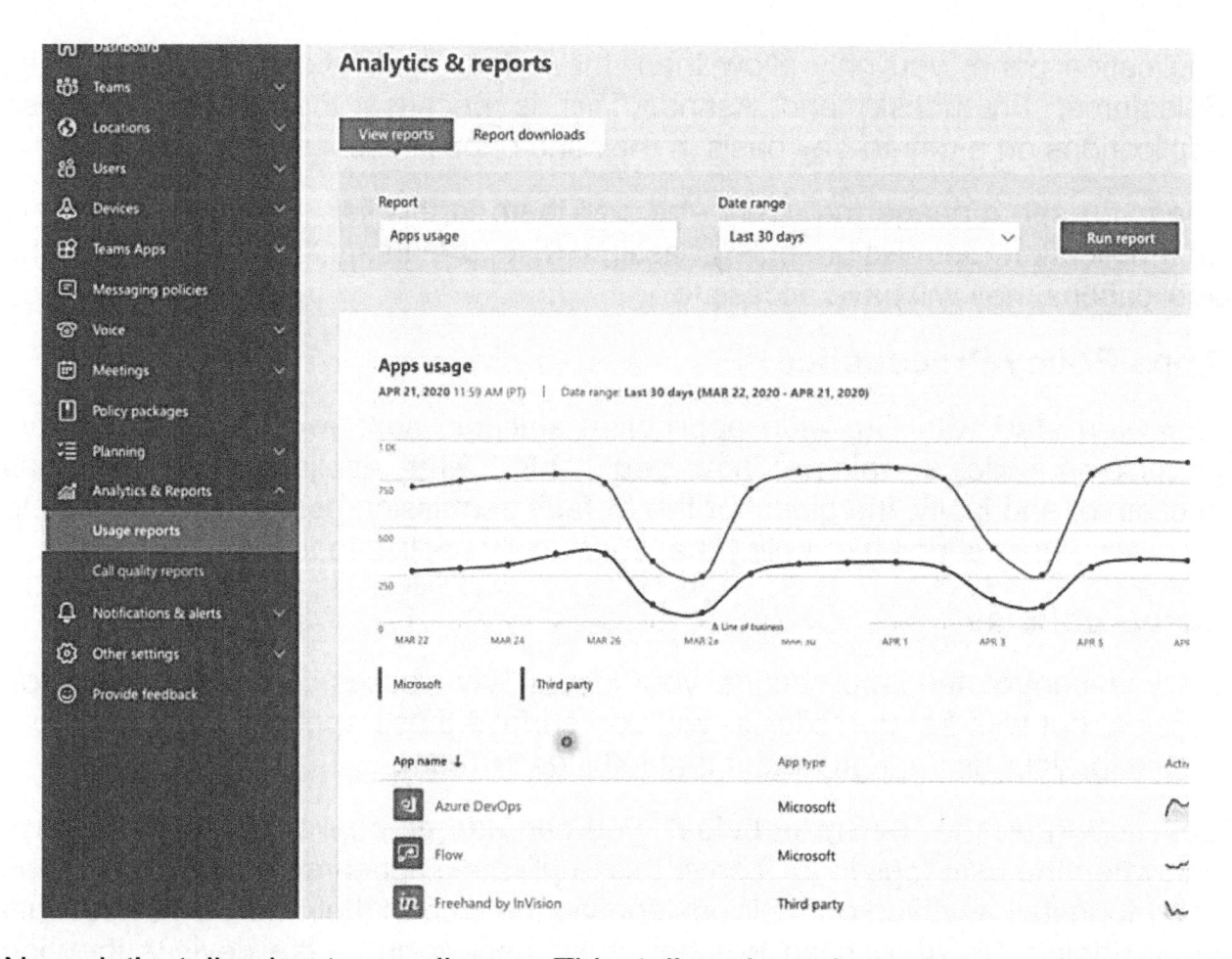

Now, let's talk about compliance. This talks about how the capabilities you deploy, what application has these capabilities, and how the data is handled by that application.

For example, Bots only receive messages in which they are explicitly

mentioned by users. This data can and does leave the corporate network. A bot can retrieve and might store the list of channels in a team, and this data also leaves the network. The Bot needs to know where it's installed in an organization in the team's channel construct.

When using connectors, no data leaves the corporate network. So all the connector does is post messages to a channel.

When using an application in a tab, the risk profile is similar to what a web application has. So, running that same application in a web browser, you authenticate to the application, the application knows who you are, so it gets the sign-in name and UPN of the current user, the Office 365 Group in which it resides (If it's a team), and the tenant ID of the current user.

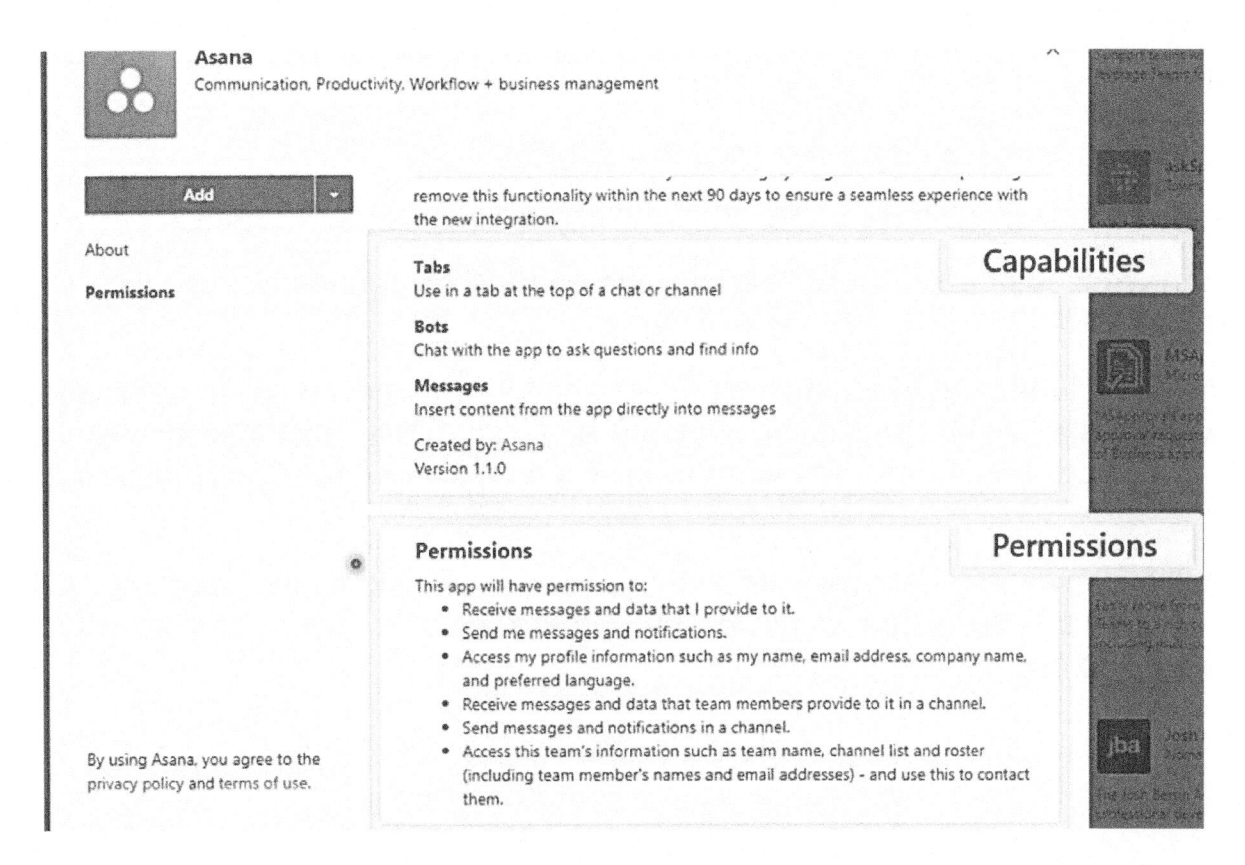

[Screenshot of Asana app details showing Capabilities and Permissions sections]

Let's look at an application. Before you install the application, you can look at what its capabilities are. It could work as a tab, a bot, and a message extension. You need to understand how your users are going to use this. You can also look at the permissions this application requires to operate. Very straightforward, right upfront, all the information is there. You can review it and analyze it.

Managing Third-party apps in Teams

To enable an application for your organization, there are some steps to follow and things to consider. First, you should look at the architecture of the application, such as privacy, security, compliance features within Teams, and what is enabled for this application. Then you can look at what the application can do (Bots, tabs, message extensions). You can also analyze the scope (where this application can be installed; Teams, channels, chat, personal context), look at the application permission (what this application requires to operate), what you know about the developer, what security and compliance standards they meet, and if they have already been through an internal approver. Then you can talk to your procurement and InfoSec about that application to be allowed for the users to be used in Teams. And lastly, you can look organization-wide at what applications my users are using and focus on those applications to enable them for users in Teams.

Summary

In this chapter, we discussed apps in Teams.

First, we looked at some common myths about using apps in Teams.

Then we looked at the apps' background and the categories of apps with some examples.

We went further to discuss how you can publish and discover applications, dwelling also on the extensibility points and capabilities of these applications. You also got some help with what to look out for when creating or installing an app.

Lastly, we covered how you can manage your applications, including third-party applications. We looked at the policy permissions for apps and how you can create and apply these policies.

Chapter 10: Enhancing Teams With Bots

In this chapter, you'll learn how to work with Bots. Bots are available to more than just the Microsoft Team's applications, so you may have already experienced them and didn't quite even know it.

The first thing you need to do with Bots in the Microsoft Team's application is to find out if they're even available for your use.

Checking Availability

So, you go to the general channel of your team, but to see if this has been enabled by the administrator of your organization you need to go in and take a look at where you would find those team members that are already a part of this particular team. For that, you're going to go to the three dots (that's the more options menu) just to the right of the team, and you go into **"View team"**. Now, this is a great place for you to see who else is a member and you're also able to see who has access to this team.

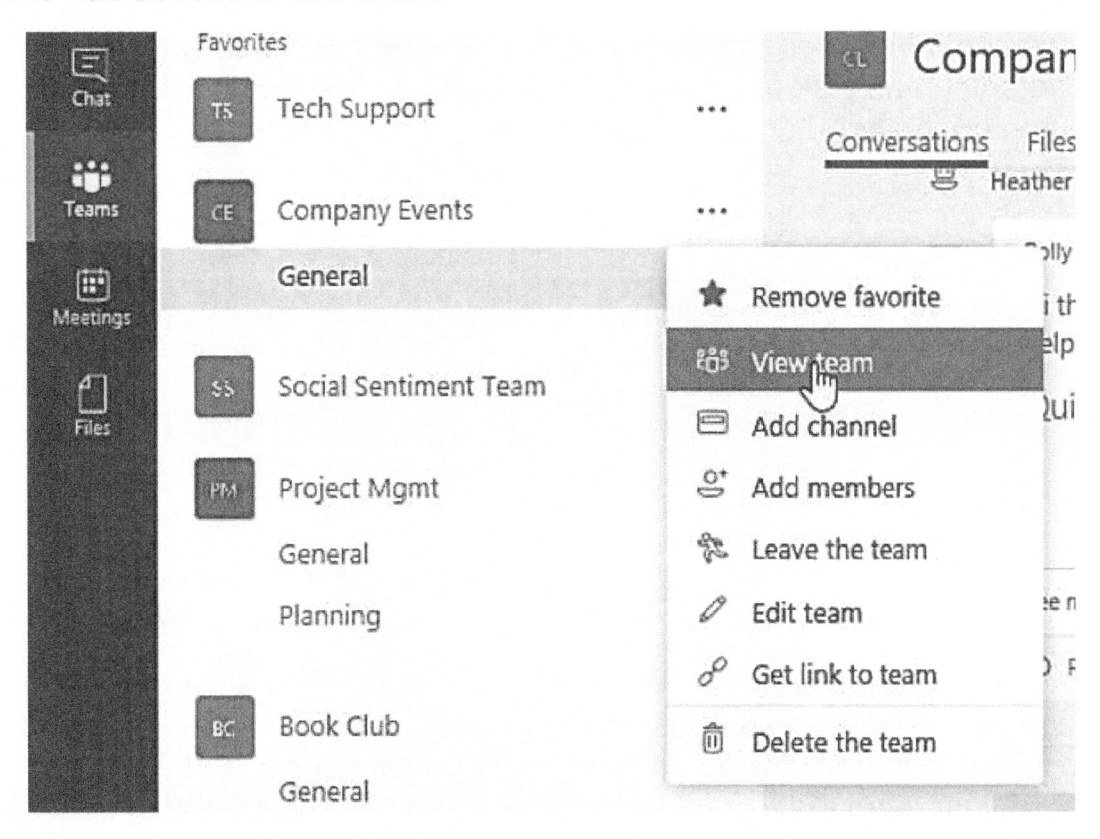

If you take a look at the names of the tabs at the top you can see in blue the members' area, and over to the right you can see those channels and manage each of those channels, as well as the settings overall for this team. To the right of that is where you'll see bots. If you are following along on your computer or later on you go back and you check the team that you're in and you don't see Bots there as a tabbed area that means it has not been enabled by your administrator, so you might want to check in with them at your organization and see if that is something that they can make happen.

Bots in a Conversation

Let's go ahead and take a closer look at these Bots. Think of this as another member of your team, it's just that they're not a member like you and me; they're an artificial intelligence or what's known as an AI type of a member. So it is someone that you can communicate with and get answers back from that particular bot and there are all sorts of Bots that you can use for many different reasons within your Team.

There are a couple of these bots enabled within different teams, the most common ones being Hipmunk and Polly, and you'll see that there is a description next to each of those telling you what these bots can help you out with. If you'd like to see what other bots are available, this is another great place for you to check out from time to time as they add more.

If you click on **"Discover bots"** over to the right, you will see a gallery listing of all the bots you can pick from again. If you want to add another bot, click on the plus button on the right.

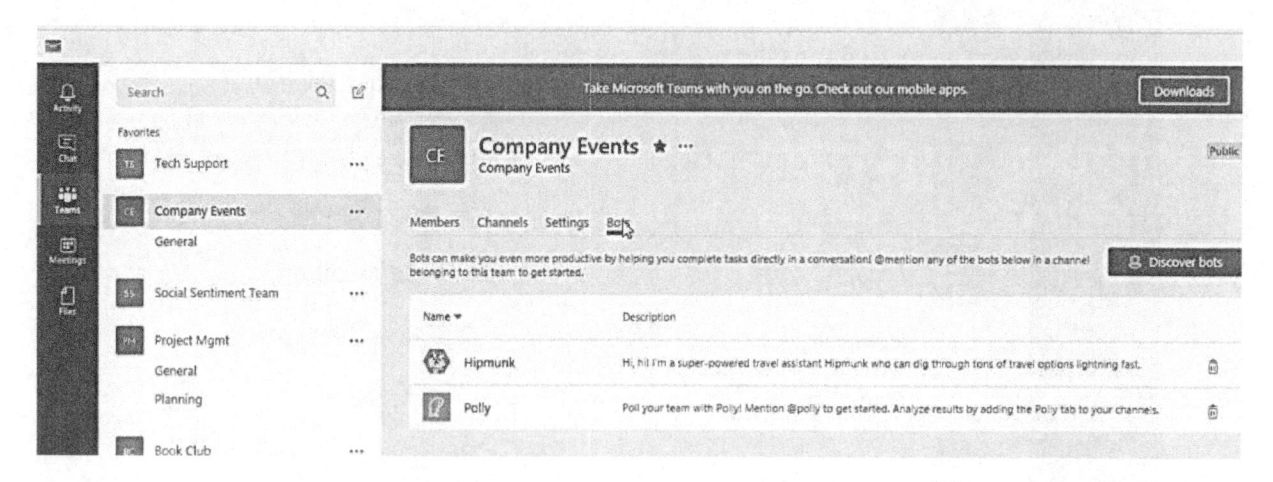

One thing you will need to do before you're able to enable and use these bots is you do need to permit these bots to communicate back and forth within the channel of your team that you're setting this up for. It needs to be able to receive messages that are sent, and it needs to be able to send messages and notifications back, so if you're asking a question, you're going to want to get something back from that bot. This is just a security parameter and you can go ahead and approve this capability for this bot so you go ahead, agree to those terms and click **"Done"**, and there you can see that you've now added the new bot.

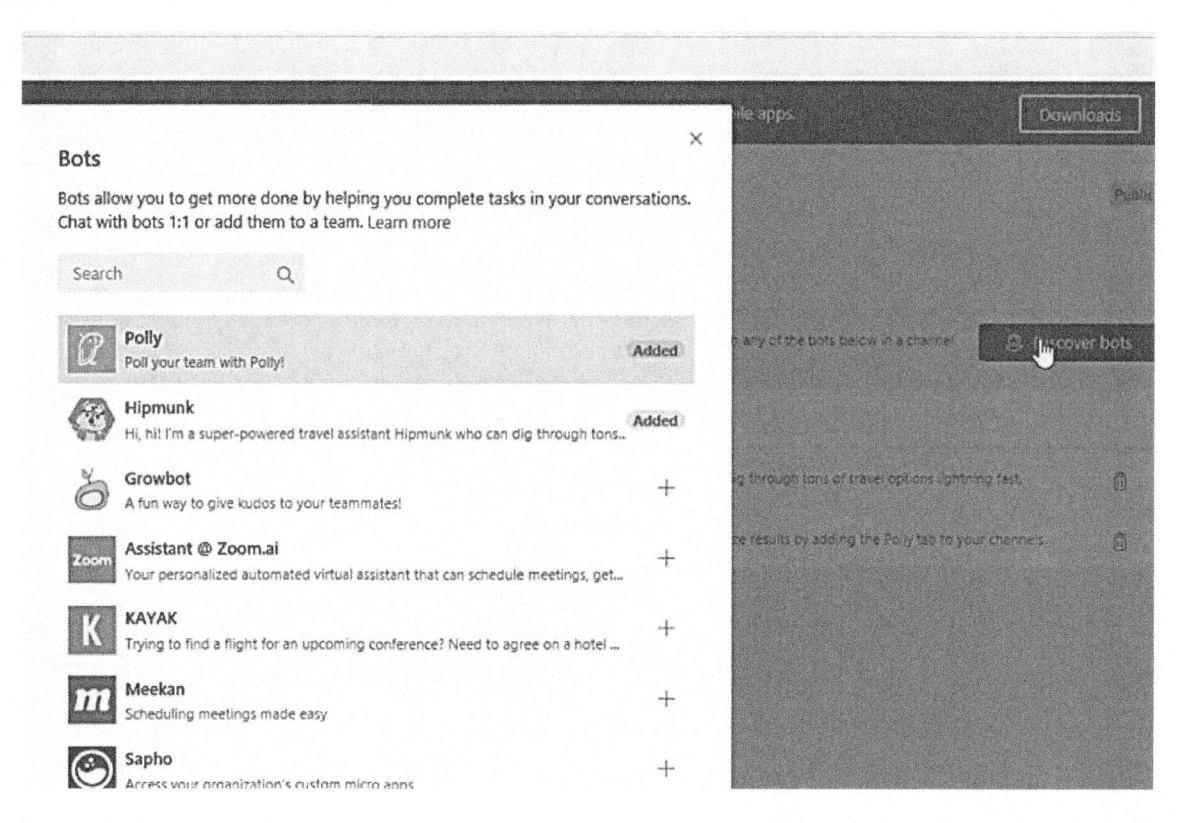

Back to the general channel of your team, and you'll notice that below your last message, it'll mention that you've added the new bot to the team and as you hover over the bot's names it gives information about what this bot can do.

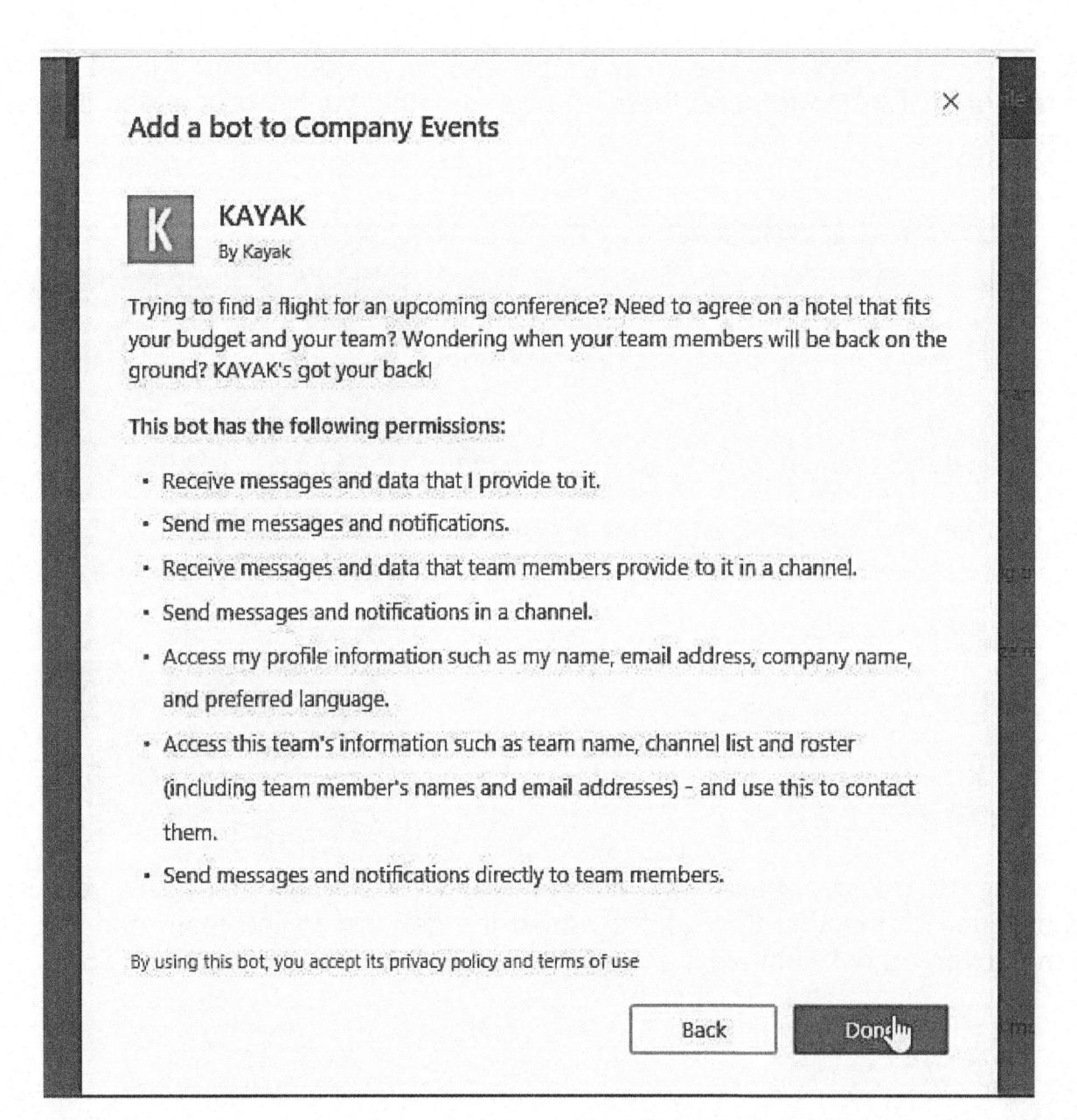

Add a bot to Company Events

KAYAK
By Kayak

Trying to find a flight for an upcoming conference? Need to agree on a hotel that fits your budget and your team? Wondering when your team members will be back on the ground? KAYAK's got your back!

This bot has the following permissions:

- Receive messages and data that I provide to it.
- Send me messages and notifications.
- Receive messages and data that team members provide to it in a channel.
- Send messages and notifications in a channel.
- Access my profile information such as my name, email address, company name, and preferred language.
- Access this team's information such as team name, channel list and roster (including team member's names and email addresses) - and use this to contact them.
- Send messages and notifications directly to team members.

By using this bot, you accept its privacy policy and terms of use

[Back] [Done]

You can go ahead and reply to the chat, just to let everyone know in your team once you add new members to this particular team in this channel. Whenever you're working with a bot, you'll always need to start your communication with that bot as an "**@ mention**", so if you enter the @ symbol and then the name of the bot you'll see that the suggestion list is showing it recognizes who that is, you can click on that or press **"Enter"** to also accept that that is the person that you want to talk to you.

For most bots, all you have to do is frame what it is you're asking as you normally would as a question while typing that out. There is an exception with the Polly bot where that is creating a poll and you're saying this is the question and these are each of the answers, in that case, you'd have to use quotations around all of that for it to work properly.

Some other bots are coming out soon so be on the lookout for; **Whobot**, which is a great way for you to type in a project name, customer, or vendor name that you're looking for more information around and it's going to show you who else in the team has mentioned that a lot or is quite popular and working on those particular subjects, and **Spacebot** (another one you might look for here in the new future or you might want to look and see if you can give it a try), which is a great way for you to add pictures from NASA to your team channels.

Here, you'll know how to build a bot for Microsoft teams, and if you follow these steps, you'll build your first bot for Microsoft teams.

Features of A Bot

The first one is obvious, and that is chat. This could either be a one-on-one chat, a group chat or you can add a bot to a team or respective channel, so you can have the conversation in that channel with the bot as well.

You've got messaging extensions, both search-based and action-based, which always consists of a bot in the back end doing the logic for you in most cases.

You could have a task module built using a bot using the bot framework and a lot more things.

As you can imagine, for all of that you would need to at least write some code, but right now there's a new feature or a new tool called Programming Composer which is a kind of visual Interface for building bots so you have two options, to build a bot or use for free, mainly within the Microsoft space. So you either go with the panoramic SDK or go with power virtual agents from the power platform or use bot member composer which is a visual interface for building bots using the SDK underneath.

Without further ado let's jump into a little demo.

Building a Bot

When you download the Bot Framework Composer tool, it's an installable tool, so you can install it on whatever Operating System you'd like to and if you open it up you get a lot of choices for either grabbing resources which are out there or published by the Teams platform and then you have the most recent version installed.

You have a lot of templates to be selected, so you could go with a Blank bot that consists of nothing, and also, you can have an Enterprise assistant which already comes with a lot of business logic and dialogues in there and it acts as a kind of starting point which you can use to develop your Enterprise assistant. You can also make use of skills, such as People or calendaring skill, which is available and published by Microsoft, and both template versions are either available in **"C#"** or **"Node"** as a preview.

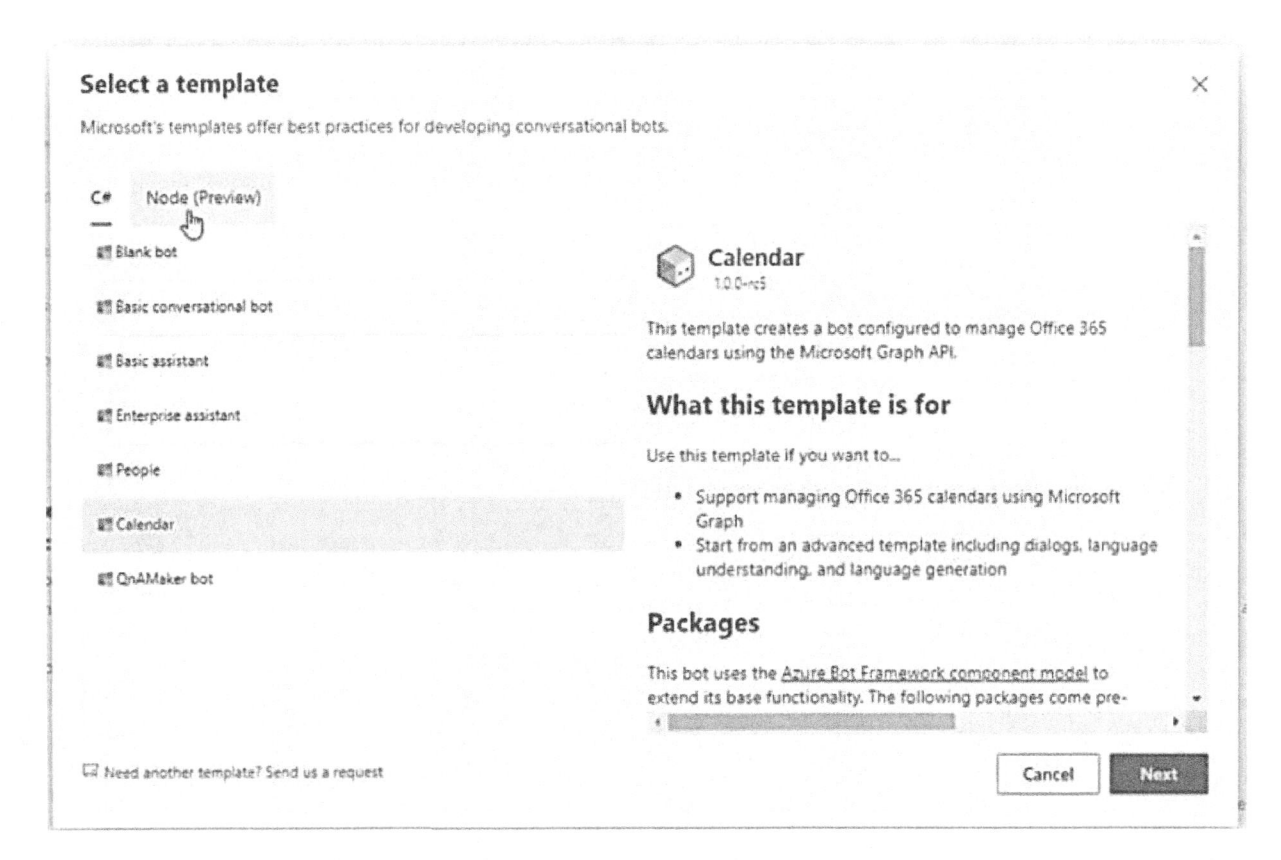

In the past, if you want to create a team bot, you had two options; you either go with a Q&A Maker to establish a set of FAQ knowledge base where you have questions and answers and then create a bot from that knowledge base which just answers the questions you have in the knowledge base, and the other option would be to develop your bot using code which is either **"C#"** or **"Node"**, and for all of the team's specific functionalities like task modules, messaging extensions, and others, you would need to write code to achieve that.

Recently, this has changed. After choosing your bot template, this opens up an interface to work with. On the left-hand side, you have the option to do all that without writing real code.

So to make your bot aware of any kind of knowledge base or language understanding piece, you just enable the features within the app settings so you need to insert your hostname, your knowledge base ID and of course the columns; and if you restart your bot you'll see how fast and simple that process is because. If after creating a bot and after asking a question it still gives you a notification saying "sorry I didn't find the answer", this is because the user intent isn't clear, so you get that response.

```
         Advanced Settings View (json)

      "enablePrebuiltEntities": true,
      "enableRegexEntities": true
    },
    "luis": {
      "authoringEndpoint": "",
      "authoringRegion": "westeurope",
      "defaultLanguage": "en-us",
      "endpoint": "",
      "environment": "composer",
      "name": "conversational_core",
      "authoringKey": "eea97ba4823748f683cff09a40a8664d",
      "endpointKey": ""
    },
    "MicrosoftAppId": "160ff09d-1472-4967-adf1-db94aec613b3",
    "publishTargets": [],
    "qna": {
      "hostname": "https://sb-qnamaker-us.azurewebsites.net/qnamaker",
      "knowledgebaseid": "b3ff9f81-6949-40d0-8adb-16ca777e16d4",
      "qnaRegion": "westus",
      "endpointKey": "d453ead0-fec2-40e7-844e-f1c5e4033cfb",
      "subscriptionKey": ""
    },
    "runtime": {
      "command": "dotnet run --project conversational_core.csproj",
      "customRuntime": true,
      "key": "adaptive-runtime-dotnet-webapp",
      "path": "../"
    },
    "runtimeSettings": {
      "adapters": [],
      "features": {
        "removeRecipientMentions": false,
        "showTyping": false,
        "traceTranscript": false,
        "useInspection": false,
        "setSpeak": {
          "voiceFontName": "en-US-AriaNeural",
```

You can replace that by connecting to your Q&A knowledgebase to answer the user's questions right away and there's a pre-configured action to that, so it just grabs the Q&A Maker settings and just queries the Q&A Maker knowledge base with that and after the restart, it should use the question you ask the bot go to the Q&A Maker in your knowledge base, query your knowledge base to see if there's any question in there which might be applicable and if so it just gives it back to you in within the one-on-one chat in Microsoft Teams.

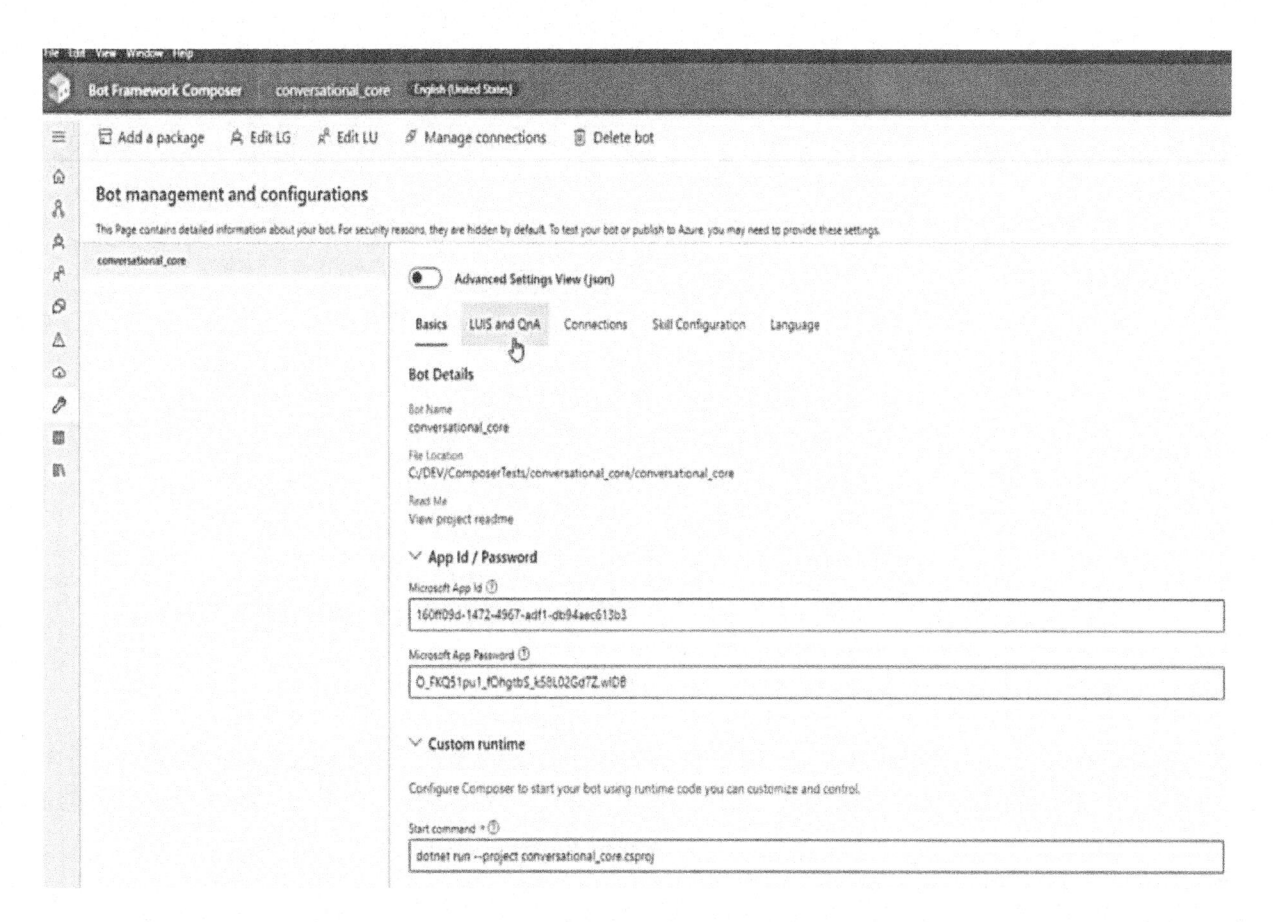

This shows you how easy it is with Composer to use all of that team's functionality without writing code, so these days you can easily build task modules or messaging extensions without the need of being a real developer or hardcore developer. So, what you need to do to make that work is getting the Composer **Package Management** solution which consists of the **Welcome**, **Graph**, **HelpAndCancel**, **Teams**, and **AdaptiveCards packages**.

And if you install the Teams package, for example, you get a lot of Microsoft team-specific options either for trigger management, so you have a trigger type or category in there and then you can select which kind of teams event should your bot listen to and as you can see in here there are a lot of events for messaging extensions, and task modules. So if the user wants to fetch the task module or if the user submits the task module, there is a certain event triggered.

Summary

This chapter was focused on you getting familiar with Bots.

We started by helping you understand what bots are and how to check if it is available in your Teams.

Then we went further to explain the unique features of a bot and in the latter part of the chapter, we provided some guidance on how you can create your first bot if you want to do so.

Chapter 11: Synergizing With Teams Integration

In this chapter, we will look at the ways you can interconnect Microsoft Teams with other platforms to get benefits from both of them to the one collaboration environment.

Connecting Microsoft Teams with SharePoint Online

Working with Microsoft Teams is something normal for all office 365 users globally, but what do you do when you want to bring SharePoint experience and work with SharePoint data on Teams?

When you want to bring teams to existing SharePoint site, you need to remember that when you're creating the modern SharePoint site, you have two types of sites you can create; one is the **Communication site** which is more connected with the Intranet, the project site or an application site and the other is the **Team site**. The Team site almost always is connected with the Microsoft 365 group which is required to have the teams created in Microsoft Teams.

Create a site
Choose the type of site you'd like to create.

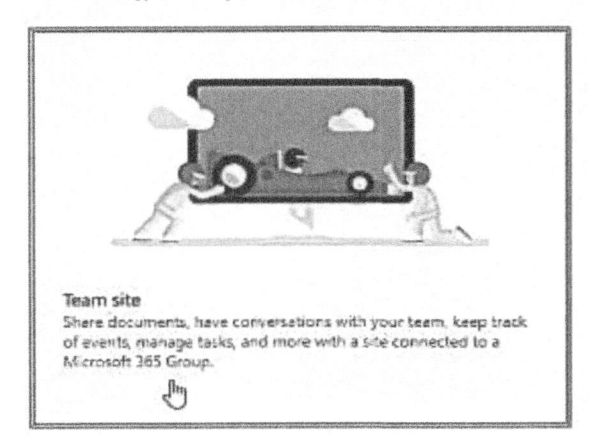

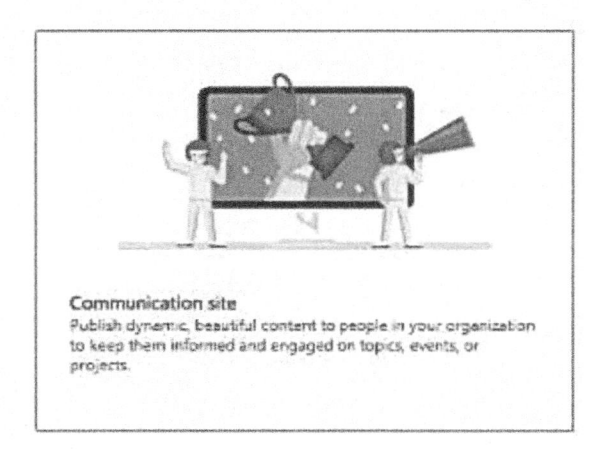

Team site
Share documents, have conversations with your team, keep track of events, manage tasks, and more with a site connected to a Microsoft 365 Group.

Communication site
Publish dynamic, beautiful content to people in your organization to keep them informed and engaged on topics, events, or projects.

There is a slight change in your environment that there are two options to create the team site on SharePoint, the one with the Microsoft 365 group and the one without it, so please check that because the possibility to bring Teams experience to SharePoint online is only possible when you're thinking about the SharePoint site with Microsoft 365 group.

When your SharePoint site is created you will see on the right top corner there is a private group created behind it and if you go to **"Site permissions"** and **"Site owners"**, you will also see that kind of group with dedicated email accounts. So this will be the sign for you that there is a Microsoft 365 group behind the SharePoint site and you can bring Teams' experience to that site. Bringing the Microsoft Teams team to that existing SharePoint site is very easy, the only thing you have to do is to locate that button and select **"Add Microsoft Teams"**. It will take a few moments and the Microsoft Team experience will be created behind your SharePoint site and you will be able to get Teams' experience connected with your already existing SharePoint site. You will see on your screen there will be an additional Teams tab on the left navigation and in the documents, you can see there is a general channel folder for your documents.

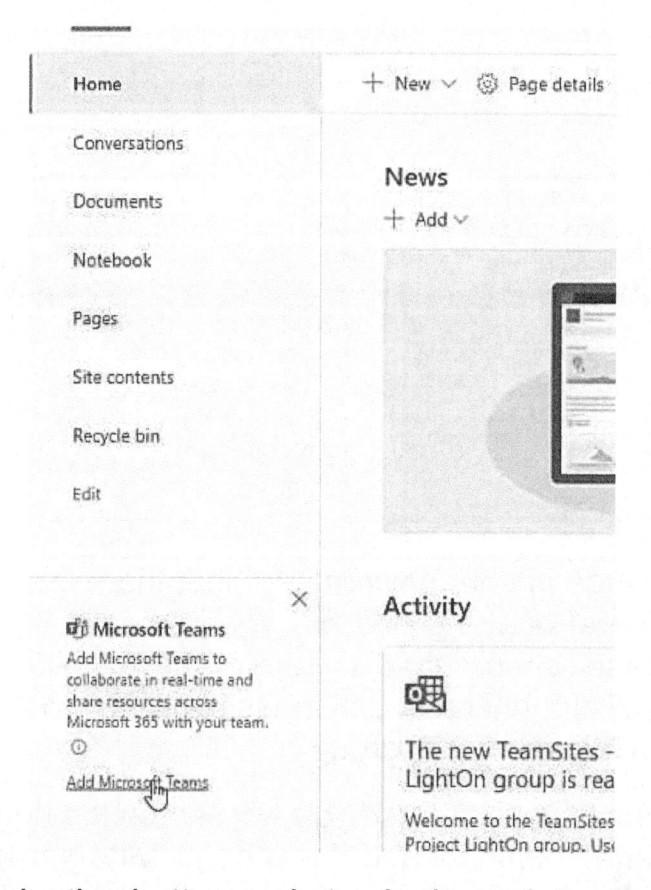

If you select this navigation button and stay in the web browser you will see that you will be navigated to Microsoft Teams which is connected directly with your existing SharePoint site.

This is a very easy process, but remember that you need to have Microsoft 365 group connected with your Teams site.

When you're working with Microsoft Teams you should always remember that every Team contains the SharePoint site behind it. If you would like to check this site, it's very easy to locate it. Just go to the Files tab and there you will find the **"Open in the Sharepoint"** button.

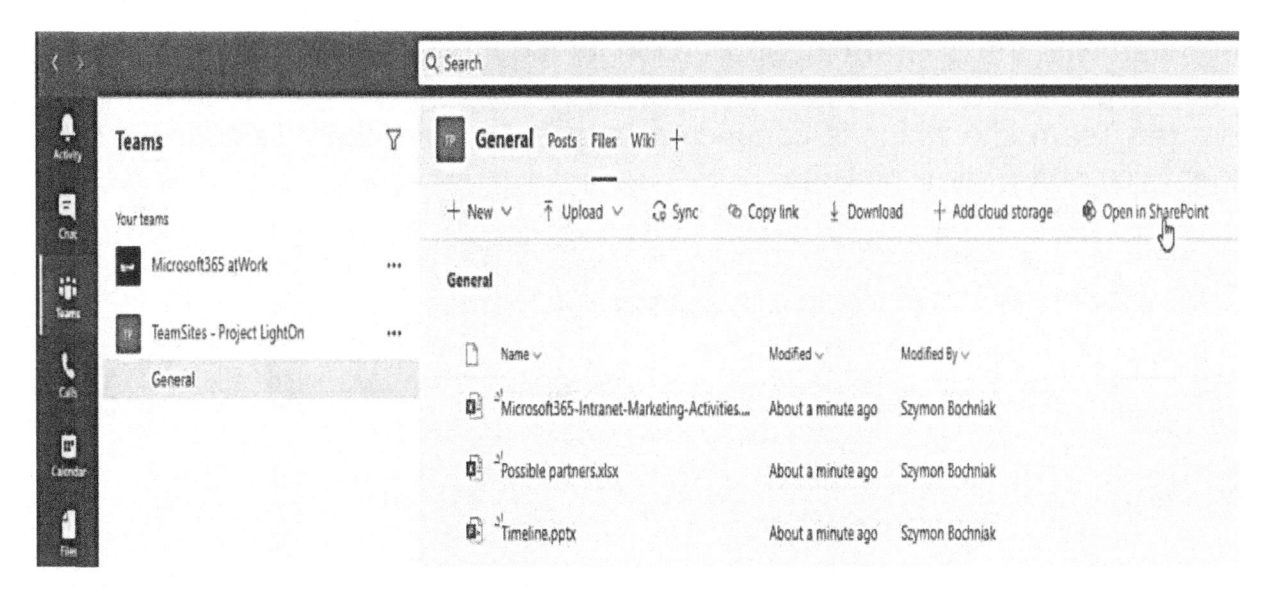

This will open the browser and navigate you to your SharePoint site which is created behind the Microsoft Teams. On this level you have access to all files, you can extend them and use them whenever you want. It's good to know about it because you can interconnect these two platforms both ways.

If you're working with Microsoft Teams, there is also an additional way to bring the SharePoint experience to your collaboration in the Teams. To do that, go to **"Add a tab"** and select the application.

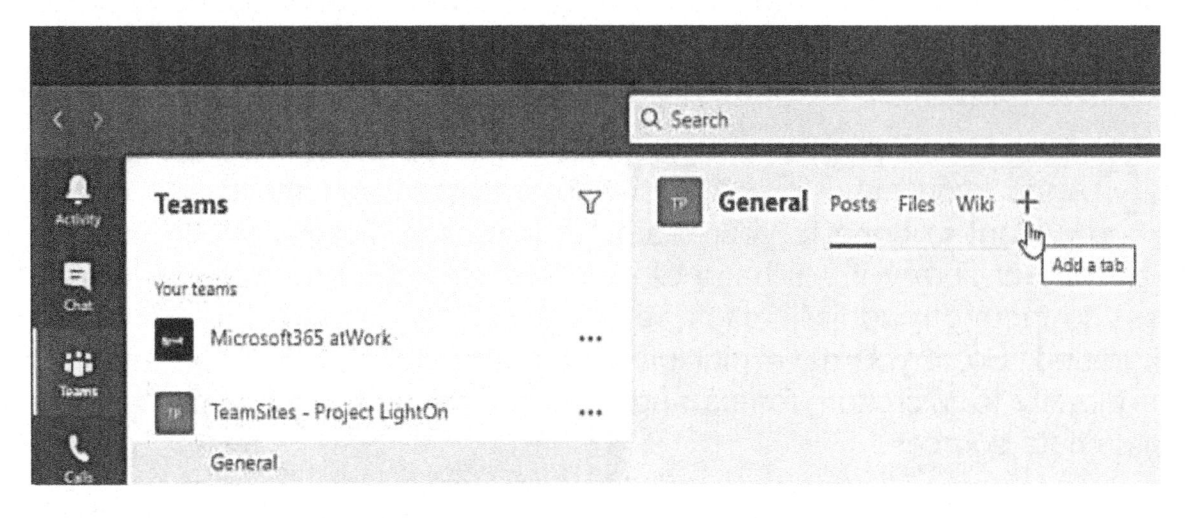

You have a few applications you can use that will bring SharePoint directly to your Microsoft Teams team. You can use **"Document library"**, which will connect the SharePoint hosted Document library as the additional tab, you can use **"Lists"**, and bring List which is created on OneDrive or SharePoint to your Microsoft Teams or you can use SharePoint and SharePoint Pages to create a connection to Lists, Libraries or Pages.

Let's start with the SharePoint application as it contains most of the features you need. If you click on the application, you can decide if you want to load the data from the Team site which is connected behind or if you want to connect to any other Microsoft SharePoint site.

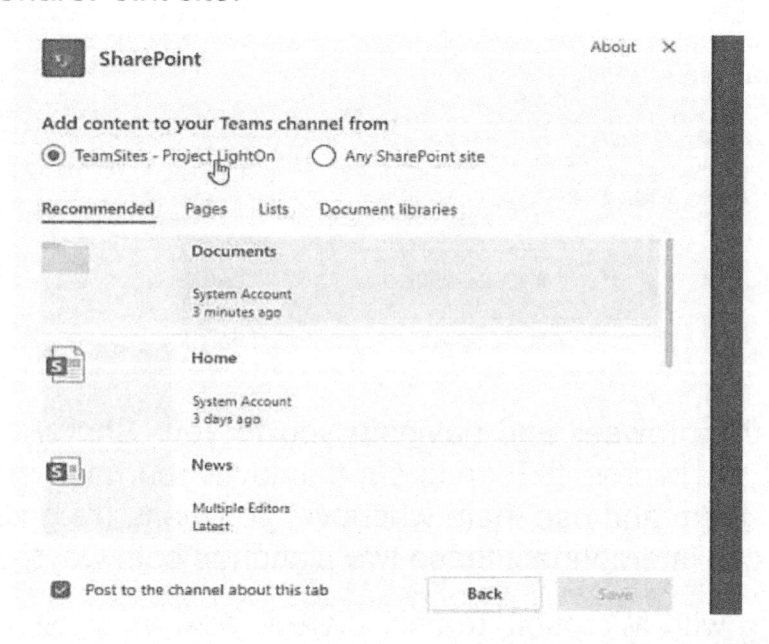

In this case, you will also have access to all components present there, if you want to bring the new page, you can select it and save it. Thanks to that you can bring content from SharePoint and embed it directly to Microsoft Teams; it is something like building the application through Teams using SharePoint components. You can see that with just a few clicks you can manage the content behind it and just bring that experience directly to Microsoft Teams.

Another thing which you can also consider is to **connect with the Document library**. Again, you have to select the **"TeamSites"** and the Document library which you want to bring to your teams in Microsoft Teams. When you publish this document library it will bring all the files stored there. You can easily get access to them through Microsoft Teams and host them in SharePoint in their background. So, if you have multiple Document libraries you can interconnect them directly to Microsoft Teams and work on the files on multiple tabs on the multiple data sources.

Pick a document library   About X

    TeamSites - Project LightOn

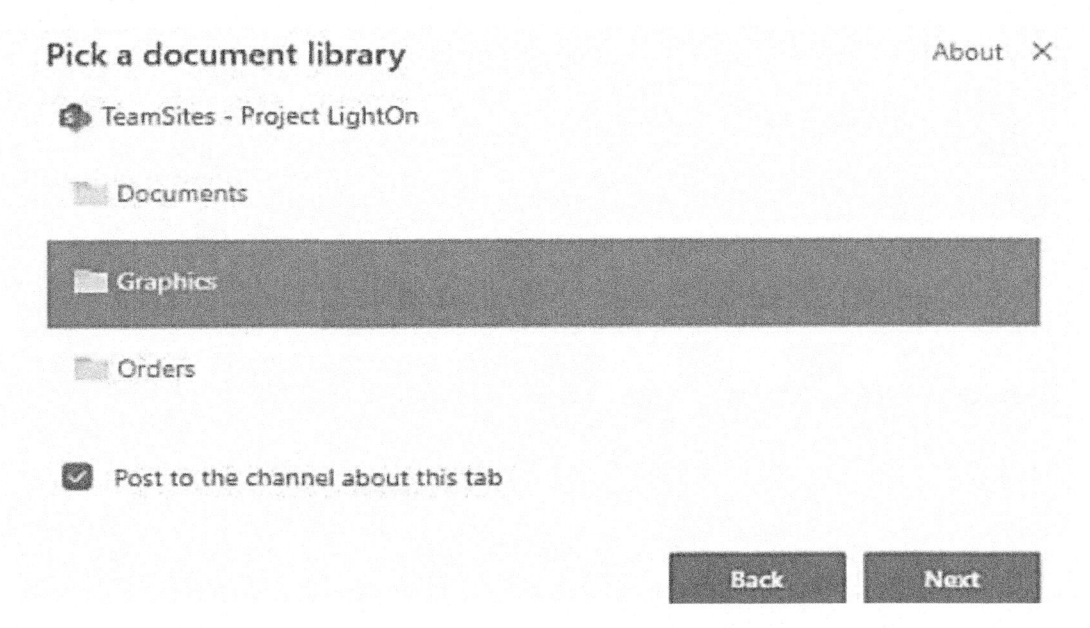

       Documents

       Graphics

       Orders

    ☑ Post to the channel about this tab

                                                Back   **Next**

Another application that you can bring to your Microsoft Teams is Lists, hosted on SharePoint. If you select the **"List"** then you can bring a List as an additional tab and deliver it to your colleagues working the same thing.

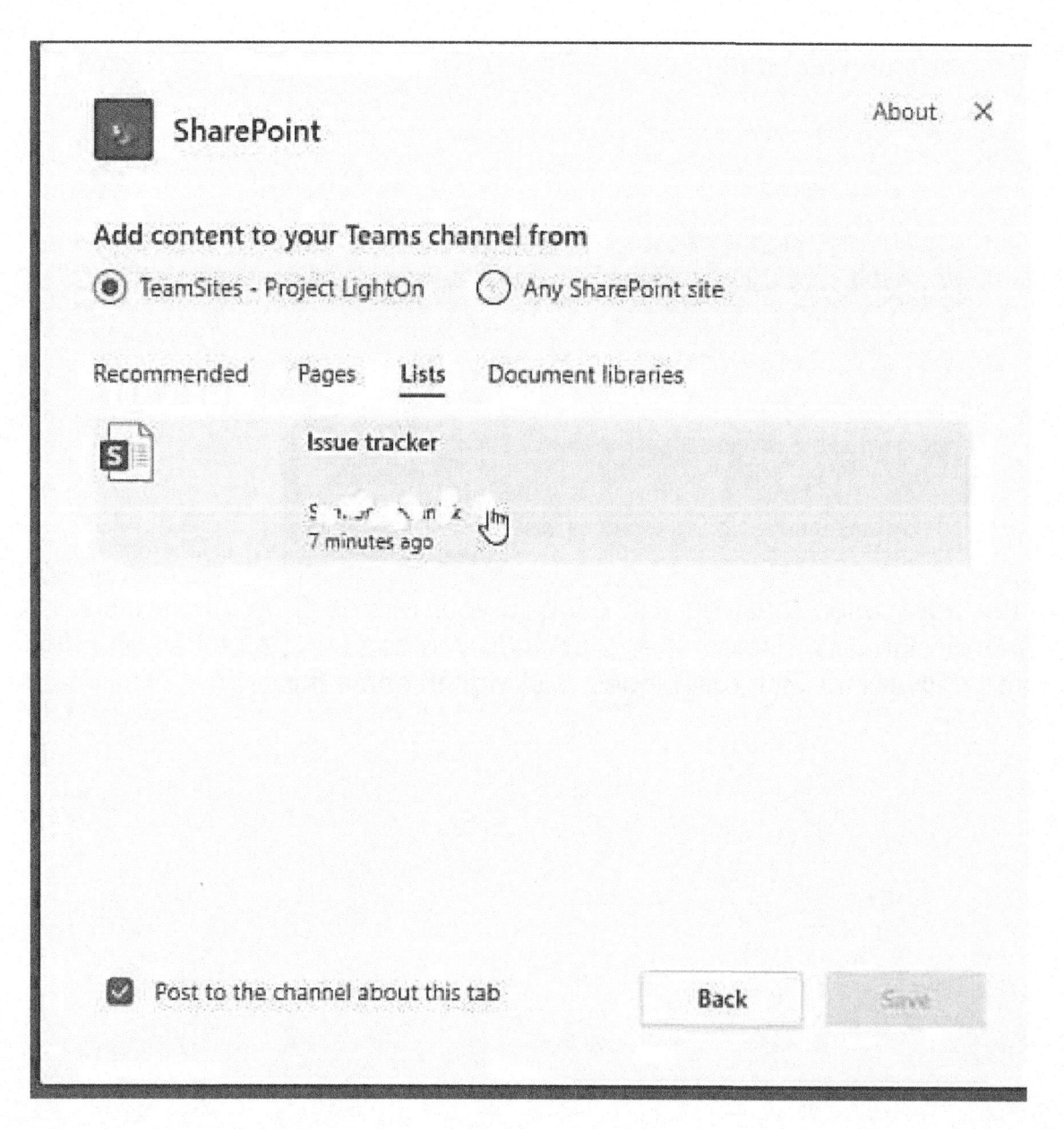

You can see that you have the whole Microsoft List experience added to Microsoft Teams, so if you're hosting that kind of data on SharePoint and your users are working mostly on Microsoft Teams, you can bring all those elements as additional applications on channels or in general team level and make it much easier for your colleagues to work on SharePoint components using Microsoft Teams.

You can see that connecting Microsoft teams with SharePoint online is very easy. Both of these platforms are already interconnected, so behind every team created in Microsoft Teams there is a SharePoint site behind it, so the only thing you have to do is to bring experience from SharePoint to Teams to get that added value.

Using Power Automate with Teams

Here, we're going to look at how you can make yourself more productive in Microsoft Teams using Power Automate. We're going to create a flow with a selected message in Microsoft Teams and push that into Microsoft To-Do. You'll see how to do that and what you need to be aware of when you're building flows like this for personal productivity.

In the Microsoft Teams app, you'll notice that if you click on the "more options menu" of a message, and go to "more actions", you can "**Create Work item**".

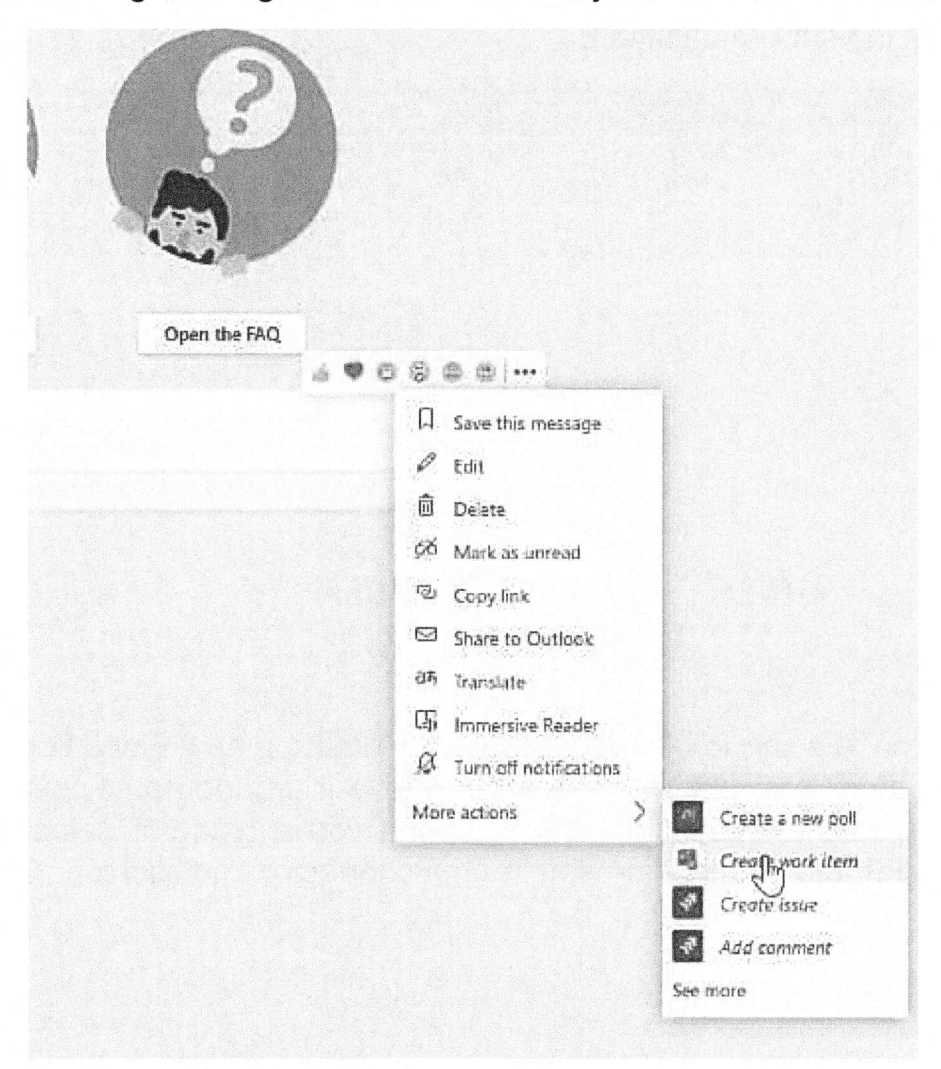

What's interesting is this can be a Flow that you can pick up data from your context of the message, as well as data that you input when you run the Flow. This is helpful because a lot of times in Teams you end up with these conversations where people talk about a lot of things and somewhere in there you agree to do something and if you don't get it onto your to-do list, you forget about it. So, what you're going to do is build a real simple Flow that allows it to show up on here as "**Add To-do item**" and you'll push that item into Microsoft To do.

So, let's switch over to the Flow portal and get started building this. The first thing you should know is that you have to be in the default environment for it to show up on that context list. So if you build a flow in a custom environment, it's just going to let you build it but it's not going to show up in the team's context menu. One way to ensure that you're doing that is you can start from the Teams app, so if you have the Power Automate app installed in Teams and you build the Flow from there, it's automatically going to create it in your default environment in your organization.

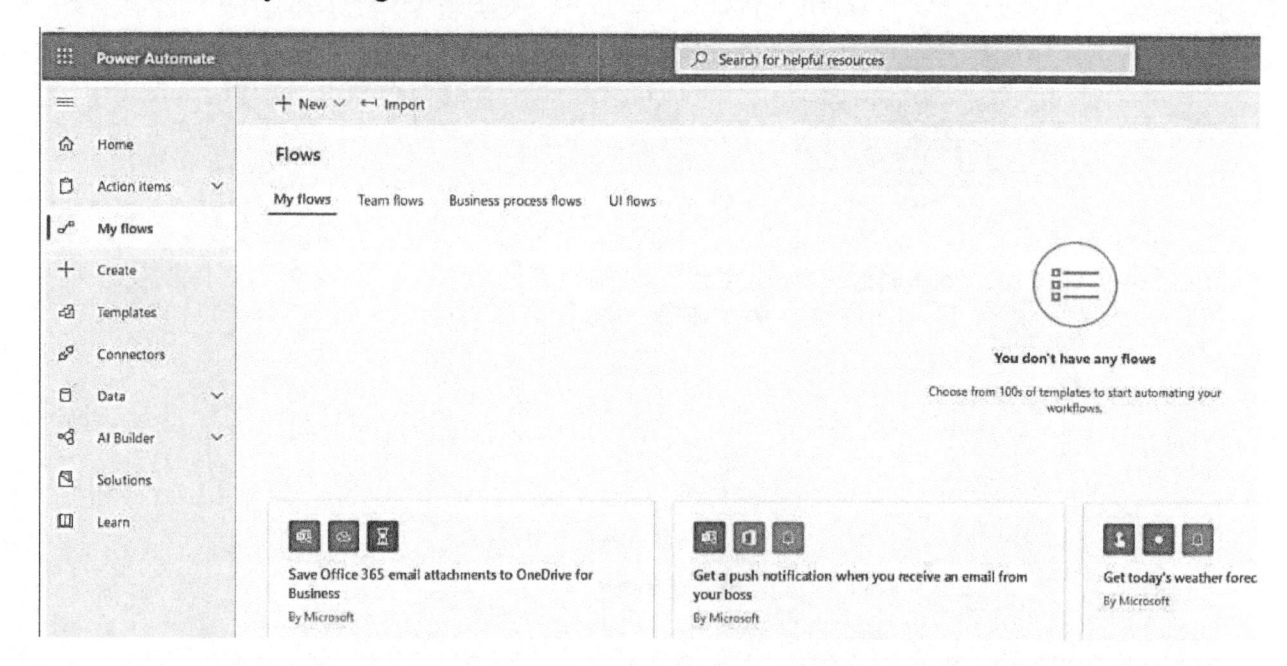

Now what you're going to do is go ahead and create a new Flow. You're going to create an instant from blank. Make sure to give it a good name because this is what's going to show up in the context menu you're going to select the "**For a selected message**" in the Microsoft Teams connector and click on "**Create**".

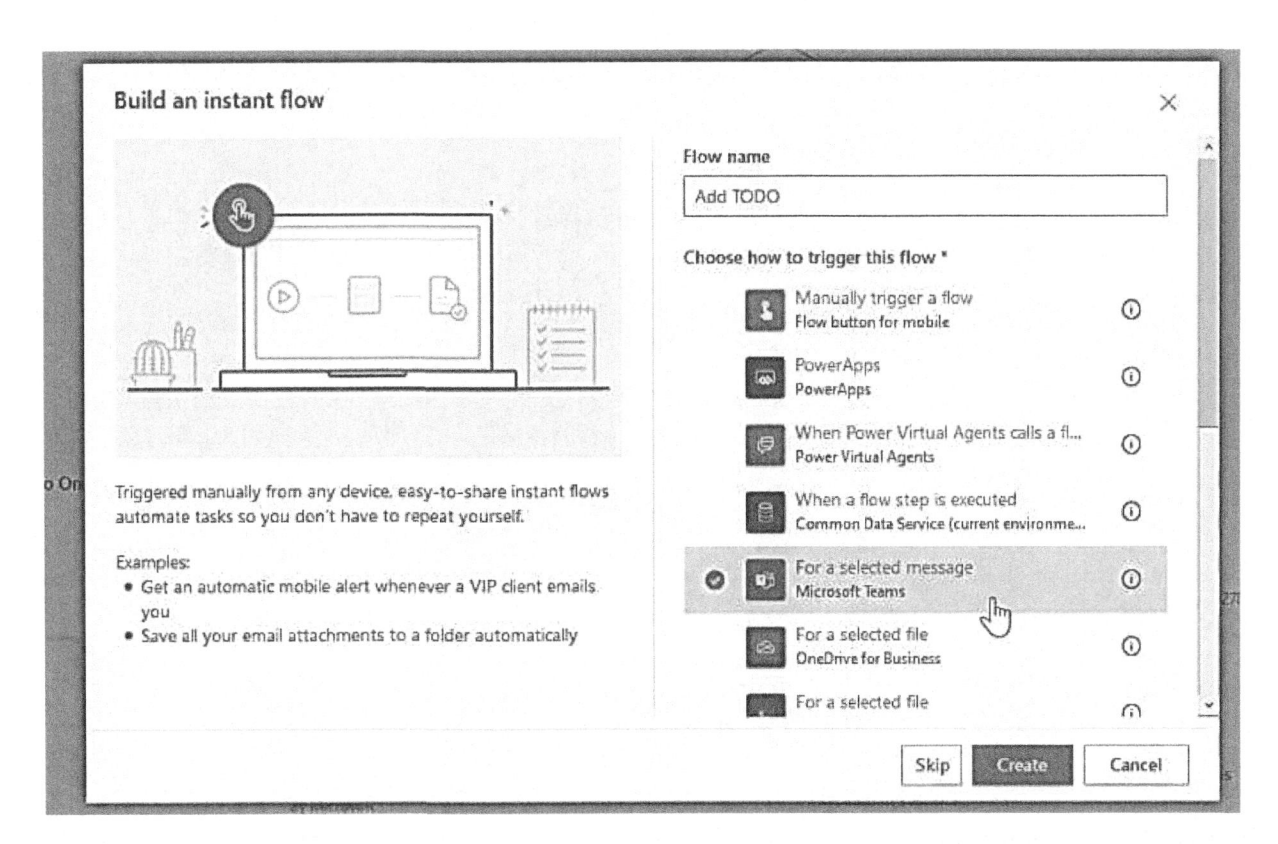

What you should do next is go ahead and allow the user or yourself to be able to give a custom title to the to-do that you're going to add in case the message itself wasn't appropriate for the title of the to-do task or maybe you wouldn't remember it. So, what you're going to do is come in here and click **"Create Adaptive Card"**.

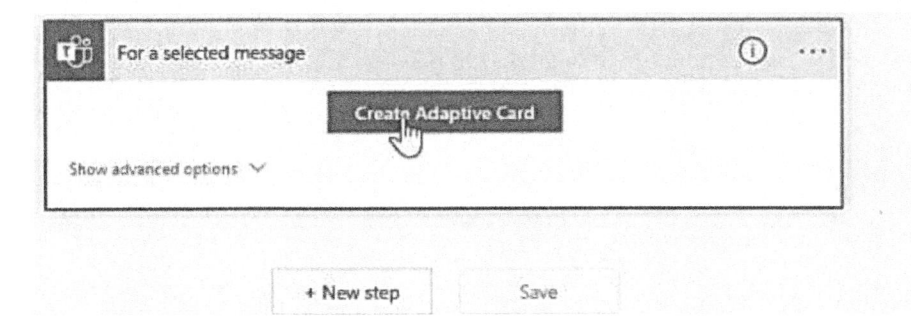

This allows you to use adaptive cards as the way to describe what you want to get as input, this is like parameters that you would have on a button flow but it's described using an adaptive card. If you haven't built these, they're just kind of a fancy way of marking up and describing what input fields and display fields you want to have and it's independent of how it's going to be rendered, and in this case, it's going to be rendered in the Teams' app.

You'll see a default one here that's asking you to tell us about yourself. If you don't want to use this, go ahead and click **"New card"** and you're going to go ahead and choose "**Blank card**" because you just want to start with an empty canvas.

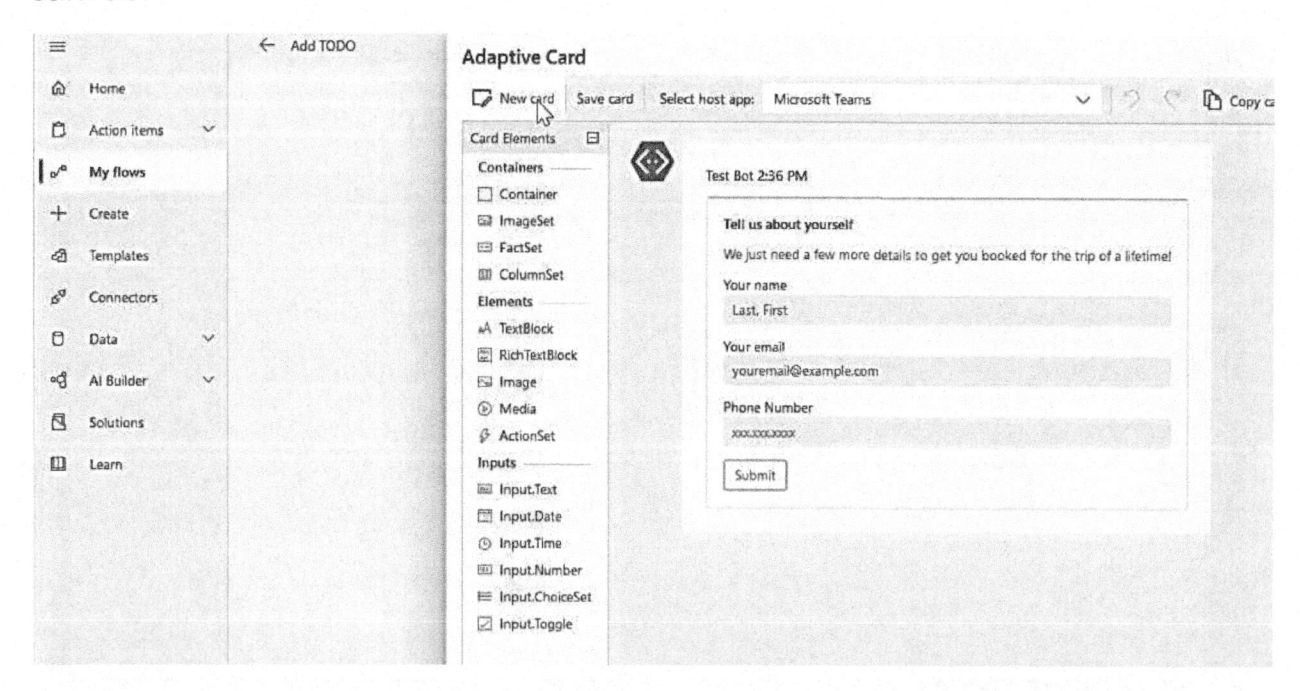

In the Card Elements, there are different things that you can use, but you're going to keep this simple because you want to focus on the core concept. You can dive into adaptive cards on your time a little bit further. So you're going to come up here, grab the input text and drop it on the area you want it, go over to the right and give it an ID, then you go ahead and save the card.

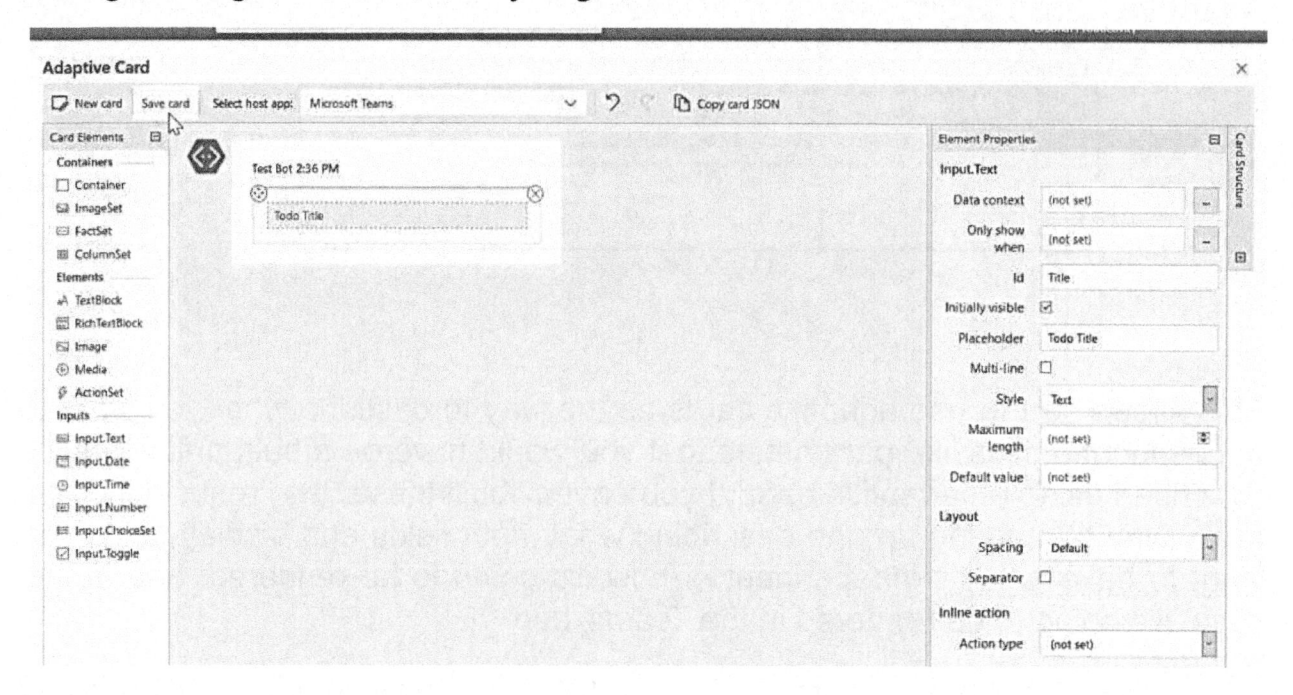

So now, you've set the stage and you'll see this when you go run the Flow from the context of the team message, it'll pop up a dialog box and in the advanced options, you'll see that you can control the height and the width of that you're so inclined.

Simply go ahead and click on **"Next step"** to add a reference to creating the to-do item.

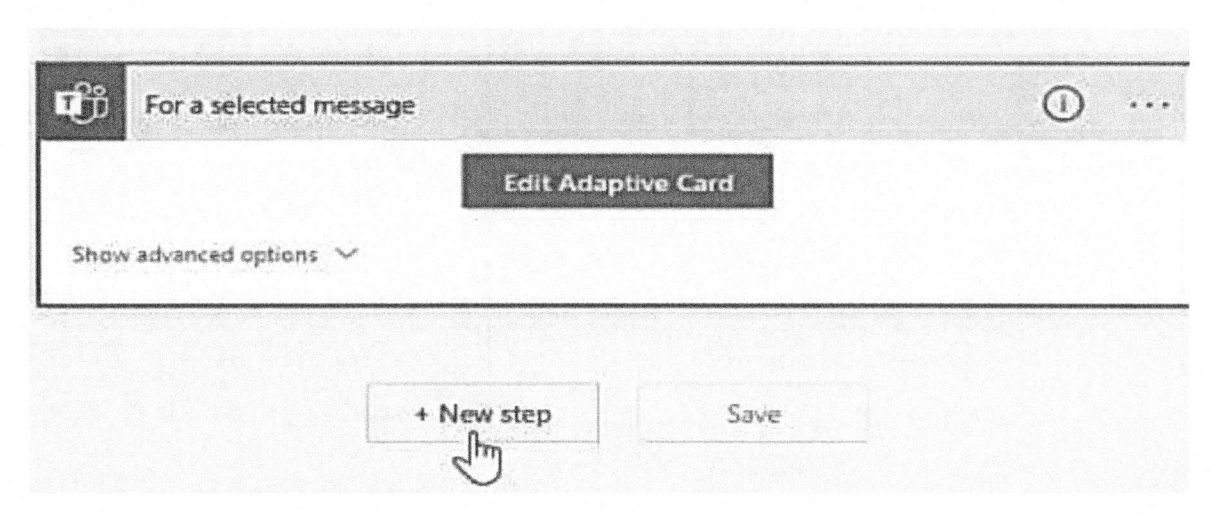

You're going to come down and get the to-do connector, so you're going to **"Add a to-do"**.

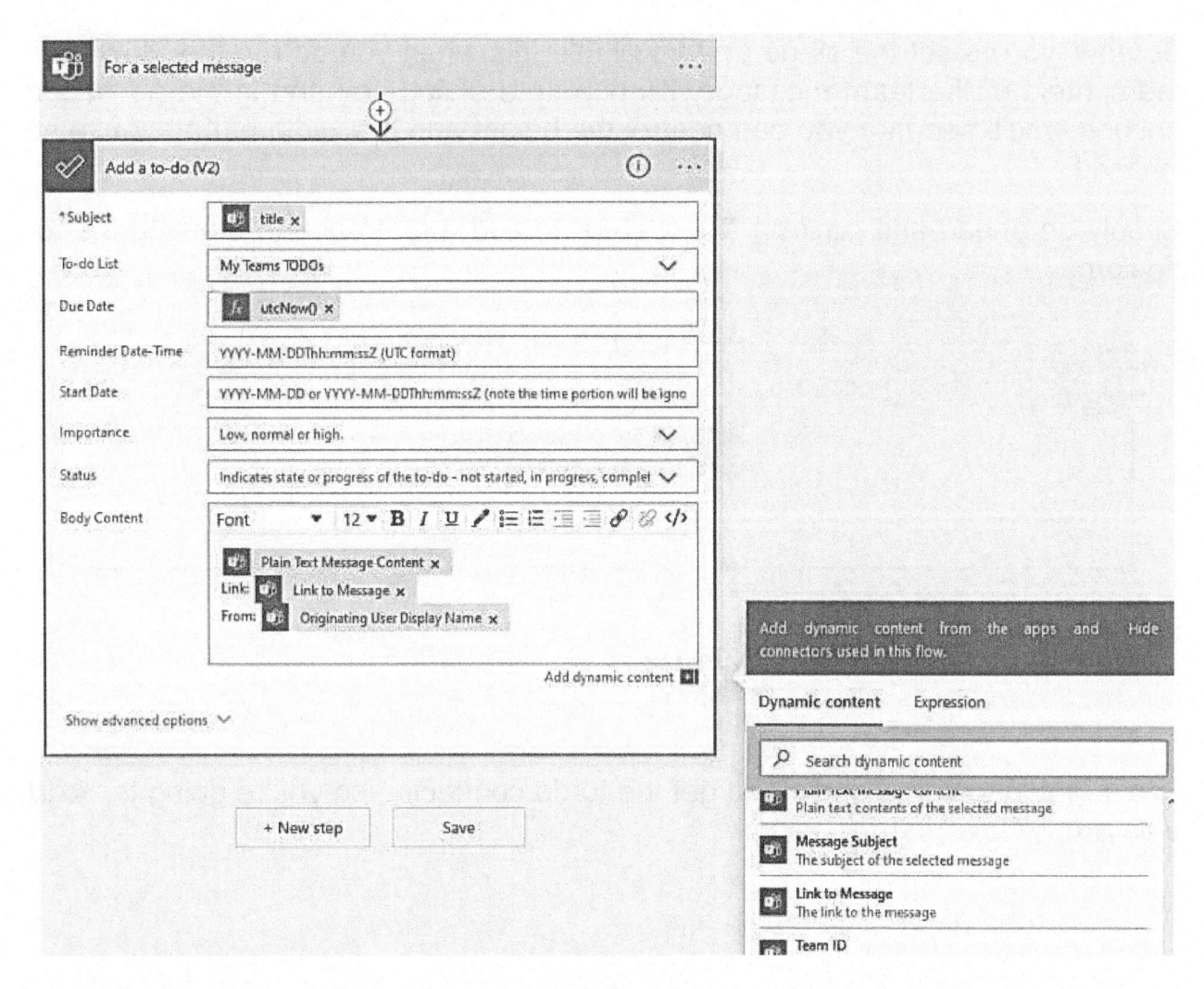

If you've already created a list in Microsoft To-Do, you'll notice that this comes in when you pick a to-do list. The subject is where you can do the conditional but if you scroll down, you'll see that on the card that the input text field you had created is showing up here and you can go ahead and bind to that real easily on there. The other thing you're going to do is go ahead and pick the due date because you want to make sure that it gets your attention and you can then reallocate it to when you want it to do. You could also prompt for a due date on the adaptive card; that would be another good field to add on there if you want to.

The other thing you're going to do is to pick up some text from it, and one of the nice things they do because Teams' messages can be rich text is they have a plain text message content that you can drop in there. You can do other things, for example, you can go ahead and add in a link to the message using the "**Link to Message**" display name and who sent the original message, that comes in the "**Originating User Display Name**". So, you don't even have to bother with the Office 365 connector to look up a user that sent it; this gives you some context so you can just fill this out. So, you'll go ahead and save this.

Now that it's saved, you're going to go ahead and jump back over to your Teams client, come over to the message, go to the "more actions" menu and you'll notice that your **"Add ToDo"** has shown up on the list and you can tell that its power automate by the icon that shows up on there

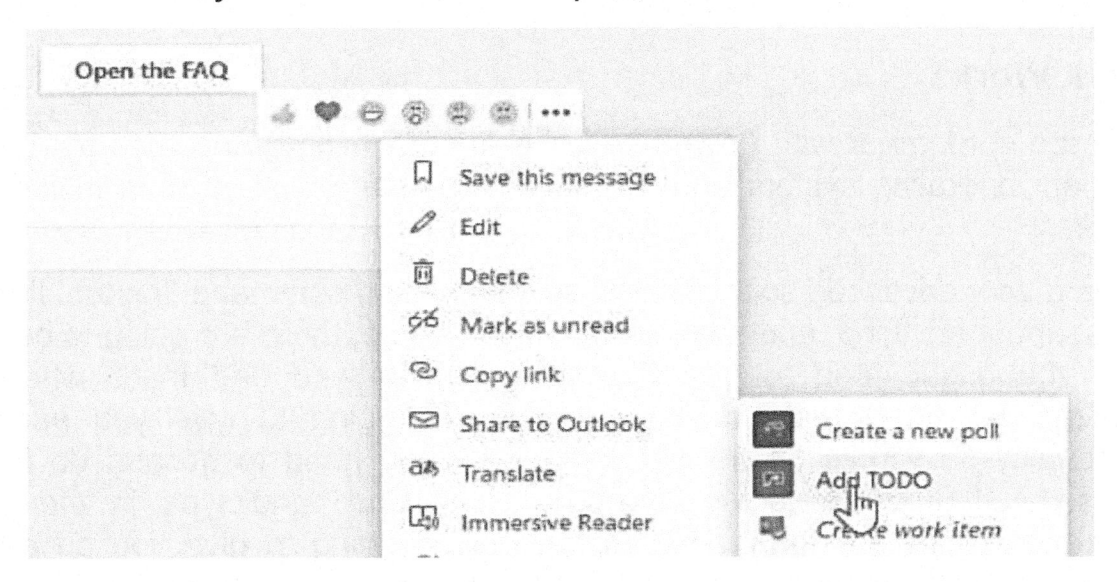

Go ahead and click it, enter the dialog title that you want in it and submit it, and that will cause your Flow to go ahead and run in the background and add your item to your to-do list. If you go back to your to-do, and there you have your task that's shown up on your list.

With that, you've successfully built a context-sensitive message Flow that can make you more productive and keep you from forgetting something that you say you're going to get done.

Summary

At the beginning of this book, we mentioned that Teams is a collaboration app and that you could connect and utilize other apps here as well.

So, in this chapter, we went deeper to explain step-by-step, how you can integrate apps in Teams. We focused on the SharePoint and Power Automate apps, and these were covered extensively. However, please note that you can integrate other apps in teams and whichever app you feel is useful for your business, you can integrate that in teams, using the steps provided.

Chapter 12: Advanced Teams Management With Powershell

This chapter is focused on PowerShell. First, you will see how to install the PowerShell module and after that, we're going to be exploring some of the other PowerShell cmdlets that are available.

How It Works

If you are not familiar with PowerShell, this is something that comes out on both the client operating system and the server operating system, it is included by default.

This is a very advanced sophisticated scripting slash command-line tool that can do just about anything, and even though it can do so, there are going to be times when you might need to give it a little helping land and that's where the **"cmdlets"** or **"modules"** comes into play. It's going to give you additional functionality so you might be wondering why you need to go and do this for Teams. Well, if you're going to go to PowerShell and type in the partial commands which are for Teams, PowerShell is going to give you an error in most cases, at least by default it will, and in short, this is just because it doesn't understand the command; you need to help it along. So what you're going to do is install a module that is for Microsoft Teams and this is going to give your PowerShell additional functionality.

This is going to make your PowerShell smarter and it's going to help you understand when you type in a partial command which is not specific to Teams. This applies to a lot of cloud platforms; it applies to Teams, SharePoint, Exchange, there are a lot of platforms that you can manage via PowerShell but not by default; you might need to install a module first before you can go and manage these platforms.

It's worth noting that if and when you should go and install one of these modules, install them as the administrator, to run your PowerShell as the administrator, right-click on PowerShell and **"Run as admih**

Once you've installed these modules, remember to restart that machine. If it's a virtual machine, the same applies, restart the machine because for some reason it doesn't always kick in until you restart the physical machine or the virtual machine.

Installing Teams PowerShell Module

First things first, you need to open PowerShell, so you can start by just typing it in at the bottom; remember to run this as an administrator since there's a good chance it's not going to work unless you run it as administrator. Also, once you're completely done remember to restart the machine.

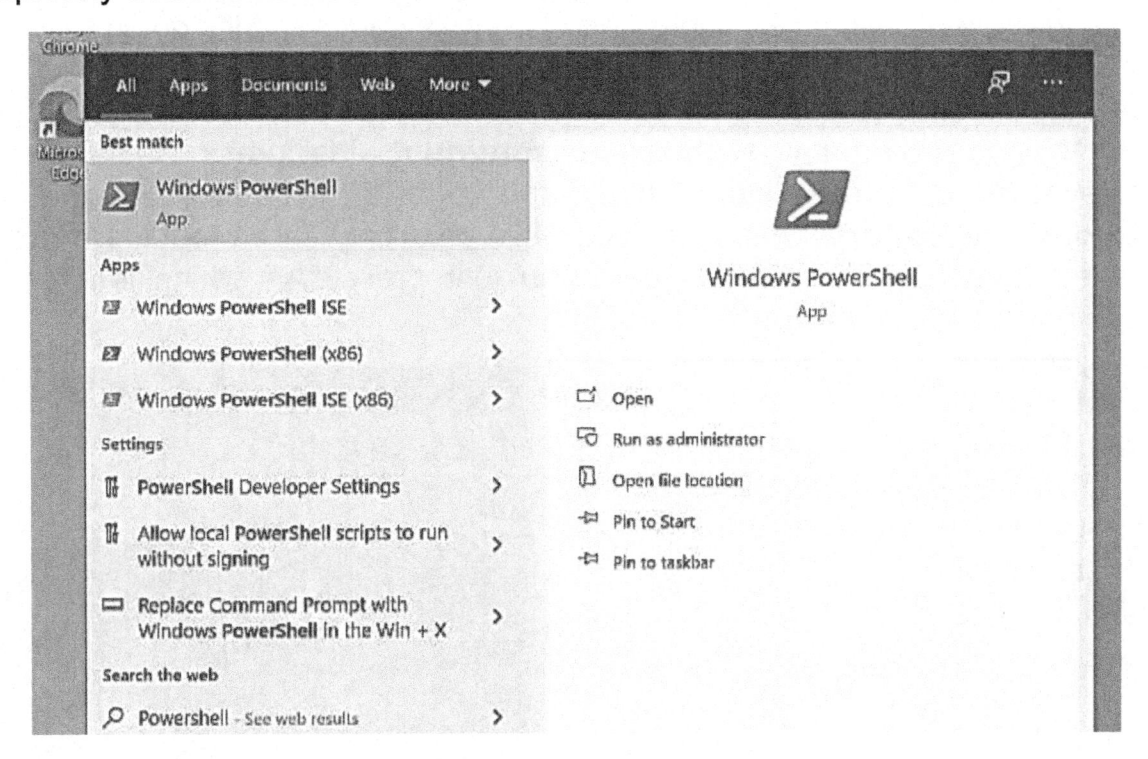

What you need to type in first is **"Set-ExecutionPolicy"**. What this is going to do is that it is going to prevent you from getting blocked or restricted when you try to run any of your PowerShell scripts.

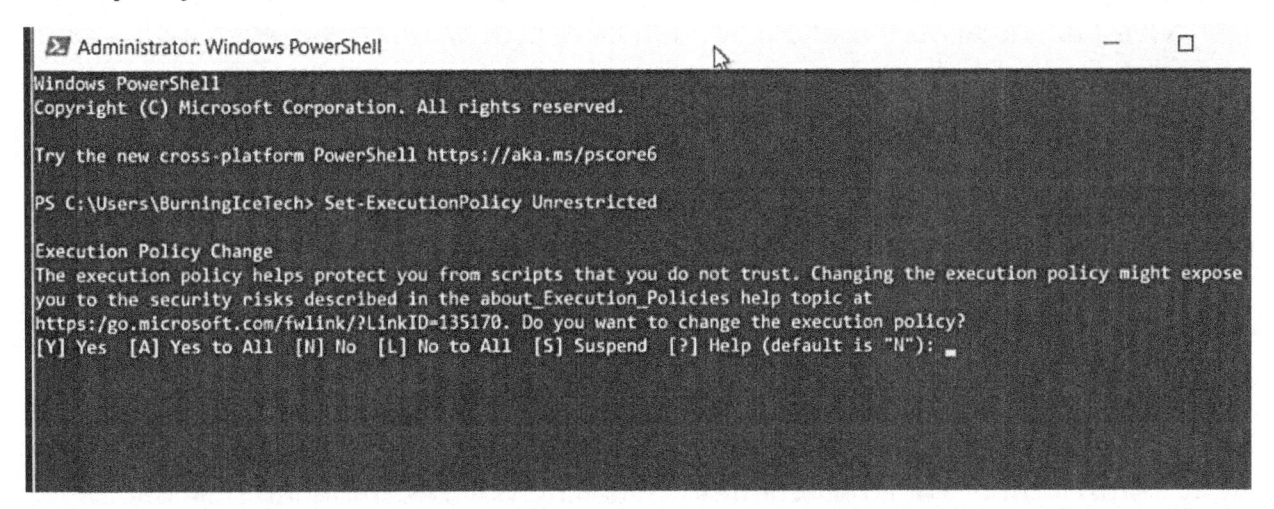

So you're just going to start things off by running this small little script that says **"Set Execution Policy"** to **"Unrestricted"**. Hit the **"Enter"** button and a message pops up, asking if you want to proceed. The next thing you're going to do is to say **"A"** and that means **"Yes"** to all.

Now, you're going to install the PowerShell module for Microsoft Teams. So, what you need to do to install the module is type in **"Install-module -Name MicrosoftTeams"**. Where it's going to get this from is that it includes your operating system, so there's a very large repository built into your Windows Operating System, and when you go and type this command it's going to go and extract that and install that onto your machine. Hit the **"Enter"** button, this might take a few seconds to pop up on your site, after which you'll get this next menu saying **"Nuget provider is required to continue"**. Just press the **"Y"** key on your keyboard and press enter. You're going to get this little message that says **"Untrusted repository"** meaning you are installing the modules from an untrusted repository. I would suggest you just press **"A"**, which is **"Yes"** for everything.

```
Copyright (C) Microsoft Corporation. All rights reserved.

Try the new cross-platform PowerShell https://aka.ms/pscore6

PS C:\Users\BurningIceTech> Set-ExecutionPolicy Unrestricted

Execution Policy Change
The execution policy helps protect you from scripts that you do not trust. Changing the execution policy might expose
you to the security risks described in the about_Execution_Policies help topic at
https:/go.microsoft.com/fwlink/?LinkID=135170. Do you want to change the execution policy?
[Y] Yes  [A] Yes to All  [N] No  [L] No to All  [S] Suspend  [?] Help (default is "N"): A
PS C:\Users\BurningIceTech> Install-Module -Name MicrosoftTeams

NuGet provider is required to continue
PowerShellGet requires NuGet provider version '2.8.5.201' or newer to interact with NuGet-based repositories. The NuGet
 provider must be available in 'C:\Program Files\PackageManagement\ProviderAssemblies' or
'C:\Users\BurningIceTech\AppData\Local\PackageManagement\ProviderAssemblies'. You can also install the NuGet provider
by running 'Install-PackageProvider -Name NuGet -MinimumVersion 2.8.5.201 -Force'. Do you want PowerShellGet to install
 and import the NuGet provider now?
[Y] Yes  [N] No  [S] Suspend  [?] Help (default is "Y"):
```

You have just installed the latest version of Microsoft Teams PowerShell Module from the PowerShell gallery repository. So now, if you were to go and use PowerShell to type Teams-related commands, it's going to understand and know what you are talking about, and from here you can manage your Teams that operate in the cloud. But even though it's going to recognize the commands, your PowerShell is not going to know which Teams it needs to connect to the cloud, so from this point forward, you need to go and connect to your company or your personal Team's environment first. That's going to be the first step before you can go and type any PowerShell commands you need to connect to your Team's environment in the cloud otherwise your PowerShell is not going to know which Teams environment it needs to connect to, and if you're going to try and apply some form of settings, whether it's calling policies, meeting policies, or just team settings in general via PowerShell, it will not know which team's environment to apply this to. So you need to go and connect it first and lastly it's also just to make sure that you're allowed to connect to the specific teams' environment. They need to know you're not trying to hijack or intercept the communication here, so to avoid that from happening you need to prove that you are the owner of this team's environment or at the very least that you're an employee or a member of this team's environment that's authorized to go and work on it.

Now let's see how you can connect to your specific team's environment once you've installed the Microsoft Teams PowerShell module. This next command that you're going to type will not work if you have not installed the Team's PowerShell module, so every command that you're going to be typing from this point forward will not work unless you've installed the PowerShell module for Teams. So, you need to go and do that first, and once you've done it you don't have to go and do it again; you only do it once then it's done.

Once you've got it installed, kindly type the following command **"Connect-MicrosoftTeams"** and what this command is going to do is ideally it'll pop up a little window and ask you for your credentials to your Microsoft Teams environment; this is just to prove once again that you are an owner or a member of that team's environment that's authorized to go and connect to it.

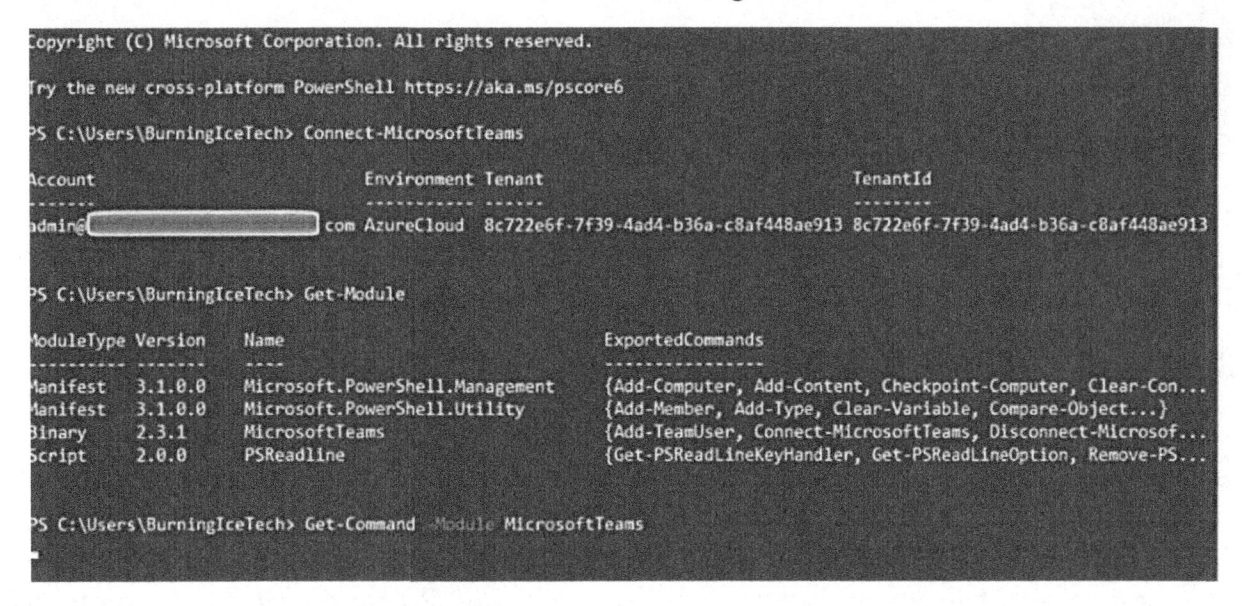

```
Copyright (C) Microsoft Corporation. All rights reserved.

Try the new cross-platform PowerShell https://aka.ms/pscore6

PS C:\Users\BurningIceTech> Connect-MicrosoftTeams

Account                                    Environment Tenant                                TenantId
-------                                    ----------- ------                                --------
admin@███████████████████ com AzureCloud  8c722e6f-7f39-4ad4-b36a-c8af448ae913  8c722e6f-7f39-4ad4-b36a-c8af448ae913


PS C:\Users\BurningIceTech> Get-Module

ModuleType Version   Name                           ExportedCommands
---------- -------   ----                           ----------------
Manifest   3.1.0.0   Microsoft.PowerShell.Management {Add-Computer, Add-Content, Checkpoint-Computer, Clear-Con...
Manifest   3.1.0.0   Microsoft.PowerShell.Utility   {Add-Member, Add-Type, Clear-Variable, Compare-Object...}
Binary     2.3.1     MicrosoftTeams                 {Add-TeamUser, Connect-MicrosoftTeams, Disconnect-Microsof...
Script     2.0.0     PSReadline                     {Get-PSReadLineKeyHandler, Get-PSReadLineOption, Remove-PS...


PS C:\Users\BurningIceTech> Get-Command -Module MicrosoftTeams
```

So when you press **"Enter"** you'll see the little window, and as long as you don't get an editor you're good to go. So what you need to go and do now is you need to provide your live ID that's associated with your subscription which is in the cloud; specifically, the one that's associated with your teams in this case. So you need to provide some sort of credentials to an admin account or an account that's got a role assigned to it that gives you permissions to go and manage your team's environment. It needs to be Teams administrator, Teams communications administrator, Teams communications engineer, Teams communications specialist, or Teams device administrator. So you go ahead and type in your email address and go to the next menu which is going to be your password.

After that, you will see that your subscription has been added and you've just logged on.

```
Windows PowerShell
Copyright (C) Microsoft Corporation. All rights reserved.

Try the new cross-platform PowerShell https://aka.ms/pscore6

PS C:\Users\BurningIceTech> Connect-MicrosoftTeams
```

[Microsoft Sign in dialog box]

In a nutshell, simply just go and install the Teams Microsoft module and once you've done that go and type in the connect command as you've just seen and there you go.

Cmdlets

Now from this point forward, it's just a matter of typing your usual good old-fashioned Teams PowerShell commands and you should be able to go and manage your teams via Powershell if you happen to know the commands. If you don't know the partial commands Microsoft Teams don't be confused, there are a lot of people out there including people that's got 20 years of experience that don't know PowerShell, so a lot of people just go to a search engine to search for the PowerShell script that they're looking for and you can go and copy-paste in some cases. Just go take those scripts; sometimes you could use them as-is, other times you just need to go and there you go. It's going to make your life so much easier.

Now, let me show you what it looks like when we view some of the other modules. If you type in an extra command such as **"Get-Module"**, this is going to get you the available modules. So, when your sign-in was successful some information about the signed-in user and the tenant are displayed.

```
opyright (C) Microsoft Corporation. All rights reserved.

ry the new cross-platform PowerShell https://aka.ms/pscore6

PS C:\Users\BurningIceTech> Connect-MicrosoftTeams

Account                         Environment Tenant                                    TenantId
-------                         ----------- ------                                    --------
admin@[REDACTED]         com AzureCloud  8c722e6f-7f39-4ad4-b36a-c8af448ae913  8c722e6f-7f39-4ad4-b36a-c8af448ae913


PS C:\Users\BurningIceTech> Get-Module

ModuleType Version  Name                            ExportedCommands
---------- -------  ----                            ----------------
Manifest   3.1.0.0  Microsoft.PowerShell.Management {Add-Computer, Add-Content, Checkpoint-Computer, Clear-Con...
Manifest   3.1.0.0  Microsoft.PowerShell.Utility    {Add-Member, Add-Type, Clear-Variable, Compare-Object...}
Binary     2.3.1    MicrosoftTeams                  {Add-TeamUser, Connect-MicrosoftTeams, Disconnect-Microsof...
Script     2.0.0    PSReadline                      {Get-PSReadLineKeyHandler, Get-PSReadLineOption, Remove-PS...


PS C:\Users\BurningIceTech>
```

To confirm the Microsoft Teams module is loaded correctly, just enter the following command that was just typed in a few seconds ago and that's going to show you whether it was installed correctly.

So, to get an overview of the available Teams PowerShell cmdlets which are from Microsoft Teams, you need to go and type in the following command and this is going to give you an overview of the cmdlets that you have available. So just type in **"Get-Command -Module MicrosoftTeams"** and enter. You'll get a big list of the available cmdlets that you can work with.

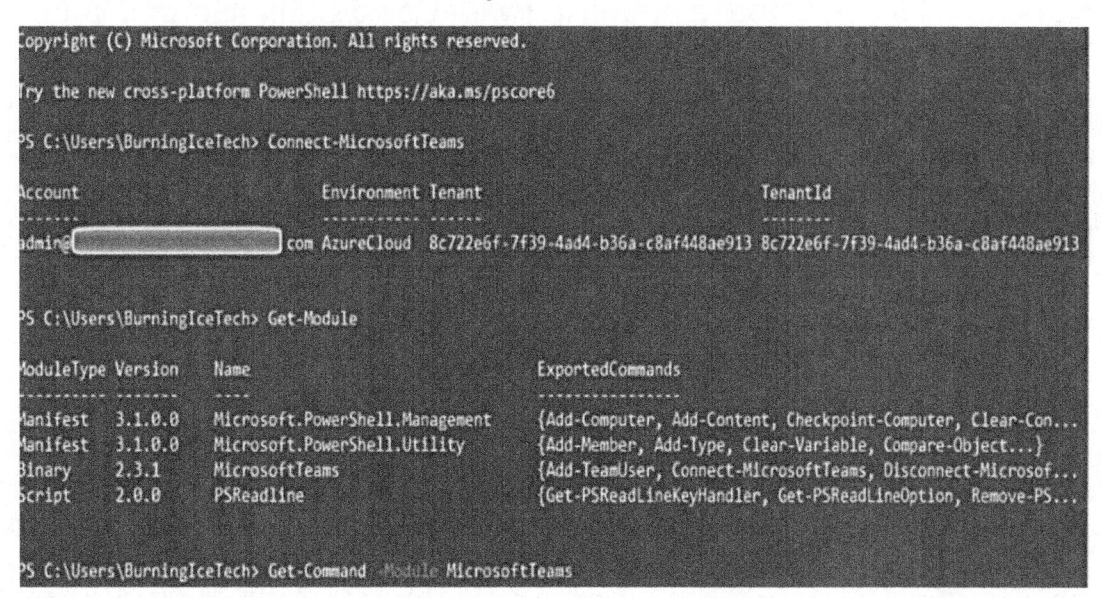

```
opyright (C) Microsoft Corporation. All rights reserved.

ry the new cross-platform PowerShell https://aka.ms/pscore6

PS C:\Users\BurningIceTech> Connect-MicrosoftTeams

Account                         Environment Tenant                                    TenantId
-------                         ----------- ------                                    --------
admin@[REDACTED]         com AzureCloud  8c722e6f-7f39-4ad4-b36a-c8af448ae913  8c722e6f-7f39-4ad4-b36a-c8af448ae913


PS C:\Users\BurningIceTech> Get-Module

ModuleType Version  Name                            ExportedCommands
---------- -------  ----                            ----------------
Manifest   3.1.0.0  Microsoft.PowerShell.Management {Add-Computer, Add-Content, Checkpoint-Computer, Clear-Con...
Manifest   3.1.0.0  Microsoft.PowerShell.Utility    {Add-Member, Add-Type, Clear-Variable, Compare-Object...}
Binary     2.3.1    MicrosoftTeams                  {Add-TeamUser, Connect-MicrosoftTeams, Disconnect-Microsof...
Script     2.0.0    PSReadline                      {Get-PSReadLineKeyHandler, Get-PSReadLineOption, Remove-PS...


PS C:\Users\BurningIceTech> Get-Command -Module MicrosoftTeams
```

```
Function      Set-CsTenantPublicProvider                            2.3.1    MicrosoftTeams
Function      Set-CsTenantTrustedIPAddress                          2.3.1    MicrosoftTeams
Function      Set-CsTenantUpdateTimeWindow                          2.3.1    MicrosoftTeams
Function      Set-CsUCPhoneConfiguration                            2.3.1    MicrosoftTeams
Function      Set-CsUser                                            2.3.1    MicrosoftTeams
Function      Set-CsUserAcp                                         2.3.1    MicrosoftTeams
Function      Set-CsUserPstnSettings                                2.3.1    MicrosoftTeams
Function      Set-CsUserServicesPolicy                              2.3.1    MicrosoftTeams
Function      Set-CsVideoInteropServiceProvider                     2.3.1    MicrosoftTeams
Function      Set-CsVoiceNormalizationRule                          2.3.1    MicrosoftTeams
Function      Start-CsExMeetingMigration                            2.3.1    MicrosoftTeams
Function      Switch-CsOnlineApplicationEndpoint                    2.3.1    MicrosoftTeams
Function      Sync-CsOnlineApplicationInstance                      2.3.1    MicrosoftTeams
Function      Test-CsEffectiveTenantDialPlan                        2.3.1    MicrosoftTeams
Function      Test-CsInboundBlockedNumberPattern                    2.3.1    MicrosoftTeams
Function      Test-CsOnlineCarrierPortabilityIn                     2.3.1    MicrosoftTeams
Function      Test-CsOnlineLisCivicAddress                          2.3.1    MicrosoftTeams
Function      Test-CsOnlinePortabilityIn                            2.3.1    MicrosoftTeams
Function      Test-CsVoiceNormalizationRule                         2.3.1    MicrosoftTeams
Function      Unregister-CsHybridPSTNAppliance                      2.3.1    MicrosoftTeams
Function      Unregister-CsOnlineDialInConferencingServiceNumber    2.3.1    MicrosoftTeams
Function      Update-CsAutoAttendant                                2.3.1    MicrosoftTeams
Function      Update-CsCustomPolicyPackage                          2.3.1    MicrosoftTeams
Function      Update-CsOrganizationalAutoAttendant                  2.3.1    MicrosoftTeams
Function      Update-CsTeamTemplate                                 2.3.1    MicrosoftTeams
Function      Update-CsTenantMeetingUrl                             2.3.1    MicrosoftTeams
Cmdlet        Add-TeamUser                                          2.3.1    MicrosoftTeams
Cmdlet        Connect-MicrosoftTeams                                2.3.1    MicrosoftTeams
Cmdlet        Disconnect-MicrosoftTeams                             2.3.1    MicrosoftTeams
Cmdlet        Get-MultiGeoRegion                                    2.3.1    MicrosoftTeams
Cmdlet        Get-Team                                              2.3.1    MicrosoftTeams
Cmdlet        Get-TeamChannel                                       2.3.1    MicrosoftTeams
Cmdlet        Get-TeamsApp                                          2.3.1    MicrosoftTeams
Cmdlet        Get-TeamUser                                          2.3.1    MicrosoftTeams
```

Lastly, there's one last command you can go and type in, this is not compulsory but it's just to help you if you're struggling with PowerShell and that is the "**Get-Help**" cmdlets. This is used to explore the available cmdlets.

```
PS C:\Users\BurningIceTech> Get-Help New-Team

Do you want to run Update-Help?
The Update-Help cmdlet downloads the most current Help files for Windows PowerShell modules, and installs them on y
```

For example, to get more information about how to create a team with PowerShell, enter the following cmdlet "**Get-Help New-Team**".

```
PS C:\Users\BurningIceTech> Get-Help New-Team

Do you want to run Update-Help?
The Update-Help cmdlet downloads the most current Help files for Windows PowerShell modules, and installs them on your
computer. For more information about the Update-Help cmdlet, see https:/go.microsoft.com/fwlink/?LinkId=210614.
[Y] Yes  [N] No  [S] Suspend  [?] Help (default is "Y"):
```

You will get an instruction afterward, and if that is something you would like press "**Y**".

Summary

In this chapter, you learned what PowerShell does and you saw that it does come by default with the client and the server operating system. You also learned that you need to go to installers to do something on Teams in the cloud as you're not going to be able to go and do something on teams by default unless you install the module first and that's going to give your PowerShell additional functionality.

You also saw how to connect to your team's environment in the cloud, what cmdlets are, and as an added extra, you saw the different cmdlets you can use and how to apply them.

Chapter 13: Keyboard shortcuts in Teams

Windows

General

To do this	In the Desktop app, press	In the Web app, press
Show keyboard shortcuts.	Ctrl+Period (.)	Ctrl+Period (.)
Go to **Search**.	Ctrl+E	Ctrl+Alt+E
Open filter.	Ctrl+Shift+F	Ctrl+Shift+F
Start a new chat.	Ctrl+N	Left Alt+N
Start a new popped out chat.	Ctrl+Shift+N	Alt+Shift+N
Open **Settings**.	Ctrl+Comma (,)	Ctrl+Shift+Comma (,)
Open **Help**.	F1	Ctrl+F1
Close.	Esc	Esc
Zoom in.	Ctrl+Equals sign (=)	No shortcut
Zoom out.	Ctrl+Minus sign (-)	No shortcut
Reset zoom level.	Ctrl+0	No shortcut
Pop out existing conversation.	Cltrl+O	No shortcut
Report a problem.	Cltrl+Alt+Shift+R	No shortcut

Navigation

To do this	In the Desktop app, press	In the Web app, press
Open **Activity**.	Ctrl+1	Ctrl+Shift+1
Open **Chat**.	Ctrl+2	Ctrl+Shift+2
Open **Teams**.	Ctrl+3	Ctrl+Shift+3
Open **Calendar**.	Ctrl+4	Ctrl+Shift+4
Open **Calls**.	Ctrl+5	Ctrl+Shift+5
Open **Files**.	Ctrl+6	Ctrl+Shift+6
Open **7th App on App bar**.	Ctrl+7	Ctrl+Shift+7
Open **8th App on App bar**.	Ctrl+8	Ctrl+Shift+8

To do this	In the Desktop app, press	In the Web app, press
Open **9th App on App bar**.	Ctrl+9	Ctrl+Shift+9
Move focus to Left rail item.	Ctrl+L	Alt+Shift+L
Move focus to message pane.	Ctrl+M	Alt+Shift+M
Move focus on top toast.	Ctrl+Alt+T	No shortcut
Open the **History** menu.	Ctrl+H	No shortcut
Go to previous section.	Ctrl+Shift+F6	Ctrl+Shift+F6
Go to next section.	Ctrl+F6	Ctrl+F6
Go to an open application.	Ctrl+F6	Ctrl+F6
Go back.	Alt+Left arrow key	No shortcut
Go forward.	Alt+Right arrow key	No shortcut
Move focus to notification.	Win+Shift+Y	No shortcut

Messaging

To do this	In the Desktop app, press	In the Web app, press
Go to compose box.	Ctrl+R	Alt+Shift+R
Expand compose box.	Ctrl+Shift+X	Ctrl+Shift+X
Send a message.	Ctrl+Enter	Ctrl+Enter
Attach a file.	Alt+Shift+O	No shortcut
Start a new line.	Shift+Enter	Shift+Enter
Mark a message as important.	Ctrl+Shift+I	Ctrl+Shift+I
Open video recorder.	Alt+Shift+F	Alt+Shift+F
Jump to last read/latest message.	Ctrl+J	No shortcut
Search current chat or channel messages.	Ctrl+F	Ctrl+F
Insert link.	Ctrl+K	Ctrl+K

Meetings and calls

To do this	In the Desktop app, press	In the Web app, press
Accept video call.	Ctrl+Shift+A	Alt+Shift+A
Accept audio call.	Ctrl+Shift+S	Alt+Shift+S

To do this	In the Desktop app, press	In the Web app, press
Decline call.	Ctrl+Shift+D	Ctrl+Shift+D
Start audio call.	Alt+Shift+A	Alt+Shift+A
Start video call.	Alt+Shift+V	Alt+Shift+V
End audio call.	Ctrl+Shift+H	Ctrl+Shift+H
End video call.	Ctrl+Shift+H	Ctrl+Shift+H
Toggle mute.	Ctrl+Shift+M	Ctrl+Shift+M
Temporarily unmute.	Ctrl+Spacebar	Ctrl+Spacebar
Announce raised hands (screen reader).	Ctrl+Shift+L	Ctrl+Shift+L
Raise or lower your hand.	Ctrl+Shift+K	Ctrl+Shift+K
Toggle video.	Ctrl+Shift+O	No shortcut
Decline screen share.	Ctrl+Shift+D	No shortcut
Accept screen share.	Ctrl+Shift+A	No shortcut
Admit people from lobby notification.	Ctrl+Shift+Y	No shortcut
Open the **Background settings** menu.	Ctrl+Shift+P	No shortcut
Schedule a meeting.	Alt+Shift+N	Alt+Shift+N
Save or send meeting request.	Ctrl+S	Ctrl+S
Join from meeting details.	Alt+Shift+J	Alt+Shift+J
Go to suggested time.	Alt+Shift+S	Alt+Shift+S
Join from meeting started toast.	Ctrl+Shift+J	No shortcut
Open meeting chat.	Ctrl+Shift+R	No shortcut
Zoom into shared content.	Alt+Shift+=	Alt+Shift+=
Zoom out from shared content.	Alt+Shift+-	Alt+Shift+-
Reset zoom for shared content.	Alt+Shift+0	Alt+Shift+0
Pan shared content up.	Alt+Shift+Up arrow key	Alt+Shift+Up arrow key
Pan shared content down.	Alt+Shift+Down arrow key	Alt+Shift+Down arrow key

To do this	In the Desktop app, press	In the Web app, press
Pan shared content left.	Alt+Shift+Left arrow key	Alt+Shift+Left arrow key
Pan shared content right.	Alt+Shift+Right arrow key	Alt+Shift+Right arrow key

Debug

To do this	In the Desktop app, press	In the Web app, press
Download diagnostic logs.	Ctrl+Alt+Shift+1	Ctrl+Alt+Shift+1

CONCLUSION

As we reach the end of the "Microsoft Teams Quick Start 2024 Guide," it's important to reflect on the journey we've undertaken together. Throughout this guide, we've explored the multifaceted nature of Microsoft Teams, delving into its many features and capabilities that make it a standout tool in the realm of digital collaboration and communication.

The Evolution of Teams

From its early days as a simple communication tool to its current state as a comprehensive collaboration platform, Microsoft Teams has continually evolved to meet the changing needs of businesses and individuals alike. This guide has covered everything from the basics of setting up and getting started with Teams to the more advanced aspects of leveraging its integrations, managing teams, and automating processes.

Key Takeaways

One of the key takeaways from this guide is the importance of effective communication in the digital workspace. Microsoft Teams offers a plethora of tools and features to facilitate this, from chat and video conferencing to live events and integrations with other Microsoft 365 applications. We've seen how mastering these tools can lead to more efficient, streamlined, and productive workflows.

The Future of Work

Another crucial aspect we've touched upon is the future of work. The digital transformation, accelerated by global events like the pandemic, has reshaped how we work, communicate, and collaborate. Microsoft Teams is at the forefront of this transformation, offering solutions that cater to remote, hybrid, and in-office work environments. This guide has equipped you with the knowledge and skills to navigate these changes and leverage Teams to its full potential.

Empowering Through Integration and Automation

We also delved into the power of integration and automation within Teams. By integrating with a wide array of apps and services and leveraging bots, Teams becomes more than just a communication tool; it becomes a central hub for your work. The guide provided insights into how these integrations can automate mundane tasks, freeing up time and resources for more critical work.

Advanced Management and Customization

For the IT professionals and power users, the guide presented advanced management techniques using PowerShell and detailed customization options. These skills are crucial for managing Teams effectively in complex environments and ensuring that the platform aligns with the specific needs and culture of your organization.

A Tool for Everyone

Perhaps most importantly, this guide has emphasized that Microsoft Teams is a tool for everyone. Whether you are a beginner, a seasoned professional, an IT administrator, or a casual user, Teams has something to offer. With its user-friendly interface and extensive help resources, anyone can start using Teams and gradually explore its more advanced features.

Looking Ahead

As we conclude, it's important to remember that the world of technology is constantly evolving, and so is Microsoft Teams. What we've covered in this guide is just the tip of the iceberg. Microsoft is continuously adding new features and capabilities to Teams, and keeping up with these changes is crucial for maximizing the benefits of the platform.

Revisiting the Core Strengths of Teams

At its heart, Microsoft Teams is more than just a tool; it's a platform that brings people, conversations, and content together, enabling users to achieve more together than they could individually. This guide has illustrated how Teams bridges the gap between people working remotely and those in the office, fostering a sense of community and collaboration regardless of physical location. By integrating chat, video, and file sharing in one platform, Teams breaks down the barriers of traditional communication, paving the way for a more inclusive and dynamic way of working.

Customization and Flexibility: A Platform for Every Need

One of the most significant advantages of Teams, as detailed in this guide, is its vast customization and flexibility. From setting up channels tailored to specific project needs to creating automated workflows with Power Automate, Teams offers an unprecedented level of customization. This guide has provided you with the knowledge to tailor Teams to your specific needs, whether you're managing a small team or an entire organization, ensuring that Teams works for you, and not the other way around.

Security and Compliance in the Forefront

In a world where data security and compliance are paramount, Microsoft Teams stands out as a platform that takes these concerns seriously. We have explored the various security features and compliance protocols that Teams adheres to, ensuring that your data is safe and your communications meet the necessary regulatory standards. This aspect is crucial for businesses in sensitive industries, and Teams provides the peace of mind that comes with top-tier security.

The Role of Teams in Fostering a Collaborative Culture

Another critical point that this guide has highlighted is the role of Teams in fostering a collaborative culture within organizations. Teams is not just a tool for communication; it's a platform that can transform the way teams interact, share ideas, and work towards common goals. We have discussed how features like Teams live events, Yammer integrations, and shared workspaces can create an environment that encourages open communication and collaborative problem-solving.

Staying Ahead in the Teams Journey

As we emphasized earlier, the journey with Microsoft Teams is an ongoing one. The technology landscape is ever-changing, and Microsoft Teams continues to evolve with new updates and features. This guide has equipped you with a solid foundation, but the learning doesn't stop here. Staying updated with the latest developments, exploring new features as they are released, and continuously adapting your Teams environment to suit your evolving needs will ensure that you remain at the forefront of digital collaboration.

Empowerment Through Knowledge and Skills

The ultimate goal of this guide has been to empower you with knowledge and skills. Whether you're a business leader looking to enhance your team's productivity, an IT professional tasked with managing a complex Teams environment, or an individual user seeking to improve your collaborative efforts, the insights and tips provided in this guide are designed to elevate your Teams experience to the next level.

Concluding Thoughts: A Gateway to the Future of Collaboration

In conclusion, the "Microsoft Teams Quick Start 2024 Guide" is more than just a comprehensive manual; it's a gateway to understanding and harnessing one of the most powerful collaboration tools available today. As you continue your journey with Microsoft Teams, remember that the platform is a living, evolving entity, and your engagement with it should be dynamic and proactive. Embrace the changes, explore the possibilities, and let Teams be the catalyst for a more connected, productive, and innovative way of working in your organization.

Final Thoughts

In closing, the "Microsoft Teams Quick Start 2024 Guide" is more than just a manual; it's a roadmap to navigating the ever-changing landscape of digital collaboration. As you continue to use Teams, keep exploring, learning, and adapting. The future of work is bright, and with Microsoft Teams, you're well-equipped to be a part of it.

Printed in Great Britain
by Amazon